HITLER´S NAVY

OSPREY
PUBLISHING

HITLER'S NAVY

NAVY

THE KRIEGSMARINE IN WORLD WAR II

GORDON WILLIAMSON

OSPREY PUBLISHING
Bloomsbury Publishing Plc
Kemp House, Chawley Park, Cumnor Hill, Oxford OX2 9PH, UK
29 Earlsfort Terrace, Dublin 2, Ireland
1385 Broadway, 5th Floor, New York, NY 10018, USA
E-mail: info@ospreypublishing.com
www.ospreypublishing.com

OSPREY is a trademark of Osprey Publishing Ltd
First published in Great Britain in 2022
© Osprey Publishing Ltd, 2022
Gordon Williamson has asserted his right under the Copyright,
Designs and Patents Act, 1988, to be identified as Author of this
work.

This book is based on previously published Osprey books in the
New Vanguard, Elite, Warrior, Campaign, Raid and Duel series,
with new chapters written by the author. For a complete list of the
source books, see Further Reading.

A catalogue record for this book is available from the British
Library.
ISBN: HB 9781472847928;
eBook 9781472847935;
ePDF 9781472847942;
XML 9781472847911

22 23 24 25 26   10 9 8 7 6 5 4 3 2 1

Maps by www.bounford.com
Index by Angela Hall
Design and layout by Stewart Larking

Printed and bound in India by Replika Press Private Ltd.

Osprey Publishing supports the Woodland Trust, the UK's leading
woodland conservation charity.

To find out more about our authors and books visit
www.ospreypublishing.com. Here you will find extracts, author
interviews, details of forthcoming events and the option to sign up
for our newsletter.

DEDICATION

This book and those individual volumes that preceded it would not
have been possible without the gracious assistance of Horst Bredow,
founder of the U-Boot Archiv, now known as the Deutsches
U-Boot Museum. Herr Bredow and his wife Annemarie were a
gracious host on my visits to the Archiv in Cuxhaven, allowing me
not only access to the Archiv, but to reside in the Archiv building
during my trips. Horst provided much help and encouragement
and made available the photographic collection for my work. The
U-Boot Museum is the world's foremost repository of information
and photographs on the subject not only of the U-Boats of the
Kriegsmarine but also of their forerunners in the Kaiserliche
Marine of Imperial Germany and other aspects of the Kriegsmarine
in World War II.

Horst Bredow sadly passed away on 22 February 2015 and is
greatly missed.

ACKNOWLEDGEMENTS

Noted U-Boat and Kriegsmarine historian Jak P. Mallmann-
Showell has been, for many years, a good friend and great source of
inspiration and support and was instrumental in introducing me to
the U-Boat Archiv.

I would also like to express my thanks to the following individuals
for their assistance:
Dave Bloor
Chris Boonzaier
Josef Charita
Thomas Huss
Detlev Niemann
Francois Saez

PHOTO ACKNOWLEDGEMENTS

DUBM   Deutsches U-Boot Museum
NHHC   Naval History and Heritage Command

CONTENTS

INTRODUCTION

Unlike other maritime nations such as Great Britain, Germany's emergence as a major sea power did not occur until the late 19th century. Its access to the sea is of course along its northern borders, with its most important ports being those of the Hanseatic League, cities such as Hamburg, Lübeck, Bremen etc. Prussia, the most powerful of the Germanic nations, had its own navy, founded in 1701, this giving birth in 1867 to the so-called North German Federal Navy (*Norddeutsche Bundesmarine*) when Prussia, primarily a land power, joined the North German Federation. Naval forces, such as they were, were primarily concerned with protection of the merchant fleet though there were some small scale skirmishes with French naval vessels during the Franco-Prussian War of 1870–71.

The successful war against France led to the formation of the new German Empire, the Second Reich, on 18 January 1871, with Wilhelm I becoming King of Prussia and Emperor (*Kaiser*) of all Germany. The small German Navy now became the *Kaiserliche Marine*. Though the task of the Imperial Navy, in the early part of its existence, was predominantly the role of a coastal defence force to deter any potential enemy nation from attempting a seaborne invasion, encouraged by the Kaiser, senior naval commander Admiral Alfred von Tirpitz began a ten-year programme of expansion and modernization of the Kaiserliche Marine.

In 1888, Kaiser Wilhelm II became emperor. With an overwhelming ambition to match or surpass the maritime strength of the British, Wilhelm II ploughed vast amounts of money into the building of new warships, in particular heavy units such as battlecruisers and battleships. The opening of the new Kiel Canal in 1896 gave Germany direct access from the Baltic to the North Sea, connecting both of its major naval commands.

In 1897 Tirpitz was appointed Secretary of State for the Navy, and in this powerful position he had influence to continue to push the expansion of the navy. By the outbreak of war in 1914 the Kaiserliche Marine possessed 22 pre-dreadnought battleships, 14 dreadnoughts and four battlecruisers with more modern heavy units under construction.

Despite the desire to compete with the Royal Navy in terms of sea power, during World War I the Kaiserliche Marine never made full use of its fleet of heavy warships. The only major engagement between the battleships of both sides occurred in 1916 when, on 31 May, the German High Seas Fleet set sail in an attempt to lure part of the

Grossadmiral Alfred von Tirpitz, largely responsible for the rise in German sea power prior to World War I. Often thought of as the 'father' of the German Navy, his name would be carried by Germany's biggest and most powerful battleship. (NHHC)

Royal Navy's Grand Fleet into a trap and destroy it. In the event, intelligence intercepts forewarned the British that the German fleet was about to set to sea and allowed a much larger British force to be assembled to meet them. In heavy units (battleships, battlecruisers and armoured cruisers) the Royal Navy force numbered 45, supported by 106 other vessels. The German fleet had only 27 heavy units with 72 other vessels. In the battle that ensued, the Royal Navy lost six heavy units and eight destroyers whilst the Germans lost two heavy units, four light cruisers and five torpedo boats. In terms of ships, the Royal Navy's losses (just over 113,000 tons) was significantly larger than the Germans' (just over 62,000 tons). In personnel losses the Royal Navy also suffered more (6,768 killed or wounded as opposed to the 3,058 killed or wounded for the Kaiserliche Marine). However, it was the German High Seas Fleet which broke off the action and returned to port. Thus, both sides claimed victory, the Germans in sinking more enemy ships than they themselves had lost, and the Royal Navy for forcing the High Seas Fleet to retire from the battleground. The High Seas Fleet though never put to sea en masse again, whilst the Grand Fleet grew in strength throughout the remainder of the war. Germany's *Unterseeboot* (U-boat) fleet, however, would see phenomenal success during World War I; but the continuing British naval blockade of Germany, together with the entry into the war of the United States, meant that the defeat of Germany became inevitable.

SMS *Elsass*, a pre-dreadnought of the Braunschweig class, one of the vessels that Germany was permitted to retain after the end of World War I. Although it survived into the Kriegsmarine era, it saw no active service and was broken up for scrap in 1936. (NHHC)

The end of World War I left the German Navy in the position of not having been defeated, but at the same time not having achieved any major victory despite the performance of the U-boats. The fleet was ordered to be surrendered to the Allies and the Grand Fleet interned at the Royal Navy's anchorage at Scapa Flow. There, determined to avoid the ignominy of the ships ending up in enemy hands, the crews scuttled their vessels under the very noses of the British.

The abdication of the Kaiser meant the end of the Kaiserliche Marine, though the Imperial flag would not be lowered on Germany's few remaining ships until December 1921.

In the meantime, on 1 January 1921, the navy, now severely limited in size by the terms of the Treaty of Versailles, was formally renamed as the *Reichsmarine*. As far as battleships were concerned, only six, plus two in reserve, were permitted, and no submarines whatsoever. These battleships, however, were obsolete and no longer fit for purpose. Five of the eight were soon decommissioned and one converted to a radio-controlled target ship. Only two, the *Schlesien* and *Schleswig-Holstein*, saw service in World War II.

Not only was the number of ships strictly limited, but so was their size. An attempt to bypass these restrictions saw the emergence of the so-called 'pocket-battleships' *Graf Spee*, *Deutschland* and *Admiral Scheer*. Classed by the Germans as *Panzerschiffe* or

armoured ships, they were the last major ships to be launched before, in 1935, the Navy was re-christened as the *Kriegsmarine*.

With Hitler in power, production of both capital ships and submarines began in earnest. Once again it was hoped that in time the German Navy could reach a size that would mean it had nothing to fear from the Royal Navy, though Hitler's determination on military expansion and conquest well before the Kriegsmarine was ready or able to challenge the British would mean disaster for the German Navy once again.

THE DEVELOPMENT OF THE KRIEGSMARINE

With the end of World War I and the scuttling of the Grand Fleet at Scapa Flow, Germany ceased to be a sea power. Left with no submarines and no major warships other than a handful of obsolete dreadnoughts, the *Reichsmarine* had the capability to do little more than offer some small measure of defence to its own coastline. The terms of the Treaty of Versailles were clearly designed to ensure that Germany's navy could never pose a threat to world peace again. A total of only 15,000 men were permitted to the Reichsmarine, of whom just 1,500 would be officers. These totals also included land-based personnel, leaving even fewer to potentially man any warships.

In terms of ships, Germany was permitted: six obsolete 'dreadnought'-type battleships with two in reserve; six cruisers with two in reserve; 12 destroyers with four in reserve; 12 torpedo boats with four in reserve (the German designation of 'torpedo boat' referred to smaller destroyer escort types); plus smaller vessels such as minesweepers.

Germany was also severely restricted in terms of what type of coastal defence fortifications it could construct, and even this vastly reduced navy was only permitted in order to offer some limited defence against possible expansionist moves westwards by the Russians in the aftermath of the Revolution.

It would not be long, however, before Germany moved to bypass many of these restrictions. With a total ban on owning submarines, Germany simply set up a submarine design bureau in Holland, posing as a Dutch shipbuilding concern, the NV Ingenieurskanntor voor Scheepsbouw. A significant amount of experience in design and construction of submarines was gained and U-boats were built for Turkey whilst others were constructed in Finland under German instruction. These early designs were the direct precursors to the Type I, Type II and Type VII U-boats used by the Kriegsmarine.

Although the nascent U-boat arm was equipped with boats of a high quality, their numbers were small. On the outbreak of World War II, only 65 U-boats had been completed and of these only 24 were ready for operational use. Although this compared reasonably well with the Royal Navy's submarine strength at the time, it was nowhere near the number that Grossadmiral Karl Dönitz, as *Führer der Unterseeboote* (Flag Officer U-Boats), considered was necessary before undertaking a war against the British. Dönitz reportedly felt he could bring Britain to its knees with a fleet of 300 U-boats. Instead, more than half of the 56 boats he had were the small Type II vessels intended only for use in coastal waters.

As with the U-boats, design and development of fast motor torpedo boats (*Schnellboote* or *S-Boote*, generally known to the Allies as E-boats) was carried out in secret, behind the guise of several commercial 'front' businesses. One such was the civilian firm of Navis GmbH in Berlin, actually run by naval officer Kapitän zur See Lohmann, who arranged for the 'private' purchase of several partially completed boats by civilians acting as front-men for the navy, to prevent their being taken over by the Allies. Yacht manufacturing concerns and boating clubs such as Travemünder Yachthafen AG, were also set up, the latter being tasked with development of fast motor torpedo boats under Korvettenkapitän Beierle, whilst giving the appearance of simply producing civilian sporting craft.

These boats were used in the mid-1920s, albeit unarmed, on secret training exercises with larger surface warships to prove the concept of the fast, manoeuvrable, torpedo-carrying motor boat. The potential for such boats was not lost on the

Grossadmiral Erich Raeder, Oberbefehlshaber der Kriegsmarine until 1943, seen here in formal dress and carrying his admiral's baton. Following his resignation in 1943, he held the honourary position of Admiral Inspector of the Kriegsmarine. Although convicted at the Nuremberg trials, he was released on health grounds in 1955 and died in 1960. (DUBM)

Reichsmarine. The Lürssen firm was heavily involved, as were others such as Abeking and Rasmussen in Bremen and the Kasparwerft in Travemünde. With their intended use hidden behind the designation UZ(s) – *U-Boot Zerstörer* (*schnell*) or fast sub-chaser – development continued.

By 1925, the 'K' class of modern light cruisers (the *Königsberg*, *Köln* and *Karlsruhe*) had been added to the fleet, joined in 1927 by the *Leipzig*. By this point, however, there were still no new heavy units under construction. A further treaty, the London Naval Agreement of April 1930, divided the cruiser class into two types, the heavy cruiser and the light cruiser. As both types were to be restricted to a 10,000-ton limit, the classification clearly referred to the armament rather than the displacement of these vessels. The light cruiser would be permitted main armament of up to 15.5cm calibre and the heavy cruiser up to 20.3cm. Existing laws, however, still set the maximum level of cruiser strength of the Reichsmarine at six light cruisers, no provision being made for the heavier type.

It was not until the conclusion of the Anglo-German Naval Treaty of June 1935 that such restrictions were set aside, with new restrictions simply setting the Kriegsmarine's total strength at 35 per cent of that of the Royal Navy, but no longer with any restriction on the numbers of individual warship types. The treaty effectively left Germany able to plan for the construction of five heavy cruisers, totalling just over 50,000 tons, within the terms of the London Naval Agreement. Shortly thereafter, the keel of the first unit, eventually to be known as the *Admiral Hipper*, was laid down at Hamburg.

One of the most significant developments during this period was the advent of the so-called 'pocket battleship'. The Washington Agreement of February 1922 had imposed restrictions on warship construction in an attempt to prevent an arms race. All the major powers had signed, and although Germany had not been invited to attend, it was clear that it would be held to the same terms.

The Agreement classified ships into two categories: capital ships with guns greater than 20cm calibre, and smaller ships with guns of a lesser calibre and with a maximum displacement of 10,000 tons. German ingenuity was to create a hybrid formula from these restrictions – a vessel meeting the displacement limits set by the Agreement (effectively a large cruiser), but mounting guns of the calibre of a capital ship. The Reichsmarine elected to divert from the usual layout of two turrets forward and two aft bearing medium-calibre guns, usually around 12cm, and go for a heavier armament of one turret forward and one aft, each bearing three 28cm guns.

The new Deutschland-class ships were classified as armoured ships or *Panzerschiffe*. This name was carefully chosen. Although

The first of Germany's new generation of U-boats, were the diminutive Type II vessels known as *Einbäume* or 'dugout canoes' because of their small size. Shown here are U-8, U-11 and U-9 moored alongside their tender, U-Bootsbegleitschiff *Saar*. Despite their small size, they performed well in the early part of the war. (DUBM)

Panzerschiff *Deutschland*, the first of the 'pocket battleships' and most powerful ship in the Kriegsmarine at the time of its launch. Serving on non-intervention patrols during the Spanish Civil War, 31 of its crew were killed when it was attacked by Republican bombers. Its sister, *Admiral Scheer*, bombarded the port of Almería in retaliation. (Author's collection)

in French terms this effectively represented a battleship, in German terms a Panzerschiff was classed below the old battleship classification of 'ship of the line' or *Linienschiffe*. The impression given by this classification, therefore, was that Germany was developing a more modest design of warship fully commensurate with the terms of the Treaty of Versailles.

In October 1928, the contract for construction of Panzerschiff A was awarded to Deutsche Werke of Kiel. The day of the 'pocket battleship' had arrived.

Following the Panzerschiffe came the Scharnhorst class (*Scharnhorst* and *Gneisenau*), classified by the Germans as *Schlachtschiffe* or 'battleships'. These came about due to the Germans deciding against producing a fourth Deutschland-class vessel and opting instead to increase the size of the next two ships to double the displacement of *Deutschland*, at 19,700 tons. In the event, these proposed new vessels were broken up in 1934 whilst still on the stocks. In 1935, they were replaced by two even bigger vessels, planned at 25,600 tons and with the main armament increased from six to nine 28cm guns, in triple turrets of almost identical design to those in the Deutschland class. These ships were coded 'D' and 'E', the three *Panzerschiffe* being vessels 'A', 'B' and 'C' in the new construction programme. Although these ships were designed partly with the restrictions of the Treaty of Versailles in mind, by the time work had commenced Hitler had openly announced his intention to rearm and no attempt was

Although classed by the Germans as a battleship, *Scharnhorst* could be more accurately considered a battlecruiser. Though more than adequately armed for its intended role as a commerce raider facing only moderately powerful escort warships, it could never have faced a true battleship of the Royal Navy on anything like even terms. (NHHC)

Bismarck, and its sister *Tirpitz*, were the only true battleships possessed by the Kriegsmarine which could compare favourably with the firepower of their Allied equivalents. Only *Bismarck* would eventually face enemy capital ships in direct combat however, and the sheer weight of numbers facing it would ensure its doom. (NHHC)

It would be the U-boats, and particularly the Type VII shown here, which would bear the brunt of the war at sea. Eventually, however, they would reach the limit of upgrading and modification of which they were capable and suffered badly from constantly improving enemy anti-submarine warfare methods. (Author's collection)

subsequently made to adhere to the original tonnage limit. Subsequent negotiations between Germany and Great Britain, resulting in the Anglo-German Naval Agreement, retrospectively agreed the construction of these much larger warships. Although extremely large and relatively powerfully armed, with nine 28cm guns, they would not be able to hold their own against 15in.-gun battleships of the Royal Navy, nor indeed was it ever intended that they should. These vessels were more akin to a battlecruiser but nevertheless were officially classified by the Germans as battleships. Finally, of course, came the most powerful warships ever to have been commissioned into the Kriegsmarine: the *Bismarck* and its sister the *Tirpitz*.

By the time *Tirpitz* was launched on 1 April 1939, Germany had the nucleus of a very powerful fleet with the most powerful battleships in the world at that time, supported by modern pocket battleships and heavy cruisers equal to anything in any other navies.

Germany still faced a major problem, however. In any potential future conflict its most likely enemy at sea would be the Royal Navy. In 1939 the Royal Navy possessed 15 battleships, some of which were admittedly elderly, but with five modern King George-V class ships under construction, over 60 cruisers and a number of aircraft carriers. In addition, Britain could call upon the support of the Commonwealth whose navies could, and indeed did, contribute to the war effort.

Germany may have had a modern fleet, but it was still quite small. It was clearly incapable of besting the Royal Navy in battle. It had failed to do so in World War I and could not hope to do so in any future conflict.

Indeed, the *Oberbefehlshaber der Kriegsmarine* (Commander in Chief of the Navy), Grossadmiral Raeder, had told Hitler on a number of occasions that the navy could not compete against any major sea power in the event of war, only for Hitler to respond that there would be no war against Britain in any case as this would result in the destruction of the Reich. In 1938, Hitler eventually conceded that the Kriegsmarine might have to face the Royal Navy at war, but that it would not happen until at least 1948.

One factor in favour of the Kriegsmarine was that Hitler himself admitted that naval warfare was something of which he knew and understood little, saying 'On land I am a hero, but at sea I am a coward.' Hitler always remained in control, but in naval matters, he interfered far less than he did with his army generals, so long as matters were progressing satisfactorily.

Hitler is said to have once complained: 'I have a reactionary army, a national-socialist air force and a Christian navy.' Certainly Grossadmiral Erich Raeder was a Christian, a Lutheran who sought to inculcate Christian values in his officers and insisted that anyone expecting a successful career as a naval officer must attend church regularly. He was certainly right-wing and saw the Nazis as a useful counterforce to the communism he despised. Nevertheless, he expected his men to keep out of politics. Unsurprisingly, he was not one of Hitler's inner circle and had nowhere near the influence that Hermann Göring or some of the more ambitious army generals could exert. This no doubt contributed to the navy rarely being first in the queue when it came to demands for construction materials needed for expansion. The Kriegsmarine would have no chance to reach the size it would require to be ready for war in 1939.

Grossadmiral Karl Dönitz, initially Befehlshaber der Unterseeboote and then Oberbefehlshaber der Kriegsmarine from 1943 to 1945, would maintain a close overview of the U-boat campaign throughout the war despite moving on to have control of the entire navy. He remained a U-boat man at heart and retained the loyalty of his 'Grey Wolves'. (DUBM)

STRATEGY AND DOCTRINE

One of the most important factors in the defeat of Germany in World War I was the Allied blockade which drastically reduced the supply of essential war materials and food to German ports. At the same time, the German U-boat offensive in 1917, attempting its own blockade of Great Britain in an attempt to starve the British into submission, came close to succeeding.

The Kriegsmarine in World War II, in view of its obvious weaknesses, would adopt a strategy not of challenging the Royal Navy directly, but of attacking merchant shipping. Whether it be U-boats in the Atlantic and further afield, E-boats in the Channel or auxiliary cruisers in far-off waters, merchant shipping would be the target. Even major warships such as *Bismarck*, *Tirpitz*, *Scharnhorst* and others, supported by cruisers, were to act as commerce-raiding battle groups.

In the coming war, German naval doctrine would be shaped not by plans for besting the enemy in fleet versus fleet action which would surely fail, but by repeating the anti-commerce operations against shipping bringing essential supplies to Britain which had been highly effective in World War I, and this time using all manner of surface vessels as well as U-boats.

Schnellboote, or 'E-boats' as they were known to the Allies, would play an important part in interdicting Allied merchant ships around the British coast. They were bigger, faster and more heavily armed than the British MTBs and MGBs they faced. (Author's collection)

Naval planning had assumed a 'three-front war', namely in the Baltic, the North Sea and the Atlantic. In the event, for most of the war, the Baltic was considered safe waters as none of the enemies facing Germany in the Baltic had any sizeable naval forces to threaten the Kriegsmarine. The Baltic would provide the Kriegsmarine with a perfect training area where U-boats and surface ships could be brought up to combat readiness before being committed to action in the West. Only in the late stages of the war did any significant amount of naval action take place in the Baltic.

KRIEGSMARINE ORGANIZATION

The fleet was divided into three main components:

1. *Flottenstreitkräfte* (Naval Forces)

Sometimes referred to as the High Seas Fleet, this component included all of the capital ships, light and heavy cruisers, destroyers, E-boats and auxiliary cruisers as well as supply and training vessels, under the command of the following Admirals:

Flottenchef (Chief of the Fleet):

Admiral Hermann Boehm	November 1938–October 1939
Admiral Wilhelm Marschall	October 1939–July 1940
Admiral Günther Lütjens	July 1940–May 1941
Generaladmiral Otto Schniewind	May 1941–July 1944
Vizeadmiral Wilhelm Meendsen-Bohlken	July 1944–May 1945

2. *Sicherungsverbände* (Security Branch)

All of the smaller vessels such as minesweepers, patrol boats, sub-chasers, escort vessels etc., commanded as follows:

Befehlshaber der Sicherung (Commander of the Security Branch):

Vizeadmiral Hermann Mootz	January 1939–October 1940
Vizeadmiral Hans Stohwasser	October 1940–June 1944
Konteradmiral Hans Bütow	June 1944–November 1944

3. *Unterseeboote* (Submarines)

All U-boat types, coastal and sea-going.

Befelshaber/Führer der Unterseeboote (Commander/Flag Officer of the U-Boats):

Grossadmiral Karl Dönitz	January 1936–February 1943

The *Flottenstreitkräfte* (Naval forces) and *Unterseeboote* (U-boats) would take the war to the enemy whilst the *Sicherungsverbände* (Minesweepers) would defend German- controlled waters.

The *Operationsabteilungschef* (C-in-C Operations) was Konteradmiral Eberhardt Godt (October 1939–May 1945).

The *Organisationabteilungschef* (C-in-C Organisation) was Generaladmiral Hans Georg von Friedeburg (September 1941–May 1945).

With some few exceptions (*Admiral Graf Spee, Admiral Scheer, Admiral Hipper*), the Kriegsmarine's heavy units scored few successes in their role as commerce raiders, though the mere threat they posed, especially the battleships *Bismarck* and *Tirpitz*, was sufficient to tie up huge amounts of British resources to neutralize the threat.

Where the doctrine of commerce warfare proved very successful was of course with the U-boats, and also the E-boats and auxiliary cruisers, all of which would sink huge tonnages of enemy shipping not only in the North Sea and Atlantic but in the far-off waters of the Indian and Pacific oceans.

Ultimately the Kriegsmarine – without its own air arm due to Göring's intransigence and insistence that 'everything that flew' belonged to him, and with the *Luftwaffe* incapable of fully understanding the needs of the Kriegsmarine when it came to supporting naval operations – was somewhat crippled from the outset of war. The speed of U-boat development, though initially not a major problem, soon fell behind the rate of development of Allied anti-submarine warfare measures. With insufficient ships, insufficient submarines and no air arm, the Kriegsmarine was simply too small and unable to gain control of the seas, forcing it to avoid battle and concentrate on sinking enemy merchants – so-called 'tonnage warfare'.

Taking all things into consideration, Grossadmiral Raeder's comment on the state of the navy on the outbreak of war is probably understandable, if pessimistic:

As far as the Navy is concerned, obviously it is in no way adequately equipped for the great struggle with Great Britain by autumn 1939. It is true that in the short period since 1935, the date of the fleet treaty, it has built up a well-trained, suitably organized submarine arm, of which at the moment about 26 boats are capable of operations in the Atlantic; the submarine arm is still much too weak, however, to have any decisive effect on the war. The surface forces, moreover, are so inferior in number and strength to those of the British fleet that, even at full strength, they can do no more than show that they know how to die gallantly and thus are willing to create the foundations for a future reconstruction.

TOP LEFT The Kriegsmarine's auxiliary cruisers (of which *Michel* is shown here) would spread fear and suspicion that any innocent merchant could turn out to be a heavily armed enemy warship. Compared to the massive costs of building a major battleship, these converted merchantmen were highly cost-effective. (DUBM)

ABOVE Perhaps the greatest asset the Kriegsmarine possessed was its manpower. German naval training was first class and produced seamen of a high quality. Almost to the end, morale amongst men of the Kriegsmarine remained surprisingly high, despite the Kriegsmarine being the most conservative and least politically motivated branch of service. (Author's collection)

CHAPTER ONE

OPERATIONAL OVERVIEW

1939
The Polish Campaign

The very first military operation of World War II would fall to the Kriegsmarine to execute. This came on 1 September 1939 as the obsolete dreadnought *Schleswig-Holstein* took its place in history when it fired the opening shots of the war. The ship, under the command of Kapitän zur See Gustav Kleinkamp, was sent on what purported to be a ceremonial visit to Danzig to honour the anniversary of the sinking of the German cruiser *Magdeburg* in the Gulf of Finland in August 1914. The *Schleswig-Holstein* was then towed into a well-chosen firing position opposite the Polish fortress on the Westerplatte and an assault force of Marines landed.

At 0447hrs on 1 September, *Schleswig-Holstein* opened fire at the Westerplatte fortress at a range of just 500m. Due to treaty restrictions, the Poles were forbidden from fortifying

Battleship *Bismarck*, seen in Grimstadfjord just before leaving on its fateful first war cruise. The camouflage scheme on the hull side was painted over before it departed, leaving only a small false bow wave on the hull side just forward of turret 'Anton' and a similar feature at the stern. The photograph was taken from on board *Prinz Eugen*. (NHHC)

Germany's first important naval victory came soon after the start of the war when, on 14 October 1939, Kapitänleutnant Günther Prien infiltrated the Royal Navy's fleet anchorage at Scapa Flow and sank the battleship HMS *Royal Oak*. His U-boat then escaped unscathed to reach Germany safely, where he and his crew were given a heroes' welcome. (Author's collection)

OPPOSITE A major blow for Germany's naval pride came in October 1939 when the Panzerschiff *Admiral Graf Spee*, after some success in commerce raiding, was scuttled in the River Plate near Montevideo to avoid what its captain believed was overwhelming enemy forces awaiting it. The commander, Kapitän zur See Hans Langsdorff, committed suicide. (NHHC)

the peninsula, but in fact had reinforced the walls of many buildings. Despite continued bombardment, the Polish defenders would hang on tenaciously for fully seven days. Westerplatte was sometimes called the 'Polish Verdun' due to the horrendous pounding the tenacious defenders received during the first week of fighting.

Meanwhile, the remnants of the Polish fleet were smothered by German air attack. The Polish submarine flotilla dispersed into the Baltic to lay mines and hunt for coastal transports, while the only remaining major surface combatants – the destroyer *Wicher* and the minelayer *Gryf* – began mine-laying operations off the coast. The small Polish naval air detachment was wiped out in German air raids during the first few days of fighting. On 3 September 1939, the Kriegsmarine sent two destroyers towards the Polish naval facilities, but they were damaged by gunfire from the coastal guns at Hel and gunfire from *Wicher* and *Gryf*. The Luftwaffe responded with a highly effective air raid, which sank Poland's two remaining major warships. The smaller coastal minelayers escaped the air raids but would eventually be sunk on 16 September.

At 1030hrs on 8 September, with the Westerplatte fortress reduced to rubble, the Polish garrison surrendered. Incredibly, of the 200-man Westerplatte garrison, only 15 were killed. The Germans were so impressed by the gallantry of the Poles that the attackers stood to attention as the defenders marched out to surrender.

Commerce Raiding

Meanwhile, all available U-boats had been sent to sea a few days earlier, so as to be in position to attack targets of opportunity once hostilities were opened. The U-boats lost no time in making their presence felt. Within just four months, they had sunk over 570,000 tons of Allied shipping. This tally included an aircraft carrier, the 22,500-ton HMS *Courageous* on 17 September and the 29,000-ton battleship HMS *Royal Oak* on 14 October. On 28 December 1939, U-30 spotted the British battleship HMS *Barham* off the Outer Hebrides and damaged it with a torpedo, forcing it into six months of repairs. By any standard, this was a phenomenal achievement for the small number of U-boats in action, made even more impressive by Kapitänleutnant Günther Prien's astonishing feat not just of entering the British fleet anchorage at Scapa Flow undetected to sink HMS *Royal Oak*, but then of escaping totally unscathed. Prien and his entire crew were invited to Berlin to be awarded the Iron Cross, with Prien receiving the Knight's Cross of the Iron Cross, all in a blaze of publicity. Never had the standing of the navy and the U-boats in particular been higher.

The surface fleet fared less well. The pocket battleship *Admiral Graf Spee* had put to sea on 21 August 1939 with orders to begin commerce raiding when war broke out. During its short career, it succeeded in sinking or capturing nine enemy ships totalling around 500,000 tons, but was eventually located by a force of three British cruisers, HMS *Exeter*, HMS *Ajax* and HMS *Achilles*. Cornered in Montevideo after putting in to make repairs, the commander, Kapitän zur See Hans Langsdorff, elected to scuttle

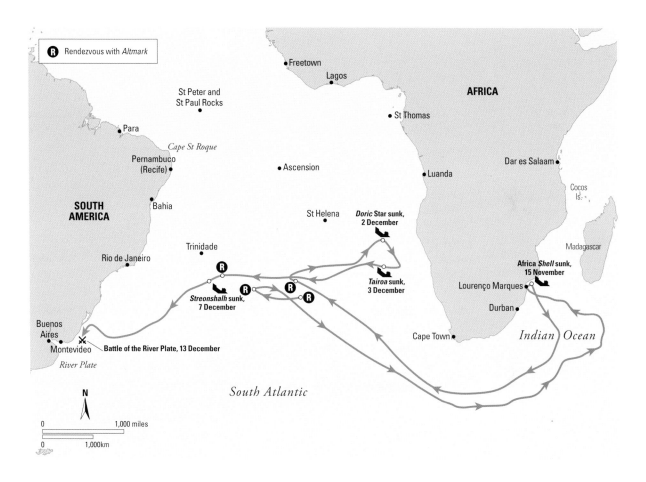

- **R** Rendezvous with *Altmark*

Freetown
Lagos
AFRICA
St Peter and
St Paul Rocks
St Thomas
Para
Cape St Roque
Pernambuco
(Recife)
Ascension
Luanda
Dar es Salaam
Cocos
Is.
SOUTH
AMERICA
Bahia
St Helena
Doric Star sunk,
2 December
Madagascar
Trinidade
Africa Shell sunk,
15 November
Rio de Janeiro
Tairoa sunk,
3 December
Lourenço Marques
Streonshalh sunk,
7 December
Durban
Buenos
Aires
Cape Town
Indian Ocean
Montevideo — **Battle of the River Plate, 13 December**
River Plate
South Atlantic

N

0 — 1,000 miles
0 — 1,000km

ABOVE The cruise of the *Graf Spee*, 26 October–13 December 1939.

the ship to prevent capture. Though it had achieved a respectable toll of enemy shipping and had tied up somewhere around 23 sorely needed enemy warships in the hunt for it, the loss of the *Admiral Graf Spee* was something the small Kriegsmarine could ill afford.

After the conclusion of the offensive in the East against Poland, a spell of relative calm ensued, though the U-boats continued their operations against Allied shipping. During this period, the so-called 'Phoney War', known to the Germans as the *Sitzkrieg*, U-boats accounted for some 238 enemy ships totalling over 800,000 tons between the beginning of October 1939 and the end of March 1940.

After some refurbishment work, in November 1939 *Scharnhorst* put to sea, in the company of its sister, the *Gneisenau*. Escorted by the light cruiser *Köln* and nine destroyers, the battleships set off to patrol the area between the Faroes and Iceland. This sortie was intended to draw out

elements of the British fleet and hopefully to ease some of the pressure on the *Admiral Graf Spee*, which was then being actively hunted by the British in the South Atlantic.

On 23 November 1939, the Germans intercepted the armed merchant cruiser HMS *Rawalpindi* and, in a brief and totally one-sided gun battle, sent the plucky auxiliary cruiser to the bottom, drawing out almost the entire Home Fleet in pursuit. The German squadron successfully evaded the British and returned to German waters without further incident.

1940
Denmark and Norway

Scharnhorst's next major sortie took place in April 1940 during Operation *Weserübung*, Germany's assault on Denmark and Norway. On 7 April 1940, in company with *Gneisenau* and the heavy cruiser *Admiral Hipper*, the *Scharnhorst* steamed north in clear weather conditions. At around 1430hrs, the German ships came under attack from RAF bombers.

Fortunately for *Scharnhorst*, the aircraft concentrated their attack on the *Admiral Hipper*, and equally fortunately for *Hipper* the quality of the British bomb-aiming was poor and no damage was done. *Hipper* was detached at 0915 hrs on 8 April and sent to provide cover for the German destroyer fleet, loaded with mountain troops en route to Narvik, that had reported engaging enemy warships. In the early hours of the next morning the German ships encountered the British battlecruiser HMS *Renown*, providing escort cover for a Royal Navy operation to lay mines in neutral Norwegian waters. *Renown* opened fire, directing its shots at the *Gneisenau*. It was *Scharnhorst*, however, that first returned fire. In extremely heavy seas, the elderly *Renown* scored the first hit, one of its 15in. shells smashing into *Gneisenau* and damaging the rangefinder/ gun director on the foretop. *Gneisenau* was hit twice more before *Renown* turned its fire on *Scharnhorst*. The superior speed of the German ships, however, allowed them to pull away gradually from their more powerfully armed adversary. Both the German sisters had suffered flood damage to their forward turret ('Anton') and were able to use only their single stern turret ('Caesar') to engage the enemy as they pulled away.

The German ships joined up with *Hipper* once again on 12 April and despite being spotted by RAF aircraft all three ships reached German waters unscathed.

The invasion of Norway, which began on 9 April, was launched ostensibly to 'protect' Norway from occupation by the British and to defend Norwegian neutrality. The real reason for *Weserübung* was to secure the port of Narvik, essential for exports of Swedish iron ore which could not cross the Baltic to Germany during the winter months due to the waters freezing over, and to give Germany ports with access into the Atlantic for the continuation of the U-boat war. This campaign saw the first use of elements of the Kriegsmarine's surface fleet. The heavy cruisers *Hipper*, *Blücher* and

OPPOSITE Naval operations off Denmark and Norway, 1940.

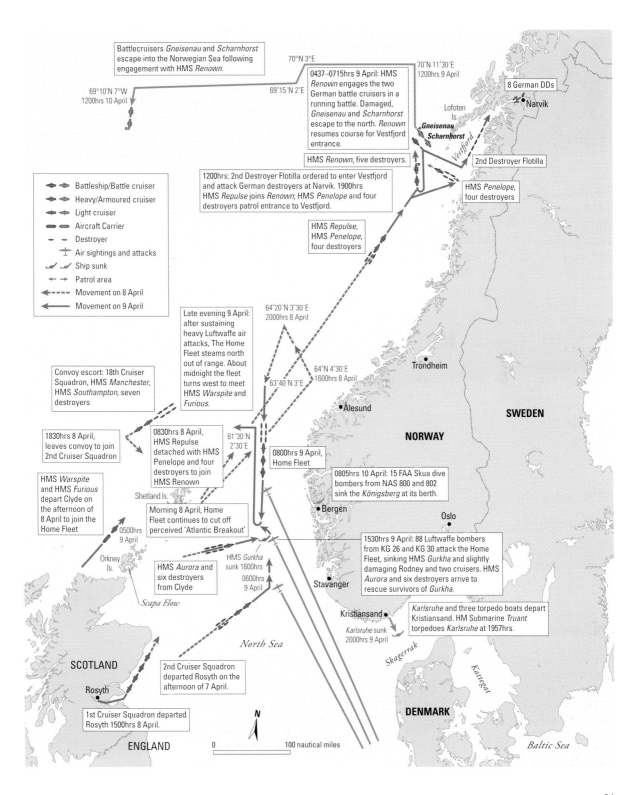

Battlecruisers *Gneisenau* and *Scharnhorst* escape into the Norwegian Sea following engagement with HMS *Renown*.

70°N 3'E

0437–0715hrs 9 April: HMS *Renown* engages the two German battle cruisers in a running battle. Damaged, *Gneisenau* and *Scharnhorst* escape to the north. *Renown* resumes course for Vestfjord entrance.

70°N 11'30'E
1200hrs 9 April

8 German DDs

Narvik

Lofoten Is.

Gneisenau
Scharnhorst

Vestfjord

69°10'N 7°W
1200hrs 10 April

69°15'N 2'E

2nd Destroyer Flotilla

HMS *Renown*, five destroyers.

HMS *Penelope*, four destroyers

1200hrs: 2nd Destroyer Flotilla ordered to enter Vestfjord and attack German destroyers at Narvik. 1900hrs HMS *Repulse* joins *Renown*; HMS *Penelope* and four destroyers patrol entrance to Vestfjord.

HMS *Repulse*,
HMS *Penelope*,
four destroyers

Battleship/Battle cruiser
Heavy/Armoured cruiser
Light cruiser
Aircraft Carrier
Destroyer
Air sightings and attacks
Ship sunk
Patrol area
Movement on 8 April
Movement on 9 April

Late evening 9 April: after sustaining heavy Luftwaffe air attacks, The Home Fleet steams north out of range. About midnight the fleet turns west to meet HMS *Warspite* and *Furious*.

64°20'N 3'30'E
2000hrs 8 April

64°N 4'30'E
1600hrs 8 April

63°40'N 3'E

Trondheim

Convoy escort: 18th Cruiser Squadron, HMS *Manchester*, HMS *Southampton*, seven destroyers

Ålesund

SWEDEN

NORWAY

1830hrs 8 April, leaves convoy to join 2nd Cruiser Squadron

0830hrs 8 April, HMS *Repulse* detached with HMS *Penelope* and four destroyers to join HMS *Renown*

61°30'N
2'30'E

0800hrs 9 April, Home Fleet

0805hrs 10 April: 15 FAA Skua dive bombers from NAS 800 and 802 sink the *Königsberg* at its berth.

HMS *Warspite* and HMS *Furious* depart Clyde on the afternoon of 8 April to join the Home Fleet

Shetland Is.

Morning 8 April, Home Fleet continues to cut off perceived 'Atlantic Breakout'

Bergen

Oslo

0500hrs 9 April

Orkney Is.

HMS *Aurora* and six destroyers from Clyde

Scapa Flow

HMS *Gurkha* sunk 1600hrs

0600hrs 9 April

Stavanger

1530hrs 9 April: 88 Luftwaffe bombers from KG 26 and KG 30 attack the Home Fleet, sinking HMS *Gurkha* and slightly damaging Rodney and two cruisers. HMS *Aurora* and six destroyers arrive to rescue survivors of *Gurkha*.

Kristiansand

Karlsruhe and three torpedo boats depart Kristiansand. HM Submarine *Truant* torpedoes *Karlsruhe* at 1957hrs.

Karlsruhe sunk 2000hrs 9 April

Skagerrak

SCOTLAND

North Sea

2nd Cruiser Squadron departed Rosyth on the afternoon of 7 April.

Rosyth

1st Cruiser Squadron departed Rosyth 1500hrs 8 April.

N

ENGLAND

0   100 nautical miles

Kattegat

DENMARK

Baltic Sea

Lützow, as well as the light cruisers *Köln*, *Königsberg* and *Emden*, supported by some lighter vessels, would sieze the ports of Trondheim, Bergen, Kristiansand and Oslo, whilst a force of minesweepers was tasked with the seizure of Egersund. Meanwhile, the main prize, the port of Narvik, would be seized by a force of ten destroyers, the bulk of the destroyer fleet, carrying a large force of *Gebirgsjäger* (mountain troops). The campaign, though ultimately successful in terms of the occupation of Norway and the gaining of all targets, would cost the surface fleet dearly.

On 9 May, the force tasked with the seizure of Oslo, comprising *Blücher*, *Lützow* and *Emden*, accompanied by smaller support vessels, was led by *Blücher* into Drøbak Sound at the opening of Oslofjord. Here the heavy cruisers came under fire from Oscarsborg Fortress. The heavy guns of the fortress, ironically German-made 28cm calibre weapons, almost immediately scored direct hits, one of which exploded in one of *Blücher*'s magazines causing catastrophic damage. Meanwhile, *Blücher*'s return fire was almost totally ineffective. The German warship's fate was finally sealed when it was hit amidships by torpedoes, something the Germans had not realized the fortress possessed. At 0622hrs the German cruiser sank, taking up to 800 of the crew with it.

As the rest of the force neared, the commander of *Lützow*, seeing the conflagration, assumed *Blücher* had run into a minefield and ordered the remainder of the force to retreat.

Further north, at Narvik, the destroyer force successfully entered Ofotfjord and landed their Gebirgsjäger. On the following day, however, a force of five British H-class destroyers caught the Germans by surprise and, in the attack, sank two of the German destroyers and heavily damaged a third. As German ships manoeuvred in the narrow fjord, two more ran aground. Half the German force had been either destroyed or rendered temporarily out of action. Two British destroyers were sunk.

ABOVE The heavy cruiser *Blücher*, ablaze and about to sink after being pounded by Norwegian shore batteries and hit with torpedoes in Drøbak Sound. To lose a brand new modern heavy cruiser at such an early stage of the war was a heavy blow to the Kriegsmarine. (Riksarkivet/Norwegian National Archives)

RIGHT German destroyers moored at Narvik, the site of two naval battles which would see half of the German destroyer fleet sunk. Though they would be replaced by more modern and better armed units, to lose so many in one campaign was a serious blow. (NHHC)

Determined to eliminate the German force, the Royal Navy returned on 13 April, this time with a battleship, HMS *Warspite*, supported by nine destroyers. During the early part of this attack a German destroyer was sunk and another scuttled after running out of ammunition. Two, which had been giving supporting fire whilst tied up in port, were destroyed by enemy fire. The remaining destroyers withdrew into Rombaksfjord which branches off the main Ofotfjord and there, low on fuel and ammunition, were scuttled.

Meanwhile, *Admiral Hipper*, en route to land a contingent of *Gebirgsjäger* at Trondheim, was diverted to locate the destroyer *Bernd von Arnim* which had encountered and engaged the British destroyer HMS *Glowworm*. The arrival of the heavier German vessel sealed the British destroyer's fate. However, pounded by the cruiser's 20cm guns and with its steering out of action, HMS *Glowworm* rammed the German cruiser, causing significant damage.

The light cruiser *Königsberg* was allocated to the forces designated to transport over 600 army soldiers along with some shore-based naval artillerymen tasked with the capture of Bergen. On 8 April, the cruiser sailed from Wilhelmshaven along with *Köln* and a number of smaller vessels. In the early hours of 9 April, it successfully transferred the first group of passengers to a number of E-boats and small launches provided by the bigger ships for shuttling to the shore. Having disembarked part of its contingent of passengers, the cruiser then attempted to run for the port itself at speed, hoping to avoid the fire of Norwegian shore batteries. Luck was not on its side, however, and when passing through Byfjord on the approach to Bergen it was fired on by the 21cm guns of the Norwegian battery at Kvarven. The first shot was a near miss. The second was a direct hit on its starboard bow.

It took further hits on its forecastle and suffered significant damage, with serious flooding and fire damage. *Königsberg* finally ended up drifting, its power out, and had to drop anchor. Eventually return fire from the heavy artillery of *Königsberg* and its sister *Köln*, supported by Luftwaffe bombers and the efforts of army troops on shore, silenced the shore batteries.

Kapitän zur See Alfred Schulze-Hinrichs, commander of the destroyer *Erich Koellner*, scuttled after being damaged beyond repair during the battle for Narvik. Note the *Narvikschild* on his sleeve. Schulze-Hinrichs went on to become a staff officer and ultimately commander of the naval war academy in Berlin. He survived the war and also served in the West German Bundesmarine. (Author's collection)

In need of repairs before it could be considered capable of putting to sea again, *Königsberg* was moored at the quay in such a position as to allow its full broadside to cover the approaches to the harbour in case of any attempt by the British to eject the German invasion force. Here, on 10 April, the Germans were taken completely by surprise by an air attack, and had no opportunity to put up an effective flak defence. *Königsberg* was damaged by at least five 100lb bombs, one of which exploded between the quay and the ship's side, and another which passed through the decks, exiting and exploding in the water alongside, tearing a huge hole in the hull and killing several crew members. Three direct hits were received, one of which destroyed the auxiliary boiler room and two near misses in the water to its stern caused another huge rent in the hull.

It was clear that there was no chance of saving it and the order was given to abandon ship. *Königsberg* was rolling over slowly, however, and the crew had plenty of time to evacuate, before it finally rolled over and sank just under three hours after the attack began.

The fighting spirit of the Kriegsmarine may not have been in doubt, but nevertheless Operation *Weserübung*, though ultimately successful, had taken a heavy toll. The navy had lost one of its new heavy cruisers with another damaged, one of its light cruisers and all of the destroyers assigned to the Narvik operation, representing fully half of the navy's entire destroyer fleet.

Meanwhile, as the Gebirgsjäger struggled to maintain their grasp on Narvik, on 9 May the German Army and Luftwaffe had launched *Fall Gelb*, the attack on France and the Low Countries. In the short-lived campaign, which was concluded by an armistice which came into effect on 25 May, the Germans siezed France, Belgium, Luxembourg and Holland in a victory which gifted the Kriegsmarine a range of strategically important ports with direct access to the Atlantic and ideal launch points for attacks on Allied shipping.

In June, *Gneisenau* and *Scharnhorst* were despatched to Norway once again together with *Admiral Hipper*, in a sortie designed to relieve the Allied pressure on German troops fighting in Norway, and especially the beleaguered mountain troops at Narvik. In fact, the Allies had already begun to withdraw from Norway and the German squadron steamed right into the midst of one small convoy of British ships comprising a troopship, a tanker and a corvette, and sank all three. At this point, *Hipper* withdrew because of a fuel shortage, leaving *Scharnhorst* and *Gneisenau* to continue. Later that same day, the two German warships encountered the aircraft carrier *Glorious*, escorted by the destroyers *Acasta* and *Ardent*. Both German ships opened fire on the carrier which was unable to launch any of its own aircraft. At 1822hrs, just 96 minutes after sighting the enemy ships, *Ardent*, badly battered by the 10.5cm secondary armament of the German ships, capsized and sank. *Scharnhorst* itself was struck on its starboard side just by turret 'Caesar', by a torpedo from *Acasta*, causing substantial flooding. Forty-six minutes later, *Glorious* was sent to the bottom and the uneven struggle finally came to an end at 1917hrs when *Acasta* was sunk.

The German ships returned to Trondheim on 9 June and repairs on *Scharnhorst* were immediately commenced. After a stay of 11 days in the Norwegian port, *Scharnhorst* set sail for Germany, only to come under attack by British torpedo bombers, but no hits on the battleship were achieved and it reached Kiel safely on 23 June. The following several months were spent on repairing and refitting the ship and carrying out extensive crew training and sea trials.

Following the action with its sister, *Gneisenau* put briefly into Trondheim; but shortly after leaving, on 20 June, was torpedoed by the British submarine HMS *Clyde*. Suffering a hit on the starboard bow, it was forced to return to Trondheim for temporary repairs.

On 26 July, *Gneisenau* set sail for home, with a sizeable escort, only to find itself the target of yet another torpedoing attempt, this time by HMS *Thames*. Fortunately for *Gneisenau*, the torpedoes missed, but regrettably for the escorts, the torpedo boat *Luchs* was hit and sank. *Gneisenau* reached Kiel safely on 30 July, and spent the remainder of the year undergoing repairs. On 28 December, it set sail, once again with *Scharnhorst*, on a raiding sortie but ran into seriously bad weather and suffered significant storm damage, forcing their return to port.

Commerce Raiding

The German capital ships took no further significant part in the war for the remainder of 1940, although the pocket battleship *Admiral Scheer* would carry out an audacious sortie into the South Atlantic and Indian Ocean, leaving port on 31 October and, in the course of a 46,000-mile war cruise, encountering and sinking 17 enemy ships totalling 113,000 tons in addition to the armed merchant cruiser *Jervis Bay*, before returning unscathed to Wilhelmshaven on 1 April 1941. Meanwhile, the *U-Bootwaffe* continued to rack up impressive scores of enemy tonnage sunk. Between April and December the U-boats sank 377 ships totalling 2,015,143 tons and damaged many others. This total included warships as well as merchants. During this phase of the war, many of the top U-boat aces, like Günther Prien, Joachim Schepke, Otto Kretschmer and Erich Topp began to make their reputations as deadly ship killers. It was a period known to the U-boat men as 'the Happy Time'.

The year 1940 also saw the Kriegsmarine unleash a new weapon on Allied shipping, the *Hilfskreuzer*, or auxiliary cruisers. These ships were converted merchantmen, heavily armed with guns, torpedoes and even aircraft. Seven were put to sea during that year: *Orion, Atlantis, Widder, Thor, Pinguin, Komet* and *Kormoran*. Most spent a year or more at sea and between them sank over 100 ships totalling almost half a million tons.

After the campaign in the West, the Kriegsmarine lost no time in establishing strongly defended bases in French, Belgian and Dutch ports, and the U-boats which would be based in France were soon joined by an equally deadly weapon, the *S-Boote* (known to the Allies as the E-boats), with 1.Schnellbootflottille in Cherbourg,

March 1941 was a difficult month for the U-boats with the loss of three top aces. Kapitänleutnant Otto Kretschmer, shown here, was captured when his boat U-99 was sunk, whilst Günther Prien and Joachim Schepke were killed in action. Kretschmer sat out the rest of the war in a POW camp in Canada. (DUBM)

25

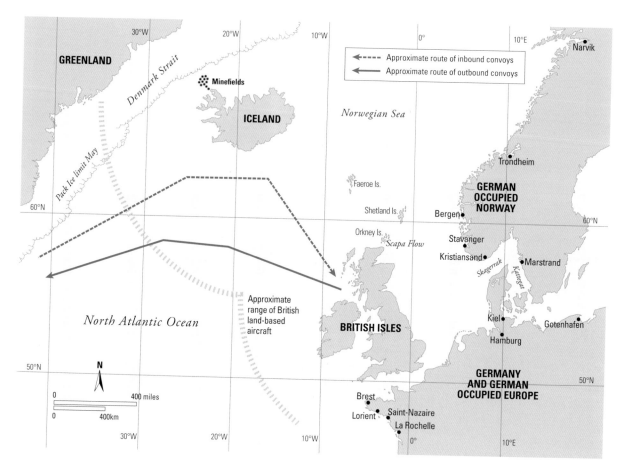

North Atlantic convoy
routes, 1941.

2.Schnellbootflottille in Ostend and 3.Schnellbootflottille in Rotterdam. These boats now had the advantage of operating from Channel ports, giving them a greater operating range than previously. They were in constant action against coastal shipping as well as British motor torpedo boats and other warships.

1941

On 22 January 1941, *Scharnhorst* put to sea, once again in the company of its sister, *Gneisenau*, the two ships successfully breaking through into the Atlantic via the Denmark Strait in early February. Due to the typically heavy seas experienced in the Atlantic at this time of year, both ships suffered constantly from breakdowns caused by them shipping large amounts of water, the Atlantic bows they had both had retrofitted providing little or no improvement to their seaworthiness. The German ships had been specifically ordered not to seek engagement with superior enemy forces and in accordance with these orders had turned away from convoys that were known to be escorted by capital ships. Nevertheless, *Scharnhorst* succeeded in sinking a total of eight enemy ships, accounting for some 48,200 tons, finally putting into the French port of Brest on 22 March 1941.

Unfortunately, while waiting to enter dry dock for an overhaul of its engines, *Gneisenau* was hit by a torpedo launched by a British aircraft and suffered serious damage. No sooner had it been taken into dry dock than it was attacked once again by enemy aircraft and suffered four bomb hits, one of which failed to explode. All non-essential crew were thereafter removed and housed in barracks on shore. Further repairs were necessitated, resulting in *Gneisenau* remaining out of action until January 1942.

The heavy cruiser *Admiral Hipper* departed port on 1 February 1941, intent on raiding Allied shipping lines. On 11 February, it encountered a convoy, SL 64, comprising 19 ships. Drawing alongside the convoy, it opened fire using its main and secondary armament as well as torpedoes. The total number of ships sunk is disputed but was at least nine, and possibly up to 14 may have been destroyed. It returned to Brest unharmed, on 15 February.

Battle of the Denmark Strait

With *Scharnhorst* and *Gneisenau* temporarily out of the picture, attention turned to *Bismarck*. In May 1941, it had been declared ready for combat service. Previously, plans had been made by the naval high command to put together a powerful force consisting of the battleships *Bismarck*, *Tirpitz*, *Scharnhorst* and *Gneisenau*. As *Scharnhorst* and *Gneisenau* had already carried out a successful raid against British shipping, one can only imagine the havoc that could have been created, and the sheer amount of Royal Navy resources that would have been required to hunt down this German force. Unfortunately for the Kriegsmarine, *Tirpitz* was not yet ready for combat service and *Scharnhorst* was undergoing an extensive overhaul of its engines. It was thus decided that *Bismarck* would sortie along with *Gneisenau* and the heavy cruiser *Prinz Eugen*. *Bismarck*'s task would be to engage any warships escorting convoys that might be intercepted, and draw them off to allow the consorts to attack the merchantmen.

The plans were changed once again, however, when *Gneisenau* was damaged by the aforementioned RAF bombing raid on the port of Brest, where it was then docked. Thus, the forthcoming sortie, codenamed *Rheinübung*, was to be carried out only by *Bismarck* and *Prinz Eugen*. Under the command of Admiral Günther Lütjens, who flew his flag on *Bismarck*, the German force would attempt to take the northern route, across the North Sea and down through the Denmark Strait into the Atlantic, undetected if possible, and then prey on convoys of merchant ships bringing essential supplies across the Atlantic from Nova Scotia in Canada.

On 25 April 1941, *Bismarck* and *Prinz Eugen* were ordered to sail, escorted by a number of destroyers. Yet more delays to the fateful mission were experienced after

Battleship *Bismarck*, seen in Grimstadfjord just before leaving on its fateful first war cruise. The camouflage scheme on the hull side was painted over before it departed, leaving only a small false bow wave on the hull side just forward of turrent 'Anton' and a similar feature at the stern. The photograph was taken from on board *Prinz Eugen*. (NHHC)

Prinz Eugen was damaged by an exploding mine. Although there was some hope that the mission might now be delayed until *Scharnhorst* and *Tirpitz* were ready for action, the Oberbefehlshaber der Kriegsmarine, Grossadmiral Raeder, decided that the mission must proceed as soon as *Prinz Eugen* was once again ready for action.

Bismarck sailed from Gotenhafen on 18 May, arriving at Grimstadfjord near Bergen in Norway where it dropped anchor. At around the same time, *Prinz Eugen* had arrived in Norway, anchoring at Kalvanes Bay, a little further north, where it topped up its fuel bunkers.

Unfortunately for the Germans, the arrival of the German ships in Norway was immediately reported to the British by members of the Norwegian underground movement. Photographs subsequently taken by RAF photo-reconnaissance aircraft confirmed *Bismarck*'s identity.

On 21 May, *Bismarck* set sail and rendezvoused with *Prinz Eugen* at Kalvanes Bay. Escorted by destroyers, the two sailed northwards. At the latitude of Trondheim the destroyer screen departed, leaving *Bismarck* and *Prinz Eugen* to continue steaming northwards, before turning west and skirting around the north of Iceland. Late on 23 May the German ships began negotiating the minefields that obstructed the Denmark Strait between the west coast of Iceland and the eastern limit of the ice fields off Greenland's east coast. It was here, on the evening of the 23rd, that contact was made with the British heavy cruiser *Suffolk*. Having spotted the German ships, *Suffolk* began to track them and was joined shortly afterwards by its sister, the *Norfolk*, alerted by signals from *Suffolk*. *Bismarck* opened fire, forcing the British cruisers to withdraw. After a brief attempt to pursuer its stalkers, *Bismarck* resumed its course.

Just before 0600hrs on the following morning, the mastheads of enemy ships were spotted on *Bismarck*'s port beam. These were the battlecruiser *Hood* and the battleship *Prince of Wales*. The British opened fire almost immediately. Two minutes later, the German ships responded. Both concentrated their fire upon *Hood*, whilst the British battlecruiser, confused by the similarity in design of the German ships, fired at *Prinz Eugen*. The *Prince of Wales* correctly judged the identity of each of the German ships and fired on *Bismarck*. Within two minutes of opening fire, *Bismarck*'s observers noted a massive fire on *Hood* just by the aft mast caused by hits from *Prinz Eugen*. Just four minutes after this, a salvo from *Bismarck* penetrated *Hood*'s decks and ignited its magazine. In a massive explosion, the British battlecruiser broke its back. Within minutes the two halves of the 48,000-ton warship had sunk, leaving but three survivors from a crew of 1,421. *Prince of Wales* withdrew under cover of a smokescreen.

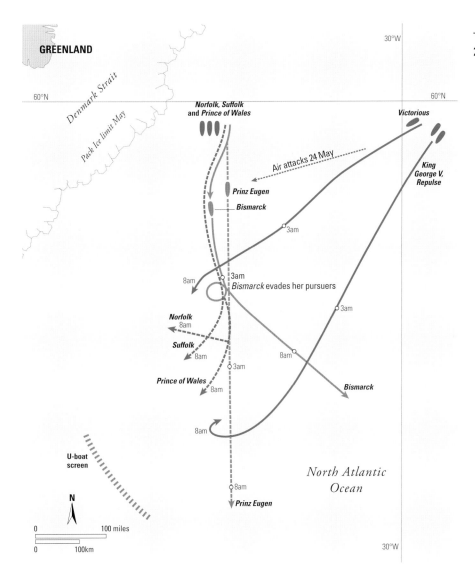

The Denmark Strait,
24–25 May 1941.

One shell from *Prince of Wales* had ripped a hole right through *Bismarck* from port to starboard, allowing over 2,000 tons of water to be shipped. Another hit caused significant flooding in one of the boiler rooms. More significantly, *Bismarck* was now suffering from an oil leak, which would make it much easier for the enemy to find and track it.

Admiral Lütjens at this time decided that *Bismarck* would make for St Nazaire whilst *Prinz Eugen* continued into the Atlantic to hunt enemy merchant ships. Accordingly, at just after 1800hrs on 24 May, *Bismarck* turned to starboard, opening fire on the British ships still shadowing it, whilst *Prinz Eugen* turned to port and into the covering curtain of a rain squall, allowing its escape.

The sinking of the *Bismarck*, 27 May 1941.

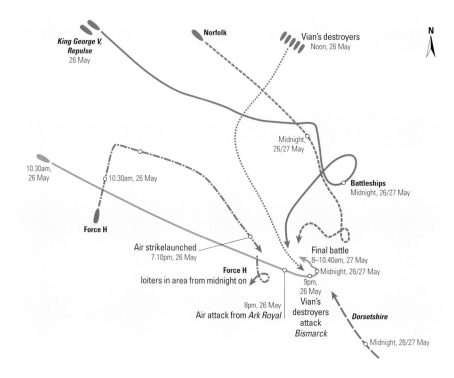

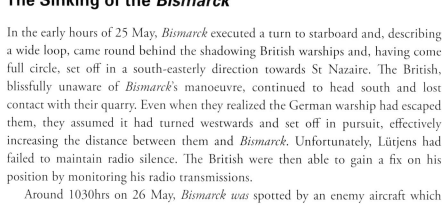

At around 2330hrs, several Swordfish, torpedo-carrying biplanes, from the aircraft carrier HMS *Victorious* appeared. One torpedo struck *Bismarck* on its starboard side, though it appeared to have struck the armoured belt and did little damage.

The British, now eager to avenge the loss of *Hood*, reassigned every available heavy unit to the pursuit of the German battleship. Before the day was out, a total of six battleships and battlecruisers, two aircraft carriers, 13 cruisers and 21 destroyers were involved in the hunt for *Bismarck*.

The Sinking of the *Bismarck*

In the early hours of 25 May, *Bismarck* executed a turn to starboard and, describing a wide loop, came round behind the shadowing British warships and, having come full circle, set off in a south-easterly direction towards St Nazaire. The British, blissfully unaware of *Bismarck*'s manoeuvre, continued to head south and lost contact with their quarry. Even when they realized the German warship had escaped them, they assumed it had turned westwards and set off in pursuit, effectively increasing the distance between them and *Bismarck*. Unfortunately, Lütjens had failed to maintain radio silence. The British were then able to gain a fix on his position by monitoring his radio transmissions.

Around 1030hrs on 26 May, *Bismarck was* spotted by an enemy aircraft which immediately signalled the battleship's position. *Bismarck* had been rediscovered.

Around ten hours later, 15 Swordfish from HMS *Ark Royal* appeared over *Bismarck*. A total of three torpedoes are believed to have hit the German battleship despite its violent manoeuvring. The first two hits were not fatal, but the third damaged and jammed *Bismarck*'s rudder, sending it into a permanent turn to starboard.

Bismarck's alarm bells began ringing just after 0830hrs on the morning of 27 May as the battleships *Rodney* and *King George V* appeared off its port bow. A few minutes later, *Rodney* opened fire, closely followed by *King George V*. *Bismarck* replied less than two minutes later.

The first hits were scored on *Bismarck* just after 0900hrs as the British battleships swiftly began closing the range. Within 20 minutes, the two forward turrets on the heavily outgunned *Bismarck* were out of action and the forward fire control position blown away. By just after 0930hrs, turrets 'Caesar' and 'Dora', and their fire control position, were also put out of action.

Though listing heavily, *Bismarck*'s hull was still intact and there was no immediate danger of sinking. The upperworks, however, had been devastated by fire from the massive guns of *Rodney* and *King George V*, and it was clearly incapable of offering further resistance. Reluctantly, the order was given for *Bismarck* to be scuttled. At 1039hrs, *Bismarck*, listing so much it was virtually on its side and down by the stern, finally rolled over and sank. Only 110 men from *Bismarck*'s crew of 2,092 were saved.

E-boats and U-boats

In the meantime, E-boats continued to menace shipping around British coastal waters occasionally operating in large numbers. One attack on shipping in March 1941 saw a force of 17 E-boats attack a convoy, sinking seven ships. Successes were sporadic, however, though mines laid by E-boats posed a constant menace.

Though the U-boats continued to exact a heavy toll on Allied shipping during 1941, it was not without loss to themselves and in March alone, three of the top aces were eliminated. Prien and Schepke were killed, and Kretschmer captured.

Not all was going the way of the Allies, however, as having already lost two battleships, HMS *Royal Oak* and HMS *Hood*, the Royal Navy suffered another blow to morale on 14 November when U-81 under Kapitänleutnant Friedrich Guggenberger torpedoed and sank the aircraft carrier HMS *Ark Royal*, gaining some degree of revenge for the loss of *Bismarck* since aircraft from *Ark Royal* had been largely responsible for its loss.

Then, on 25 November, U-331 under the command of Kapitänleutnant Hans-Diedrich von Tiesenhausen torpedoed and sank the battleship HMS *Barham* in the Mediterranean.

The year 1941 saw 461 Allied ships sunk, totalling over 2,200,000 tons. On 11 December, Hitler made the fateful decision to declare war on the USA. This would lead, for the *U-Bootwaffe*, to a second 'Happy Time' as U-boats were unleashed against shipping off the US coast.

On 25 November 1941, Kapitänleutnant Hans-Diedrich von Tiesenhausen struck another serious blow against the Royal Navy when he torpedoed and sank the battleship HMS *Barham* in the Mediterranean, earning promotion and the award of the Knight's Cross in the process. (DUBM)

1942
The Channel Dash

The danger of air attacks on the Kriegsmarine heavy units at Brest forced the Germans to consider returning them to safer ports in German waters. Only two routes were available: northwards around the west coast of Great Britain and then down through the North Sea, or by a fast run along the Channel coast and through the Dover Strait. The second and preferred option, though it would bring the ships dangerously close to British shores, would also allow the Luftwaffe to provide strong air cover. The first option would have reduced the level of German air cover and risked the German ships encountering heavy elements of the British Home Fleet.

Accordingly, on 11 February, *Scharnhorst*, along with *Gneisenau* and the Hipper-class heavy cruiser *Prinz Eugen*, heavily escorted by destroyers, E-boats and minesweepers, set sail, initially meeting no opposition from the enemy. It was not until after the German flotilla had passed Calais that the first British reaction came. Although determined attacks were made by British destroyers and motor torpedo boats, supported by torpedo bombers, the British reaction had been too late. A Royal Navy submarine tasked with monitoring movements from Brest had withdrawn to charge its batteries and had missed the departure of the German ships. By the time the British were alerted, the flotilla had reached the area in which they could be supported by a powerful presence from the Luftwaffe. The incident, known to the Germans as Operation *Cerberus* and to the wider world as the 'Channel Dash', was not without its problems for the Germans, however, as both *Gneisenau* and *Scharnhorst* struck mines.

Finally, around midday on 13 February, *Scharnhorst* arrived in Wilhelmshaven and was moved straight into dry dock for damage inspection. As well as damage to the hull, several turrets had been dislodged from their bearings and the foundations for the main engines damaged. *Scharnhorst* was then moved to Kiel where repairs were carried out, and the battleship spent the remainder of the year in training exercises and sea trials.

On 11 February 1942, the two sister ships *Scharnhorst* and *Gneisenau*, along with *Prinz Eugen* and numerous smaller ships, took part in what became known as the 'Channel Dash', and successfully avoided being bottled up in the French port of Brest, safely reaching Germany. (NHHC)

In *Gneisenau*'s case, the mine damage was slight and it was able to continue on into Brunsbüttel harbour along with *Prinz Eugen*.

On 13 February, *Gneisenau* moved to Kiel where it underwent repairs at the Deutsche Werke yard. Contrary to regulations, *Gneisenau* was taken into dry dock before its ammunition stocks were unloaded. On the night of 26 February, during a heavy air raid, one solitary bomb hit the forecastle and exploded after penetrating the armoured deck. Munitions stored in turret 'Anton' were detonated and the resultant explosion blew the massive turret from its bearings and over 100 crewmen were killed.

On 20 February, *Prinz Eugen* and *Admiral Scheer* were ordered to Trondheim from Brunsbüttel. Three days later *Prinz Eugen* was torpedoed by the British submarine HMS *Trident*, having its rudder blown off and stern severely damaged. After emergency repairs in Norway, it was forced to return to Kiel where repairs took several months. It took no further part in any major actions that year.

The spring of 1942 saw further attempts to destroy enemy shipping using *Hilfskreuzer*. *Michel* put to sea in March followed by *Stier* in May. Between them they sank 18 ships totalling over 130,000 tons but were themselves both destroyed.

Operation *Rösselsprung*

Another chance for the heavy units to make an impact on the course of the war came in mid-1942. A force consisting of *Tirpitz*, *Admiral Hipper* and six destroyers from Trondheim, and *Lützow*, *Admiral Scheer* and six destroyers from Narvik, was ordered to intercept and destroy the large convoy PQ 17, heading from Hvalfjord in Iceland to Arkhangelsk in the Soviet Union. Codenamed Operation *Rösselsprung* the undertaking faced problems from the start. On the way to the rendezvous with the Trondheim group, *Lützow* ran aground in thick fog in the Tjeldsund. Three of the destroyers suffered the same fate. *Scheer* and the remaining destroyers eventually joined *Tirpitz* and *Hipper* to continue the operation.

The battlegroup finally set off on 5 July after German intelligence had detected that the convoy had scattered, but with orders to avoid contact with any British warships. Just six hours later, after the German vessels had been spotted by a British aircraft, Grossadmiral Raeder ordered them to return to port fearing they were being lured into a trap by the British. It would be left to the U-boats, and aircraft of the Luftwaffe, to attack PQ 17. This they did with great success, sinking 23 merchantmen from a total of 34 in the convoy, representing over 140,000 tons of shipping to say nothing of the 130,000 tons of essential war supplies they carried. Though *Rösselsprung* had technically been a success, it was a disaster for the reputation of the surface fleet.

Throughout 1942, E-boats had engaged in regular battles with British MTBs in the Channel, during both mine-laying and anti-convoy operations. Though nowhere near as effective as the U-boats, they did achieve modest successes. A further large-scale attack by 17 E-boats in December saw five ships from a coastal convoy sunk.

From 1940 onwards E-boats began operating out of ports in France, Belgium and the Netherlands, and by 1942 were causing significant problems for coastal shipping. A number of these very useful vessels were used by the Norwegian and Danish navies after the war. (DUBM)

Battle of the Barents Sea

The final attempt by surface units to effect a successful strike against British shipping took place in December 1942. On 31 December, *Admiral Hipper* together with *Lützow*, and each with the support of three destroyers, set out to attack Allied convoy JW 51B in an operation codenamed *Regenbogen*, and at around 0720hrs, the German force made contact with the convoy. *Admiral Hipper*, and the destroyers *Friedrich Eckoldt*, *Richard Beitzen* and *Z24*, were to the north of the convoy, faced by an escort of five British destroyers. *Lützow* and its three destroyer escorts lay further to the south. At around 0930hrs, German destroyers opened fire on the British escorts, but without scoring any hits. Ten minutes later, *Admiral Hipper* engaged with its main and heavy-flak armament, again without scoring any significant hits.

For the next two hours, the smallest and most weakly armed of the British destroyers, *Obedient* and *Obdurate*, with only 4in. guns as their main armament, shepherded their merchant charges, protecting them against attack from the German destroyers whilst the three larger escorts, *Achates*, *Onslow* and *Orwell*, fended off the German cruiser. The heavy firepower of *Admiral Hipper*'s 20.3cm guns was too much for the enemy destroyers, however, and at around 1018hrs, a number of direct hits on *Onslow* left it burning fiercely. Shortly thereafter, *Admiral Hipper* ran into the diminutive minesweeper *Bramble*, which it quickly engaged and reduced to a blazing hulk. It was left to two of the German destroyers, *Friedrich Eckoldt* and *Richard Beitzen*, to sink the unfortunate *Bramble*.

Unbeknown to the Germans, however, two British cruisers, the *Sheffield* and the *Jamaica*, were rapidly approaching from the north, shielded by the appalling weather. Meanwhile, *Admiral Hipper* had caught up with the destroyer *Achates*, pulverising it with numerous direct hits from its main armament. *Achates* was left a blazing wreck. The remaining British destroyers now turned away from the convoy to offer assistance to *Achates*. Forced to turn to the north to avoid the threat of torpedoes from the enemy destroyers, *Admiral Hipper* sailed directly into the path of *Jamaica* and *Sheffield*, and came under heavy fire. Heeling over as it turned sharply to port, the thinly armoured lower hull was exposed and it took a direct hit which penetrated below the waterline causing extensive flooding. A mixture of having been taken by surprise, severe icing of its rangefinder equipment and smoke from the onboard fires caused by several direct hits from enemy 6in. shells all conspired to prevent *Admiral Hipper* from loosing off more than a few ineffectual salvoes at the British warships as it retired westwards at speed, away from the enemy. In view of the serious damage to *Admiral Hipper*, Kummetz ordered the action broken off, as his orders were to not risk his ship.

Even more unfortunate were the destroyers *Richard Beitzen* and *Friedrich Eckoldt*, which now strayed into the path of the British cruisers. A fatal error in identification led to *Friedrich Eckoldt* believing that the British cruisers were in fact German ships, and by the time it realized the error it was too late. The German ship was annihilated

Admiral Hipper is seen here leaving its base in Norway escorted by destroyers. In December 1942 it took part in an attack on convoy JW 51B which resulted in the loss of a destroyer and damage to *Hipper,* with not a single merchantman sunk. The shambolic operation destroyed what little faith Hitler still had in his surface fleet. (NHHC)

by the overwhelming firepower of the enemy at virtually point-blank range, and blew up and sank with all hands.

Lützow had closed with the convoy by then, but was suffering the same problems with icing to its rangefinder equipment that had dogged *Admiral Hipper*. It opened fire briefly on the convoy but did no significant damage before being ordered by the flagship to break off the action and return to base. The German force returned to its anchorage in Altafjord on 1 January 1943.

Recriminations, with far-reaching consequences, began almost immediately. Unfortunately, a signal from a U-boat attempting to monitor the action was misinterpreted, and the high command were led to believe that a victory had been gained. As the truth began to unfold, it was realized that a destroyer had been lost and the *Admiral Hipper* crippled, but no single enemy merchantman had been sunk. To cap the German misery, British accounts of the action bragged of having seen off a German force much more powerful than the escorting vessels. Hitler flew into a rage, insisting that the navy was useless and ordered that all its heavy units be scrapped and their guns transferred for use on land. The protests of Grossadmiral Raeder, were to no avail, and growing animosity between Raeder and Hitler led the former to offer his resignation, which Hitler accepted. His successor was the *Führer der Unterseeboote*, Karl Dönitz. Thankfully for the Kriegsmarine, the new *Grossadmiral* did manage to tone down Hitler's orders somewhat, and the scrapping order was rescinded, though several warships were to be taken out of active service. Hitler, however, never again put his faith in the heavy units of the Kriegsmarine.

On its return to Altafjord, emergency repairs were carried out on *Admiral Hipper* allowing it to proceed safely to Bogen Bay in late January 1943.

Although the surface fleet had not covered itself with glory, the U-boats had been wreaking havoc on Allied shipping during the second 'Happy Time' and, through the course of 1942, had sunk 1,155 enemy ships totalling almost 6 million tons. Hitler would come more and more to depend on Dönitz and the *U-Bootwaffe* to fight the war at sea.

1943

Scharnhorst's final successful sortie began on 6 September 1943 when, in company with *Tirpitz* and nine destroyers, it took part in the bombardment of Allied installations on Spitzbergen. *Scharnhorst* had until then been a highly popular ship with its crew. Through four years of war, it had been involved in a few scrapes with the enemy, but had always come safely through and was considered a 'lucky' ship. Its luck was about to run out.

Battle of the North Cape

On 22 December 1943, German aircraft reported a convoy of enemy merchantmen making its way towards Murmansk. With *Tirpitz* temporarily disabled, *Scharnhorst* was the only major unit available and, having raised steam, set sail on 25 December in consort with five destroyers.

Unknown to the Germans, two escort groups of British warships, including the battleship *Duke of York*, heavy cruiser *Norfolk*, the light cruisers *Belfast*, *Jamaica* and *Sheffield*, as well as a number of destroyers, were providing cover for convoys in this area.

Due to extremely heavy seas, the lighter vessels were released to return to port, thus leaving the *Scharnhorst* alone and unescorted. Weather conditions were appalling, and it was the British with their superior radar who spotted the enemy first. *Scharnhorst* was engaged by the group comprising *Norfolk*, *Belfast* and *Sheffield* and quickly suffered a number of hits, destroying the foretop radar. *Scharnhorst* then turned and headed south towards Norway.

At just after 1615hrs on 26 December, *Scharnhorst* was detected on *Duke of York*'s radar. At 1648hrs, the British battleship opened fire, and scored a hit on *Scharnhorst*'s turret 'Anton'. A few moments later the British cruisers joined the action and began scoring hits on the German battleship.

One of the last photographs taken of *Scharnhorst*. Seen here in Altafjord in Norway, it would be sunk during the Battle of the North Cape after enduring a severe pounding from the 14in. guns of the battleship HMS *Duke of York* on 26 December 1943. (NHHC)

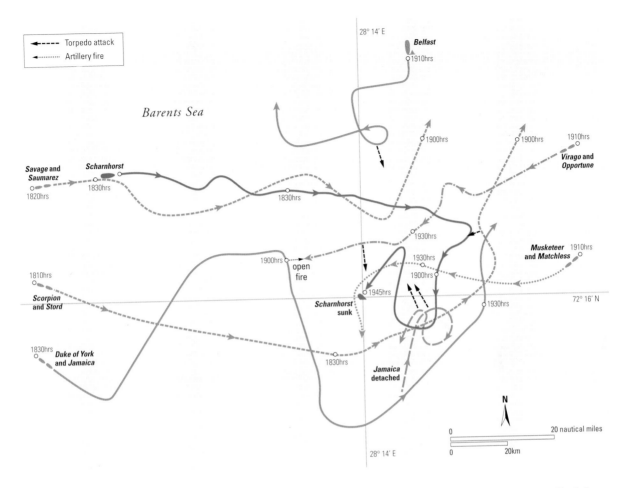

Barents Sea

Torpedo attack

Artillery fire

28° 14' E

Belfast
1910hrs

1900hrs   1900hrs   1910hrs

Virago and
Opportune

Savage and
Saumarez

Scharnhorst
1830hrs

1820hrs

1830hrs

1930hrs

Musketeer   1910hrs
and Matchless

1810hrs

1900hrs   open
fire

1930hrs

1900hrs

72° 16' N

Scorpion
and Stord

1945hrs

1930hrs

Scharnhorst
sunk

1830hrs   Duke of York
and Jamaica

1830hrs

Jamaica
detached

N

28° 14' E

0   20 nautical miles

0   20km

The Battle of the North Cape,
26 December 1943.

Forced to turn away and use the advantage of its superior speed, *Scharnhorst* pulled out of range of the accurate fire it was receiving from the British cruisers, but the 15in. guns of *Duke of York* were still scoring significant hits. Turret 'Bruno' was also put out of action.

The end came swiftly after *Scharnhorst* suffered a hit on its boiler room, causing a fatal drop in speed. British destroyers soon caught up with it and attacked with torpedoes, scoring four hits on the German ship. The crippled warship now only had its stern turret, 'Caesar', still functioning. With its speed now reduced by two-thirds, *Scharnhorst* continued to return fire, but at 1916hrs turret 'Caesar' was also put out of action, leaving *Scharnhorst* only its secondary armament. Just 14 minutes later, *Duke of York* ceased fire to allow the accompanying cruisers and destroyers to finish off the mortally wounded German ship with torpedoes. At 1945hrs, *Scharnhorst*'s magazines exploded and the battleship sank. Only 36 survivors, from a crew of 1,968, were pulled from the freezing-cold waters of the Barents Sea.

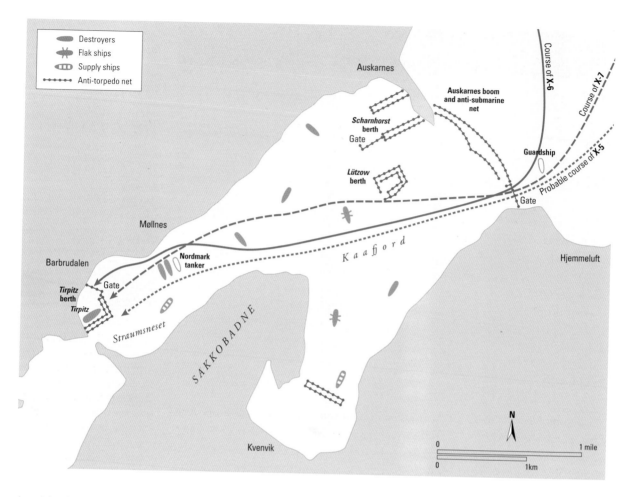

Attack by the midget submarines X-5, X-6 and X-7 on the *Tirpitz* in Kaafjord, 22 September 1943.

The Last Capital Ship: *Tirpitz*

Pronounced battleworthy in January 1943, *Tirpitz* had been moved to Altafjord where it was heavily involved in training exercises that lasted until mid-summer.

In September, *Tirpitz* took part in the brief sortie against Allied shore installations on Spitzbergen Island, using its main armament in anger for the first time, before returning safely to its anchorage. On the night of 22 September, however, the battleship was severely damaged when British midget submarines succeeded in penetrating the German anchorage. Two were successful in laying charges under the hull of *Tirpitz*. These exploded just after 0800hrs on 23 September.

Damage to the ship was extensive; turrets, rangefinders, fire control centres, aircraft catapults, rudders, main shafts, engines, generators and steam pipes were all badly affected. To all intents and purposes, *Tirpitz* was now out of commission. Fully six months were required for the most essential repairs to be carried out.

By the end of 1943, the Kriegsmarine's heavy units had been decimated.

TOP LEFT The battleship *Tirpitz*. (NHHC)

With *Gneisenau* out of commission, only *Tirpitz* and some heavy cruisers remained. Fortunately for Dönitz, his U-boats were still performing well, at least for the first half of the year. March 1943 was particularly successful with 108 ships totalling over 585,000 tons being sunk. By December, however, this had reduced to 14 ships totalling just under 69,000 tons. Too many Allied ships were evading the U-boats and losses in U-boats themselves were growing as Allied anti-submarine tactics improved. A total of 492 Allied ships, amassing 2,418,130 tons, had been sunk.

1944–45

During the Allied build up for the invasion of Normandy in 1944, the E-boats scored their greatest success. On 27 April a combined force of nine boats from 5. and 9. Schnellbootflottillen attacked a force of eight American LSTs escorted by the corvette *Azalia*. The Allied force had failed to detect the E-boats until it was too late and two LSTs were sunk and one severely damaged. The loss of life was heavy, estimated at well over 700. These LSTs had in fact been involved in a live practice exercise for the forthcoming D-Day landings and were to disembark their troops on the beaches at Slapton Sands.

ABOVE On 17 August 1942, Korvettenkapitän Erich Topp was awarded the Oak Leaves and Swords to his Knight's Cross in recognition of having sunk nearly 200,000 tons of enemy shipping, much of it off the American coast during the so-called second 'Happy Time'. (Author's collection)

LEFT E-boats scored a significant victory in 1944 when landing ships carrying out a practice run for the Normandy invasion were caught unawares by E-boats from 5. and 9. Schnellbootflottillen. Two ships were sunk, two badly damaged and over 700 Allied soldiers and sailors killed. (Author's collection)

The Kriegsmarine was, however, now just a shadow of its former self. *Bismarck*, *Scharnhorst*, *Blücher* and *Graf Spee* had been lost, while *Gneisenau* had had its upgrading cancelled and would never again be fit for service. Of the heavy cruisers, *Lützow*, *Admiral Scheer* and *Prinz Eugen* had been relegated to training duties and *Admiral Hipper* was decommissioned. Even the light cruisers had taken a hammering. *Königsberg* and *Karlsruhe* had been sunk, and *Leipzig*, after being out of commission, returned to service in September 1944 only to suffer a collision with *Prinz Eugen* in October which damaged it so much that it was rendered unfit for service. *Köln* and *Nürnberg*, along with the elderly *Emden*, had all been relegated to training duties.

On the early morning of 28 April 1944, off Slapton Sands, LST 531 is hit by a torpedo from an E-boat from 9.Schnellbootflottille based in Cherbourg. Vessels from both 5. and 9. Schnellbootflottillen were involved in the attack in which LST 531 was sunk with heavy loss of life and two others badly damaged. The LSTs, escorted by MTBs and MGBs, were on a practice exercise for the forthcoming invasion of Normandy.
(Howard Gerrard © Osprey Publishing)

The Sinking of *Tirpitz*

Tirpitz was the only heavy unit still capable of inflicting serious damage on Allied shipping, but was itself undergoing repairs after the attack by British midget submarines in September 1943.

On 3 April 1944, a mixed force of fighter aircraft and torpedo bombers consisting of over 164 aircraft attacked. After first strafing the battleship, inflicting heavy losses amongst the *Tirpitz*'s gun crews, the bombers arrived and dropped a total of 99 bombs on the battleship. Sixteen direct hits or near misses were scored.

Despite the number of bomb hits it suffered, only around a month was required for the repair workers on site to remedy the damage, and *Tirpitz* was once again ready for trials by the beginning of July 1944.

So far, attacks had been carried out predominantly by light torpedo bombers but on 15 September a force of Lancaster heavy bombers, most carrying a new, large and devastating bomb known as the 'Tallboy', packing 12,000lb of explosive reached *Tirpitz*. The battleship was well warned and had succeeded in laying a thick smokescreen over the entire area. Despite this, one direct hit was achieved on the ship's forecastle. This bomb penetrated right through the ship, exiting through the hull bottom and exploding right under the keel. Damage was serious and *Tirpitz* was once again out of commission.

In the circumstances, it was decided not to restore the ship to battleworthy condition again, but to tow it to a suitable location where it could be used as a floating gun battery. *Tirpitz* was subsequently anchored off the island of Haaköy in shallow waters where it was hoped that even if it did suffer further attacks, the worst-case scenario might be that it would simply settle on the bottom, with its armament still useable. *Tirpitz* made its own way to the new anchorage, where it arrived on 16 October.

In order to bolster its protection against air attack, two flak ships were anchored near to the ship and a number of flak positions established on shore. On 12 November, however, a further force of Lancaster bombers carried out a new attack. Two direct hits were scored right at the start of the attack, ripping a massive hole in the hull and causing a 15-degree list. Further hits over the next few minutes saw the list increase to 40 degrees and resulted in the order being given to abandon the lower decks. Within just nine minutes of the first bomb falling, the list had increased to 70 degrees, and a fire in one of the secondary armament turrets spread to the magazine for turret 'Caesar', which exploded, hurtling the massive turret into the air. Two minutes later, the battleship capsized.

ABOVE By 1944 *Tirpitz* was more noteworthy as a potential rather than actual threat, though the British made regular attempts to sink it. As a result, considerable efforts were made to camouflage the ship, as can be seen in this photo. (NHHC)

BELOW Officers stroll on the deck of *Tirpitz*, the ship covered in foliage. Such camouflage would prove to be of no avail, the leviathan eventually being sunk by Lancaster bombers using the massive 'Tallboy' bombs. (NHHC)

ABOVE In desperate attempts to intercept Allied shipping bringing supplies to the French ports after the Normandy invasion, the Germans committed a number of what would generally be termed 'midget submarines' of various types to action. This shot shows a 'Neger' manned torpedo. (DUBM)

RIGHT The conning tower emblems of a prancing devil figure clearly show how the Type VIIC boat U-552 earned the name the 'Red Devil Boat', as Topp brings his boat into port after yet another successful mission. (DUBM)

Although over 800 crewmen were saved, over a thousand others were trapped in the upturned hull. Rescue workers succeeded in cutting through the upturned hull bottom and rescued a further 82 crewmen. The final death toll was 971. Germany's last capital ship was gone.

The U-boats continued to fight on as best they could, but the 'Happy Times' were well and truly over. The summer of 1944, following the Allied invasion of Normandy, saw the Kriegsmarine lose its French bases, though U-boats continued to operate from Norway until the end of the war. Far from forging successful careers, many U-boat commanders failed to survive their first war cruise as Allied countermeasures grew in effectiveness. During 1944, a total of 210 enemy ships were sunk, less than half the number sunk in 1943; the tonnage, 789,147, was also less than that of the previous year. In 1945, the number of enemy ships destroyed more than halved once again, with 94 sunk, totalling 319,347 tons.

As the war drew to a close, the few remaining cruisers were sent into action on shore bombardment duties to assist the *Wehrmacht* (Armed Forces) on the crumbling Eastern Front. *Admiral Scheer*, returning to Kiel to have the worn-out bores of its main armament replaced, fell victim to Allied bombing and capsized on 9 April 1945. *Lützow* was bombed in port in Swinemünde on 16 April and damaged beyond repair, being reduced to a stationary gun platform. *Admiral Hipper* was also caught in port undergoing repairs and scuttled after being fatally damaged by RAF bombers on 3 May. *Prinz Eugen*, truly a lucky ship, was the only heavy cruiser to survive the war, reaching Copenhagen on 20 April and being subsequently decommissioned.

One of the 'lucky ships', *Prinz Eugen* survived the war and is seen here in Wilhelmshaven in 1946 prior to being sailed to the USA by its original German crew. It was eventually destroyed during atom-bomb tests at Bikini Atoll in the Pacific. (NHHC)

CHAPTER TWO

HITLER'S SHIPS

CAPITAL SHIPS
Pre-Dreadnoughts

Schlesien and *Schleswig-Holstein* were the last survivors of the five Deutschland-class battleships built by the Kaiserliche Marine. They were completed after the launch of the revolutionary British battleship HMS *Dreadnought* in 1906, and so were already of an obsolescent design when they entered service. Both vessels saw extensive service in World War I, and remained in service for training duties throughout the 1930s. Both ships saw limited duty during World War II, including during the invasion of Poland in 1939, and the occupation of Denmark and invasion of Norway in 1940.

The pre-dreadnought *Schlesien*, shown here in 1940 during gunnery exercises, did not play a major part in World War II, being predominantly used as a training vessel, though it often provided support to the army in the form of shore-bombardment missions. (NHHC)

Although of the same class, the two veterans were built in different yards, *Schlesien* at the Schichau yard in Danzig and *Schleswig-Holstein* at the Germaniawerft in Kiel. The ships were both built as three-stackers but during refit both had the two forward funnels trunked into a single stack. Both, as built, featured 14 x 10.5cm guns, ten of which were set into sponsons on the hull side. Although later reduced to three each side, this rather antiquated configuration was retained.

Schlesien and *Schleswig-Holstein* Specifications			
Length	125.9m	**Speed**	16 knots
Beam	7.6m	**Armament**	4 x 28cm guns in two twin turrets 6 x 15cm guns 10 x 4cm flak guns 22 x 2cm flak guns
Propulsion	3 x 17,000hp coal/oil-fired engines	**Complement**	725

Sister to *Schlesien*, the *Schleswig-Holstein* earned its place in history by firing the first shots of World War II when it opened fire on the Polish fortress of Westerplatte on 1 September 1939. Although scuttled at the end of the war it was raised by the Soviets and ended up being used as a target ship. (Author's collection)

Linienschiff *Schleswig-Holstein*

On 1 September 1939 *Schleswig-Holstein* took its place in history when it fired the opening shots of World War II, at 0447hrs, targeting the Westerplatte fortress in Danzig at a range of just 500m.

Schleswig-Holstein subsequently took part in the occupation of Denmark before once again being relegated to training duties, as the flagship of the *Befehlshaber des Ausbildungsverbandes* (Chief of Training Units of the Navy), a situation which continued until mid-1944 when its anti-aircraft armament was considerably enhanced with the intention of using it as a flak ship to provide additional anti-aircraft defences for the port of Gotenhafen. In December 1944, however, it was seriously damaged in a bombing attack and gradually settled on an even keel in Gotenhafen Harbour, in water just 12m deep. Although no longer mobile, it was still capable of using its armament, until finally a fire on board put it permanently out of action.

Linienschiff *Schlesien*

Schlesien's wartime career was less eventful than that of its sister. Used as a training ship for officer cadets until the beginning of 1940, it then spent a period of time acting as

Schlesien

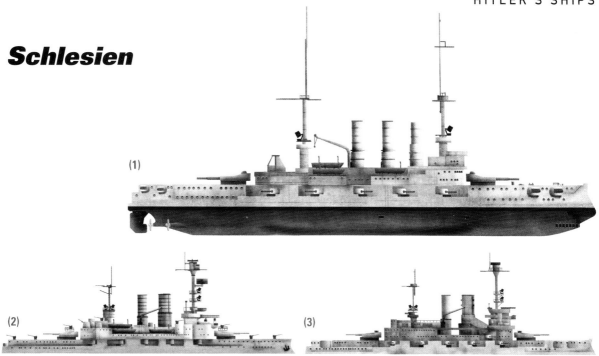

(1)

(2)

(3)

(1) *Schlesien* in pre-refit appearance. The colour scheme is the typical overall very pale grey as seen on most large, pre-war German warships, with black waterline and red lower hull. It still has the secondary armament mounted in hullside sponsons, a feature deleted on subsequent refitting, and retains the original three-funnel configuration.

(2) *Schlesien* after its major refit. The forward funnel has been removed and substantial reworking has altered the superstructure.
(3) *Schleswig-Holstein* after its first major refit. Note the trunking from the original forward funnel position leading to the centre (now the forward) funnel.
(Ian Palmer © Osprey Publishing)

an ice-breaker for the U-boat fleet. It was used briefly during the invasion of Denmark until being withdrawn from active service in July 1940 and thereafter used as an accommodation ship and occasionally as an ice-breaker.

As with its sister, in late 1944 its flak armament was significantly improved, and from early 1945 it helped provide improved anti-aircraft defence for Gotenhafen.

In April 1945, it moved from Gotenhafen to Swinemünde to restock with ammunition, and at the same time transported over 1,000 wounded soldiers back from the front for treatment. On 3 May 1945, it struck a mine north-west of Swinemünde and settled in shallow water. Like *Schleswig-Holstein*, its guns remained active and provided much needed fire support to army units.

The Scharnhorst Class

The Scharnhorst class comprised two vessels: *Scharnhorst* and *Gneisenau*. These were the first capital ships built by the Kriegsmarine,and marked the beginning of Nazi Germany's naval rearmament following the Treaty of Versailles.

ABOVE Stern view of *Scharnhorst* showing the massive bronze eagle fitted to the stern of all medium and large warships. In most cases these were removed and put into storage early in the war though some vessels lost early in the war still carried them. (NHHC)

ABOVE RIGHT *Scharnhorst* is shown here in its post-refit form, with elegant clipper bow replacing the original straight stem. It still carries the aircraft catapult atop turret 'Caesar', soon to be removed. *Scharnhorst* can be instantly identified by the location of its mainmast on the rear superstructure. (NHHC)

Schlachtschiff *Scharnhorst*

The first keel in this class to be laid down was begun at Deutsche Werke in Kiel on 6 May 1935, and the second at the Kriegsmarinewerft in Wilhelmshaven on 15 June 1936. Delays in the construction of the first vessel meant that the second hull was completed first. The vessel was launched on 3 October 1936, christened *Scharnhorst*. The launch ceremony was attended by Adolf Hitler along with the Minister of War, Generalfeldmarschall von Blomberg, and the widow of Kapitän zur See Schultz, commander of the Kaiserliche Marine's SMS *Scharnhorst*, lost off the Falklands in December 1914.

The fitting out of the new battleship took just over two years and it was not finally commissioned until January 1939. During extensive sea trials, it was discovered that the ship had a tendency to take on considerable volumes of water over the forecastle in anything much more than a flat, calm sea. This caused some flooding of the areas below deck in the forward part of the ship and also led to problems with the electrics of the forward turret. Accordingly, *Scharnhorst* was taken back into dry dock and, whilst the usual post-commissioning final shipyard work was undertaken, the opportunity was taken to make some other improvements. Most important of these works, carried out in June 1939, was the fitting of a raised 'clipper' or 'Atlantic' bow, which greatly improved the ship's graceful appearance but sadly did little to improve the problem of its shipping vast amounts of water in rough seas. This remodelling of the bow saw the forward anchors changed from two on the port side and one starboard, to one on each side. Each of the anchor hawses on the hull side was sealed and instead an anchor cluse positioned either side of the forecastle. At the same time, a raked funnel cap was fitted and the mainmast moved from abaft the funnel to a new location further astern. Its hangar was also enlarged during these modifications.

On 10 September 2000, the wreck of the *Scharnhorst* was discovered in 290m of water off the North Cape by survey vessels of the Norwegian Navy.

Scharnhorst's **Commanders**	
January 1939–September 1939	Kapitän zur See Otto Ciliax
September 1939–April 1942	Kapitän zur See Kurt Hoffmann
April 1942–October 1943	Kapitän zur See Friedrich Hüffmeier
October 1943–December 1943	Kapitän zur See Fritz Hintze

Scharnhorst

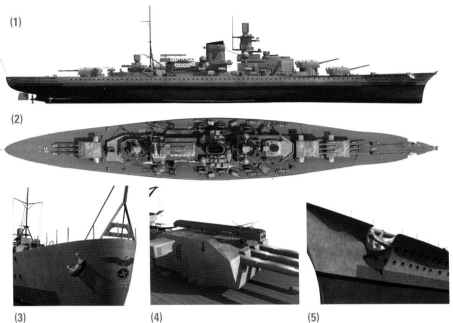

(1)

(2)

(3)   **(4)**   **(5)**

(1) *Scharnhorst* in the initial pre-war colour scheme. On the plan view **(2)**, the teak main decks can be seen. The upper decks were finished in a non-slip material seen here as a dark grey colour. **(3)** shows the original stern. Pre-war, most large German warships had a large bronze eagle and swastika fitted here. **(4)** shows the original turret-fitted aircraft catapult. **(5)** shows the redesigned *Scharnhorst* bow. The anchor now sits at a cluse on the forecastle rather than the chain emerging from a hawse-hole on the hull. (Ian Palmer © Osprey Publishing)

Scharnhorst Specifications		
Displacement	37,200 tons, loaded	• 9 x 28cm guns in three triple turrets, capable of firing projectiles weighing over 300kg to a maximum range of 42.5km at a rate of 3.5 rounds per minute per barrel
Length	235.4m	
Beam	30m	
Propulsion	3 x Brown-Boveri turbines developing a total of 160,060hp	• 8 x 15cm guns in four twin turrets, capable of firing 45.3kg projectiles to a maximum range of 23km at a rate of 8 rounds per minute per barrel • 4 x 15cm guns in single turrets, specification as above, but range of 22km due to slightly less maximum elevation
Speed	31–32 knots	• 14 x 10.5cm flak guns in twin turrets, firing a 15kg projectile to a maximum range of 17.7km at a rate of 18 rounds per minute per barrel
Endurance	7,100 nautical miles at optimum speed of 19 knots	• 16 x 3.7cm flak guns in twin turrets, firing projectiles weighing 0.75kg at a rate of 40 rounds per minute to a range of 8.5km
Fuel capacity	6,108 metric tons	• 22 x 2cm flak guns mounts in a mixture of single- and quadruple-barrel mounts, 120 rounds (single barrel) or 220 rounds (quadruple barrel) per minute to a range of 4.9km
Aircraft	3 x Arado 196 floatplanes	
Complement	1,968 (1,669)	• 6 x 53.3cm torpedoes (never used operationally)

Armament (spanning column label)

Schlachtschiff *Gneisenau*

Gneisenau, although the first of the class to be laid down, was not launched until after its sister. At the launch ceremony on 8 December 1936, the christening was carried out by the widow of the commander of the cruiser SMS *Gneisenau* of the *Kaiserliche Marine*, lost along with SMS *Scharnhorst* during the Battle of the Falklands in December 1914. It was particularly appropriate that Germany's two most modern warships were named for two contemporaries who did so much to improve and modernize the Prussian Army. Commissioned into the navy in May 1938, *Gneisenau*'s first commander was Kapitän zur See Förste.

After taking on its crew, the new battleship set sail on its sea trials. *Gneisenau* was based at Kiel. As had happened with *Scharnhorst*, it quickly became clear when on trials that *Gneisenau* had a tendency to ship significant quantities of water over its forecastle in even moderate seas. As a result, in January 1939, like its sister, it had its stem remodelled, giving it the so-called 'Atlantic' bow. As with the *Scharnhorst*, it was found that this modification made little difference and the problem was never fully solved. A raked funnel cap was also fitted. Unlike *Scharnhorst*, however, *Gneisenau*'s mainmast remained in its original place, abaft the funnel.

Gneisenau Specifications		
Displacement	37,900 tons, loaded	• 9 x 28cm guns in three triple turrets, capable of firing projectiles weighing over 300kg to a maximum range of 42.5km at a rate of 3.5 rounds per minute per barrel • 8 x 15cm guns in four twin turrets, capable of firing 45.3kg projectiles to a maximum range of 23km at a rate of 8 rounds per minute per barrel • 4 x 15cm guns in single turrets, specification as above, but range of 22km due to slightly less maximum elevation • 14 x 10.5cm flak guns in twin turrets, firing a 15kg projectile to a maximum range of 17.7km at a rate of 18 rounds per minute per barrel • 16 x 3.7cm flak guns in twin turrets, firing projectiles weighing 0.75kg at a rate of 40 rounds per minute to a range of 8.5km • 22 x 2cm flak guns mounts in a mixture of single- and quadruple-barrel mounts, 120 rounds (single barrel) or 220 rounds (quadruple barrel) per minute to a range of 4.9km • 6 x 53.3cm torpedoes (never used operationally)
Length	234.9m	
Beam	30m	
Propulsion	3 x Deschimag turbines developing a total of 154,000hp	
Speed	31 knots	
Endurance	6,200 nautical miles at optimum speed of 19 knots	
Fuel Capacity	5,360 metric tons	
Aircraft:	3 x Arado 196 floatplanes	
Complement	1,669	

Note: the **Armament** header spans the third column.

Gneisenau's Commanders	
May 1938–November 1939	Kapitän zur See Erich Förste
November 1939–August 1940	Kapitän zur See Harald Netzbandt
August 1940–April 1942	Kapitän zur See Otto Fein
February 1942–May 1942	Kapitän zur See Rudolf Peters
May 1942 – July 1942	Kapitän zur See Wolfgang Kähler

Gneisenau

Gneisenau during Operation *Berlin* in profile (**1**) and plan view (**2**). Its overall colour is still pale grey with the roofs of the main and principal secondary armament turrets painted yellow. The main difference between *Gneisenau* and *Scharnhorst* was the re-siting of the mainmast on *Scharnhorst* to the rear of the hangar and the design of the hangar itself. (**3**) shows the unique hangar installed on *Gneisenau* over the winter of 1941/42. (**4**) The sternmost door panel on the hangar slid rearwards whilst the centre and forward panels slid in the opposite direction. (**5**) shows details of the funnel and funnel platform. (Ian Palmer © Osprey Publishing)

Gneisenau is seen here as launched, with straight stem and second catapult on the stern turret. Note the mainmast is fixed to the rear of the funnel, which at this stage lacks the large funnel cap which will later be installed. (Author's collection)

Armour, gunnery and radar

In terms of armour protection, *Scharnhorst* and *Gneisenau* boasted 35cm thick side armour, capable of withstanding a hit from a 38cm shell. The main deck consisted of 5cm-thick armour plate, rather modest, but reinforced two decks below by a further armoured deck 9.5cm thick. This, it was calculated, would contain the destructive effect of any projectile exploding after penetrating the main deck above. These specifications may have been acceptable at the time it was built, but, as the war progressed and the penetrating power of Allied bombs increased, it was to prove inadequate. Protection from torpedoes, on the other hand, was excellent, with a 4.5cm-thick armoured torpedo bulkhead 4.5m inboard from the outer hull.

Post-refit *Gneisenau* showing the clipper bow which replaced the straight stem. The similarity between *Gneisenau* and its sister *Scharnhorst* is clear. Only the position of its mainmast easily identifies it as *Gneisenau* in this photo. (NHHC)

ABOVE The badge awarded to qualifying crewmen serving on battleships and cruisers. The central motif is clearly based on the Scharnhorst-class warships. Instituted in April 1941, it was awarded to those individuals who had served 12 weeks active service on a battleship or cruiser. In special circumstances it could be awarded to the entire crew. (Author's collection)

Both *Scharnhorst* and *Gneisenau* were fitted with 10.5m stereoscopic rangefinders. These were fitted in all three main turrets, with further sets on the foretop and aft fire control centre. A further 6m rangefinder was positioned on the forward fire control centre for the secondary armament, and 4m rangefinders in domed housings either side of the bridge structure and either side of the funnel.

In the late 1920s and early 1930s Germany had been active in pioneering radar, with the *Reichsmarine* being one of the keenest advocates of the new technology. In 1934, a foundation known as the Gesellschaft für Elektroakustische und Mechanische Apparate, was established to promote further development of the infant systems, and by 1935 a fully operational 48cm wavelength (630 MHz) radar set was demonstrated to the *Oberbefehlshaber der Kriegsmarine*. Shortly after being installed for the first time in an operational warship, the system was altered to 82cm (370 MHz) and this became the standard for naval use. After the outbreak of war, however, inter-service rivalry and a general feeling that the systems had been developed as far as was feasible led to a stagnation in development, allowing the Allies to overtake the Germans.

Both *Scharnhorst* and *Gneisenau* were provided with a FuMO 22 (FuMO, *Funkmessortungsgerät*) radar set in 1939, attached to a housing above that of the foretop rangefinder. This system had a large 6m x 2m 'mattress' antenna.

Gneisenau had this equipment upgraded to the FuMO 27 version, with the smaller 4m x 2m antenna, in January 1941. *Scharnhorst* also had this improvement carried out in 1942. Both ships sometime in late 1941 or early 1942 also had a FuMO 27 apparatus affixed to the stern rangefinder housing. The FuMB 4 *Samos* (*Funkmessbeobachtungsgerät*) radar array was also affixed to the foretop housing immediately below the FuMO 27 at the same time.

The Bismarck Class

One of the most famous warships of all time, the *Bismarck* was laid down at the shipyard of Blohm & Voss in Hamburg on 1 July 1936. With the lifting of the restrictions imposed by the Treaty of Versailles, Germany embarked on a major warship building programme. Though still somewhat restricted by the terms of the Anglo-German Naval Agreement of June 1935, the way was clear for the construction of at least two major battleships, powerful enough to match those in the arsenal of their most likely future adversary, the Royal Navy.

The result, the Bismarck class, would be the largest warships ever built by Germany and at over 50,000 tons fully loaded, as big if not bigger than any equivalent on the strength of the Royal Navy.

FAR LEFT *Bismarck* during fitting out at the Blohm & Voss shipyards. This is a port-side bow view. The guns have been installed in turret 'Bruno' but the roof of the turret has yet to be fitted. After launching, it would take a further 18 months of fitting out work before it was ready to be commissioned. (NHCC)

LEFT This imposing bow view shows the completed *Bismarck.* Only the rangefinders and radar fittings on the foretop and forward control centre remain to be added. Due to its short service life, no major modifications were made before its loss. (ullstein bild via Getty Images)

Schlachtschiff *Bismarck*

The *Bismarck* was launched at the Blohm & Voss yard in Hamburg on 14 February 1939. In the ceremony, attended by Adolf Hitler, the christening was performed by Dorothea von Löwenfeld, granddaughter of the 'Iron Chancellor' himself.

As launched, *Bismarck* featured a straight stem, but whilst it was still being fitted out, the opportunity was taken to provide it with a raked 'Atlantic' bow. On completion of the fitting out, *Bismarck* was formally commissioned into the Kriegsmarine on 24 August 1940, under the command of Kapitän zur See Ernst Lindemann.

Bismarck Specifications			
Displacement	50,900 tons, loaded	**Armament**	• 8 x 38cm guns in four twin turrets, capable of firing projectiles weighing 800kg to a maximum range of 36.5km at a rate of 2 rounds per minute per barrel • 12 x 15cm guns in six twin turrets, capable of firing 45.3kg projectiles to a maximum range of 23km at a rate of 8 rounds per minute per barrel • 14 x 10.5cm flak guns in twin turrets, firing 15kg projectiles to a maximum range of 17.7km at a rate of 18 rounds per minute per barrel • 16 x 3.7cm flak guns in twin turrets, firing projectiles weighing 0.75kg at a rate of 40 rounds per minute to a range of 8.5km • 12 x 2cm flak guns in a mixture of single- and quadruple-barrel mounts, 120 rounds (single barrel) or 220 rounds (quadruple barrel) per minute to a range of 4.9km
Length	250m		
Beam	36m		
Propulsion	3 x Blohm & Voss turbines developing a total of 150,170hp		
Speed	30 knots		
Endurance	9,280 nautical miles at optimum speed of 16 knots		
Fuel Capacity	8,000 metric tons		
Aircraft	4 x Arado 196 floatplanes		
Complement	2,092		

Bismarck's **Commander**	
August 1940–May 1941	Kapitän zur See Ernst Lindemann

Schlachtschiff *Tirpitz*

Sister to the *Bismarck*, this magnificent warship was laid down on 24 October 1936 at the Kriegsmarinewerft in Wilhelmshaven on a specially lengthened and strengthened slipway.

On 1 April 1939, the new battleship was launched at Wilhelmshaven in an elaborate ceremony attended by Adolf Hitler and a large number of former dignitaries of the Imperial German Navy. The christening was performed by Frau von Hassell, daughter of Grossadmiral Tirpitz. Final building work and fitting out was not completed until February 1941, its formal commissioning into the Kriegsmarine being performed on 25 February. This was followed by brief initial trials before *Tirpitz* sailed for the safe waters of the Baltic, docking at Gdynia.

On 5 May 1941, Hitler paid a formal visit to his latest battleship and also to its sister, *Bismarck*, which was also anchored at Gdynia.

Tirpitz was strikingly similar to *Bismarck*, just 3m longer. The major visual differences were that *Tirpitz* featured a modified design to the midships upper deck which extended over the full width of the main deck and had the ship's cranes mounted on this upper deck as opposed to on the main deck as with *Bismarck*. *Tirpitz* also carried two quadruple torpedo launchers midships on each side, not fitted on *Bismarck*.

RIGHT *Tirpitz* was a close sister to *Bismarck*, most of the differences being around the midships area and not immediately apparent in this photo. Its aircraft cranes were in a different position and unlike *Bismarck*, *Tirpitz* carried torpedo tubes amidships. (ullstein bild via Getty Images)

BELOW *Tirpitz*, c.1941, in standard grey livery with distinctive dark turret tops. During the course of its service career, it would carry a wide range of complex camouflage schemes on both hull and superstructure, and would also receive greatly enhanced anti-aircraft armament. (NHCC)

Bismarck

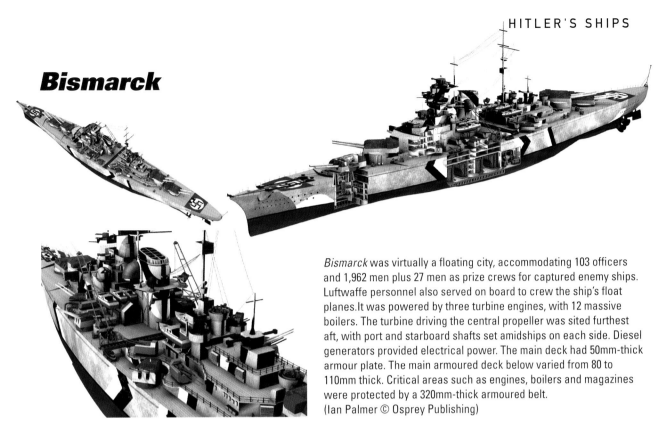

Bismarck was virtually a floating city, accommodating 103 officers and 1,962 men plus 27 men as prize crews for captured enemy ships. Luftwaffe personnel also served on board to crew the ship's float planes. It was powered by three turbine engines, with 12 massive boilers. The turbine driving the central propeller was sited furthest aft, with port and starboard shafts set amidships on each side. Diesel generators provided electrical power. The main deck had 50mm-thick armour plate. The main armoured deck below varied from 80 to 110mm thick. Critical areas such as engines, boilers and magazines were protected by a 320mm-thick armoured belt.
(Ian Palmer © Osprey Publishing)

Tirpitz Specifications		
Displacement	52,700 tons, loaded	
Length	253m	
Beam	36m	
Propulsion	3 x Brown-Boveri turbines developing a total of 150,170hp	
Speed	30 knots	
Endurance	9,280 nautical miles at optimum speed of 16 knots	
Fuel Capacity	8,000 metric tons	
Aircraft	4 x Arado 196 floatplanes	
Complement	2,608	Armament
		• 8 x 38cm guns in four twin turrets, capable of firing projectiles weighing 800kg to a maximum range of 36.5km at a rate of 2 rounds per minute per barrel
		• 12 x 15cm guns in six twin turrets, capable of firing 45.3kg projectiles to a maximum range of 23km at a rate of 8 rounds per minute per barrel
		• 16 x 10.5cm flak guns in twin turrets, firing 15kg projectiles to a maximum range of 17.7km at a rate of 18 rounds per minute per barrel
		• 16 x 3.7cm flak guns in twin turrets, firing projectiles weighing 0.75 kilo at a rate of 40 rounds per minute to a range of 8.5km
		• 78 x 2cm flak guns in a mixture of single- and quadruple-barrel mounts, 120 rounds (single barrel) or 220 rounds (quadruple barrel) per minute to a range of 4.9km
		• 8 x 53.3cm torpedo tubes in two quadruple mounts

Tirpitz's Commanders	
February 1941–February 1943	Kapitän zur See Karl Topp
February 1943–May 1944	Kapitän zur See Hans Meyer
May 1944–November 1944	Kapitän zur See Wolf Junge
November 1944	Kapitän zur See Robert Weber

Armour, gunnery and radar

The Bismarck class featured a side belt of 35cm-thick Krupp armour. The main deck consisted of 5cm-thick armour plate, reinforced two decks below by a further armoured deck 8cm thick, and 10cm-thick over critical points such as the steering room and magazines.

Each main turret in the class featured a 10.5m stereoscopic rangefinder. The set in 'A' turret was removed from *Bismarck* during the winter of 1940 and never fitted to *Tirpitz*. Further 10.5m sets were installed on the foretop and the aft control centre. A 7m rangefinder was fitted on the forward control centre and 6.5m sets fitted to the secondary armament turrets either side of the funnel. A 4m set was installed in a domed housing either side of the bridge to control the heavy flak with further sets aft of the mainmast and just forward of turret 'C'.

Bismarck and *Tirpitz* were initially provided with identical radar equipment comprising a FuMO 23 apparatus attached to the forward, foretop and stern main rangefinders. The antenna array on this type measured some 4m x 2m.

Tirpitz eventually had its forward array replaced with the FuMO 27, and the foretop set provided with a FuMO 27 housing atop the existing FuMO 23. Ultimately, the FuMO 26 array, whose larger antenna measured some 6.6m x 3.2m, was fitted on the foretop. In 1944, a FuMO 30 *Hohentweil* radar set was mounted in the topmast and a further FuMO 213 *Wurzburg* radar array on the forwardmost of its stern 10.5cm flak rangefinder housings.

RIGHT Its solitude in the remote Norwegian fjords earned *Tirpitz* the sobriquet of 'Lone Queen of the North'. This stern photo shows it in its Kaafjord lair; its vast bulk clearly evident. (NHHC)

FAR RIGHT Generaladmiral Otto Schniewind, Flottenchef 1941–44. He retired from active duty in July 1944 and survived the war. Charged with war crimes for his part in the invasion of Norway, he was acquitted and served in the US-established Naval Historical Team. He died in 1964. (Heinrich Hoffmann/ ullstein bild via Getty Images)

CRUISERS

Kriegsmarine cruisers can be considered under four categories: the pocket battleships (which were reclassified as heavy cruisers), the heavy cruisers, the light cruisers and the auxiliary cruisers. 'Pocket battleship' was never a German term, but one coined by the foreign press because of the exceptionally heavy armament carried on what was a cruiser-size vessel.

LEFT Although all three Panzerschiffen initially had the same hull design, *Deutschland* was instantly recognisable due to its unique style of foremast and bridge structure. The ship's aircraft, a Heinkel He 60 floatplane (later replaced by an Arado 196), can be seen on its catapult just forward of the funnel. (NHHC)

Camouflage Schemes

(1)

(2)

(3)

(4)

(**1**) *Lützow* in the scheme sported during its service in Norway during 1942. A pale grey base has wide curved swathes of dark grey over the hull and superstructure.
(**2**) *Admiral Scheer* in 1942, with camouflage scheme very similar to that shown for its sister, but with subtle differences to the patterning.
(**3**) *Lützow* in 1941, wearing a camouflage scheme similar to that worn by *Bismarck*, *Prinz Eugen* and other major warships at that time, for exercises in the Baltic.
(**4**) *Admiral Graf Spee* in full disguise as it appeared during its raid into the South Atlantic, with false second funnel.
(Ian Palmer ©
Osprey Publishing)

The Deutschland Class

Designed to meet the restrictions of the Treaty of Versailles, which limited German capital ships to a maximum weight of 10,000 tons, the first of Germany's so-called pocket battleships, the *Deutschland*, was one of the few pre-war German warships that genuinely did meet the restrictions on tonnage. The other *Panzerschiffe* which followed, *Admiral Scheer* and *Admiral Graf Spee*, significantly exceeded the weight limit due to the additional armour that had been fitted.

Panzerschiff *Deutschland* (*Lützow*)

The original name of Germany's first pocket battleship speaks for itself and it is no surprise that the most powerful and modern warship in the new Reichsmarine would bear the nation's name. It was renamed in November 1939, taking the name of one of Germany's most distinguished military figures, Adolf Wilhelm Freiherr von Lützow (1782–1834). The ship was completed and commissioned into the *Reichsmarine* on 1 April 1933.

Its maiden sea voyage took place through the second half of May 1933 during which speed trials suggested a top speed of around 25 knots. Further speed trials during the following month saw *Deutschland* clock up a top speed of just over 28 knots. By December 1933 *Deutschland* had completed its trials and taken its place in the German fleet. *Deutschland* and its sisters benefited from the use of electric arc welding in their construction. The use of welding eliminated the need for rivets. Whilst each rivet might not be of significant weight, when multiplied many thousand-fold they could add significantly to the overall weight of the ship. The use of welding could therefore reduce weight considerably, and in *Deutschland*'s case the weight of the hull is said to have been reduced by fully 15 per cent.

In 1938 the funnel received a minor modification in the form of a very slightly raked funnel cap, and in the following year radar was installed in its foretop. A major refit in 1940 resulted in the original straight stem being replaced by a so-called 'clipper bow', though the rake to this bow was far less pronounced than on other similarly modified German warships. As originally constructed, *Deutschland* featured two bow anchors to port and one to starboard. The new design had only a single anchor each side. During this refit, the twin 8.8cm flak mounts were replaced by much heavier 10.5cm twin stabilized units.

Deutschland's Commanders			
1933–35	Kapitän zur See Hermann von Fischel	1941	Kapitän zur See Leo Kreisch
		1941–43	Kapitän zur See Rudolf Stange
1935–37	Kapitän zur See Paul Fanger	1943*	Fregattenkapitän Biesterfeld
1937–39	Kapitän zur See Paul Wennecker	1944–45	Kapitän zur See Knoke
		1945	Kapitän zur See Ernst Lange
1939–40	Kapitän zur See August Thiele		
1940*	Fregattenkapitän Fritz Krauss	* Temporary acting commander	

Deutschland

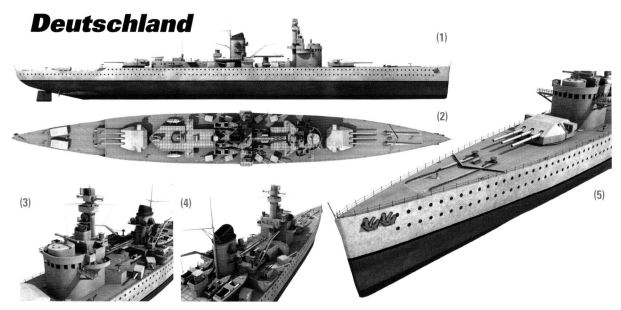

(1) *Deutschland* after its 1938 refit. Its aircraft catapult has been fitted, but no other major modifications made, other than the addition of a slightly raked funnel cap.
(2) A plan view shows the wooden planked main and quarterdeck, with other upper horizontal surfaces in a grey non-slip finish.
(3) The bridge/forward superstructure area was different from that of its sisters.

(4) The midships area also had a different searchlight platform, with the catapult carried forward rather than aft of the funnel.
(5) *Deutschland's* modified bow received less of a rake than the bows added to other warships, and retained the old anchor hawse holes at the bow.
(Ian Palmer © Osprey Publishing)

Further refits in 1942, 1944 and 1945 were principally concerned with the upgrading of the radar equipment and the addition of extra flak armament, the final 1945 refit seeing the subsidiary flak armament increased to a total of 6 x 4cm, 8 x 3.7cm and 33 x 2cm guns.

Deutschland Specifications			
Manufacturer	Deutsche Werke, Kiel	**Endurance**	10,000 nautical miles at 20 knots
Length	186m	**Armament**	• 6 x 28cm guns in two triple turrets • 8 x 15cm guns in single turrets • 6 x 10.5cm flak guns in three twin turrets • Miscellaneous additional smaller calibre anti-aircraft guns • 8 torpedo tubes, mounted in fours in rotating armoured housings on the quarterdeck, firing 53.3cm G7A torpedoes
Beam	20.7m	**Aircraft**	2 shipboard aircraft, initially Heinkel He 60, then Arado 196
Draught	5.8m	**Complement (average)**	30 officers and 1,040 men
Displacement	14, 100 tons		
Maximum speed	28 knots		

TOP RIGHT *Deutschland* on a training sortie showing its main 28cm armament at maximum elevation. The large quadruple torpedo tube housing can be seen either side of the quarterdeck. It would later be renamed *Lützow*, to avoid the possibility that a major warship bearing the name of the nation might be lost. (NHHC)

BELOW *Deutschland* passing through the Kiel Canal. A clipper bow would later replace the straight stem and an extremely tall funnel cap would be added. Its foretop would be remodelled and would carry radar fittings, and it would sport various camouflage paint schemes. (NHHC)

Panzerschiff *Admiral Scheer*

As first launched, *Admiral Scheer* was a virtual clone of its sister the *Admiral Graf Spee*. In 1940, however, it received a major rebuild. The original straight stem was replaced by a clipper bow, extending the overall length. Its original enclosed bridge was also replaced, this time by one built around an exposed tubular pole mast. A new tripod-style mainmast was installed to the rear of the funnel, which also received a lightly raked funnel cap.

Admiral Scheer now bore a closer resemblance to *Deutschland* than to the *Admiral Graf Spee*, though all three sisters had enough significant differences to make them identifiable at a glance, the most obvious being the installation of a much higher, sharply raked funnel cap in 1943.

RIGHT As completed, *Admiral Scheer* was an almost identical twin to *Admiral Graf Spee* though later modifications would change its appearance considerably. It would be given a raked bow, tall funnel cap and its pagoda-style bridge would be removed and a new remodelled bridge fitted. (Author's collection)

Admiral Scheer Specifications

Manufacturer	Marinewerft, Wilhelmshaven	Armament	• 6 x 28cm guns in two triple turrets • 8 x 15cm guns in single turrets • 6 x 10.5cm flak guns in three twin turrets • miscellaneous additional smaller calibre anti-aircraft guns • 8 torpedo tubes, mounted in fours in rotating armoured housings on the quarterdeck, firing 53.3cm G7A torpedoes
Length	186m	Aircraft	2 shipboard aircraft, initially Heinkel He 60, then Arado 196
Beam	21.3m	Complement (average)	30 officers and 1,040 men
Draught	5.8m		
Maximum displacement	14,900 tons		
Maximum speed	28.3 knots		
Endurance	10,000 nautical miles at 20 knots		

Admiral Scheer's Commanders

1936–38	Kapitän zur See Otto Ciliax
1938–39	Kapitän zur See Hans-Heinrich Wurmbach
1939–41	Kapitän zur See Theodor Krancke
1941–42	Kapitän zur See Wilhelm Meendsen-Bohlken
1942–43*	Fregattenkapitän Gruber
1943–44	Kapitän zur See Richard Rothe-Roth
1944–45	Kapitän zur See Thienemann

* Temporary acting commander

BELOW A late image of *Admiral Scheer* showing the remodelled bridge area, very tall funnel cap and complex disruptive camouflage pattern. The outline of its Arado Ar 196 floatplane can be seen on the catapult just aft of the funnel. By this stage it carried improved radar and enhanced anti-aircraft armament. (NHHC)

Panzerschiff *Admiral Graf Spee*

Admiral Graf Spee did not undergo any significant major modifications during its short life. In 1938, its twin 8.8cm flak guns were replaced by more modern and powerful 10.5cm twin units, on stabilized mounts. At the same time, a 'mattress' antenna was fitted to the experimental radar on the foretop. As initially constructed, *Admiral Graf Spee* featured a searchlight on a platform at either side of its bridge structure. These platforms and their searchlights were removed and replaced by a single platform and searchlight on the face of the bridge structure. Although a major rebuild was scheduled for *Admiral Graf Spee* around 1942, no significant changes were made before the ship met its fate.

Admiral Graf Spee Specifications			
Manufacturer	Marinewerft, Wilhelmshaven	**Armament**	• 6 x 28cm guns in two triple turrets • 8 x 15cm guns in single turrets • 6 x 10.5cm flak guns in three twin turrets • miscellaneous additional smaller calibre anti-aircraft guns • 8 torpedo tubes, mounted in fours in rotating armoured housings on the quarterdeck, firing 53.3cm G7A torpedoes
Length	186m	**Aircraft**	2 shipboard aircraft, initially Heinkel He 60, then Arado 196
Beam	21.65m	**Complement (average)**	30 officers and 1,040 men
Draught	5.8m		
Maximum displacement	16,060 tons		
Maximum speed	28.5 knots		
Endurance	10,000 nautical miles at 20 knots		

Admiral Graf Spee's Commanders	
1936–37	Kapitän zur See Conrad Patzig
1937–38	Kapitän zur See Walter Warzecha
1938–39	Kapitän zur See Hans Langsdorff

Certainly the most famous of the so-called pocket-battleships, *Admiral Graf Spee* underwent only very minor modifications which made little difference to its general appearance. The searchlight platforms either side of the bridge would be removed and replaced by a single mount on the face of the bridge. (Author's collection)

Armour, gunnery and radar

The Deutschland class, though outwardly similar in hull design, had different armour. *Deutschland* and *Admiral Graf Spee* featured 8cm upper belt armour whilst *Scheer* had only 5cm belt armour. *Scheer*, however, had 8cm lower belt around whilst *Deutschland* and *Admiral Graf Spee* had only 6cm. The upper decks had thin armour, only 1.7–1.8cm, with the lower armoured deck around 4–4.5cm. Given that these ships were intended as 'hit and run' commerce raiders and were not expected to tackle enemy heavy units, the decision to sacrifice armour in favour of speed was not unreasonable.

The main armament for the type consisted of six 28cm SK L/52 C28 guns in two triple turrets. These fired a 300kg shell for a range of 36.5km at a rate of fire of two rounds per minute. These weapons were an earlier version of the type installed on *Scharnhorst* and *Gneisenau* and had a shorter range and lower rate of fire.

Secondary armament, consisting of eight 15cm SK L/55 C28 naval guns in single turrets, was identical to those carried on *Scharnhorst* and *Gneisenau*.

A 10.5m stereoscopic rangefinder was installed in each main armament turret with a further set on the foretop and aft command centre. For the secondary armament a 7m rangefinder was positioned on the forward command centre. Flak was controlled by a 3m rangefinder in front of the bridge and one either side abaft the funnel.

Deutschland carried early experimental radar equipment known as Seetakt during the earliest part of its career, equipment that was put to good use in night movements off the Spanish coast during its Civil War non-intervention patrols. Prior to the outbreak of war, this equipment was replaced by a standard FuMO 22 set with a 6m x 2m 'mattress' antenna, fitted to the forward face of the foretop rangefinder. No radar antenna was carried on the aft rangefinder of *Deutschland*/*Lützow*.

Admiral Scheer was initially provided with a FuMO 22 set on the forward face of its foretop rangefinder in 1939. During its major refit in 1940, however, this was replaced by a FuMO 27 with the smaller 2m x 4m antenna. A further antenna for the *Timor* FuMB 7 was also added to the rear of the rangefinder in 1942. Additionally, four individual antennae (forward, aft and at each side) were fitted for the FuMB 4 *Sumatra* equipment. On the aft rangefinder was affixed a further 2m x 4m antenna for FuMO 27 equipment. This equipment was added in 1941.

Admiral Graf Spee was initially equipped with an experimental form of the FuMO 22, which was at that time designated as the FMG 39 (gO). The 'mattress' antenna at this point was smaller than the later production set, at 0.8m x 1.8m.

Admiral Graf Spee showing the camouflage scheme applied before setting off on its ill-fated war cruise in 1939. Note the false bow wave painted on the hull. Only a single searchlight is carried on the face of the bridge structure. (NHHC)

Admiral Graf Spee

The best known of all the pocket battleships is undoubtedly the *Admiral Graf Spee*. Its exploits in the South Atlantic captured the imagination of the world. It was 186m in length, with a beam of 21.7m. With a full load it displaced some 16,100 tons. Power was provided by eight MAN diesel engines, each developing 7,100bhp, four being coupled to each of the propeller shafts. These gave it an endurance of some 18,605 nautical miles at an optimum 15 knots. *Admiral Graf Spee* was also able to reach, in test, a maximum speed of 28.5 knots. (Ian Palmer © Osprey Publishing)

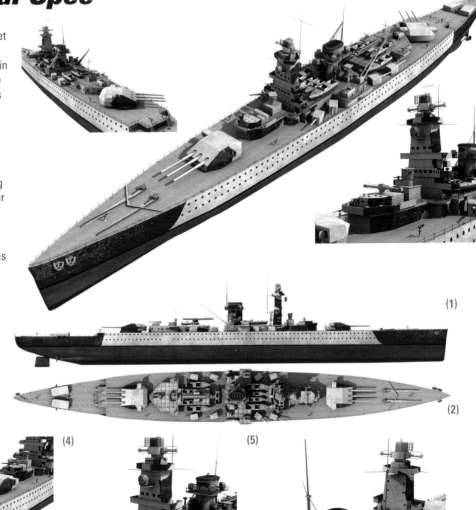

(1)

(2)

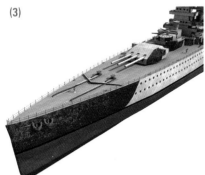

(3)

(4)

(5)

(1) *Admiral Graf Spee* in wartime guise. It was the only one to retain the pagoda-style bridge structure.
(2) Plan view.
(3) Bow detail, showing the anchor arrangement with two anchors to port and one to starboard.
(4) The massive pagoda-style bridge was wide, but not particularly deep. It was topped by a rangefinder with

mounted FuMO radar array. It is likely that had *Graf Spee* survived, its bridge would have received similar modification to that on *Admiral Scheer*.
(5) *Admiral Graf Spee* never received the angled funnel cap that was fitted to its sisters.

The Admiral Hipper Class

Schwere Kreuzer *Admiral Hipper*

This, the first of Germany's new and powerful heavy cruisers, was named for Admiral Franz Ritter von Hipper (1863–1932). As first completed, *Admiral Hipper* featured a straight stem and an uncapped funnel. Its armorial crest was fitted to the stem. In November 1939 it underwent a refit in which the straight stem was replaced by a 'clipper bow', the open bridge was enclosed and the funnel had a raked cap fitted. At the same time, its armorial crests changed from a single piece on the stem, to one each side of the bow. In reality, however, it seems that only the mounting points for these shields were fitted. After the outbreak of war, such devices were removed from all warships or painted over.

Subsequent to the outbreak of war, the only significant modifications made to *Admiral Hipper* were in terms of increases to its anti-aircraft protection. Quadruple 2cm flak mounts were added to the roof of turret 'Bruno' and turret 'Caesar' in 1942, though by the end of the war these had been replaced by 4cm Bofors-type single-barrelled weapons.

LEFT A later view of *Admiral Hipper*, with tall funnel cap fitted, enclosed and glazed bridge and a raked stem. This shot shows it in a basic grey colour scheme, but it would later carry an extensive camouflage scheme. It would also carry improved radar and upgraded anti-aircraft armament. (DUBM)

BELOW *Admiral Hipper* as built. The first of its class, it shows typical early features including the straight stem, open bridge and lack of funnel cap. It would be the last major warship to enter service still showing these early features. (Author's collection)

Admiral Hipper Specifications			
Length	202.8m	**Main armament**	8 x 20.3cm guns in four twin turrets
Beam	21.3m	**Secondary armament**	12 x 10.5cm guns in six twin turrets
Draught	7.74m	**Flak armament**	12 x 3.7cm guns in six twin turrets 8 x 2cm guns on single mounts
Maximum displacement	18,600 tons	**Torpedoes**	12 x 53.3cm torpedo tubes in four triple mounts
Fuel oil carried	3,050 tons	**Aircraft**	3 x Arado 196 floatplanes
Maximum speed	32 knots	**Complement**	50 officers and 1,500 men
Endurance	6,800 nautical miles		

Admiral Hipper's Commanders	
April 1939–September 1940	Kapitän zur See Hellmuth Heye
September 1940–November 1942	Kapitän zur See Wilhelm Meisel
November 1942–February 1943	Kapitän zur See Hans Hartmann
March 1944–May 1945	Kapitän zur See Hans Henigst

BELOW Kapitän zur See Wilhelm Meisel, commander of the *Admiral Hipper*. He was decorated with the Knight's Cross on 26 February 1941 for his command of the heavy cruiser and later reached the rank of *Admiral* while serving with naval high command as *Chef der Seekriegsleitung* (Chief of Naval Staff). (Narodowe Archiwum Cyfrowe)

FAR RIGHT An early shot of *Blücher* as built, with the typical straight stem. Due to its short operational life, it was never to have the opportunity for the degree of modification and upgrade achieved by its sisters, though a raked stem was added before it saw active service. (Author's collection)

Schwere *Kreuzer Blücher*

The second of the Kriegsmarine's new heavy cruisers was named after one of Germany's greatest military heroes, Generalfeldmarschall Gebhard Leberecht Fürst Blücher von Wahlstatt (1742–1819).

Like *Admiral Hipper*, it was originally intended to have a straight stem and indeed was launched in this form. Before commissioning into the navy, however, a raked stem, the so-called 'Atlantic bow', was fitted. Due to its short service life before being sunk, no major alterations were carried out.

Blücher

(1)

(2)

(3)

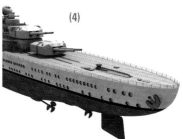

(4)

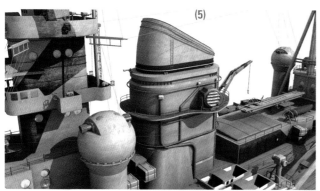

(5)

(1) *Blücher* as first commissioned, with straight stem. It still lacks the funnel cap, and has only basic rangefinder equipment, no radar having been installed.
(2) *Blücher* in its early days with anchors set into hawse holes on the hull side, two to port and one to starboard.
(3) The stem was later refitted to give the cruiser a raked bow. At this time the anchor's arrangement was altered to just one each side, set into a cluse.
(4) The stern featured an anchor on the port side only.
(5) The later raked funnel cap, fitted shortly after its completion.
(Ian Palmer © Osprey Publishing)

Blücher Specifications

Length	202.8m	Secondary armament	12 x 10.5cm guns in six twin turrets
Beam	21.3m	Flak armament	12 x 3.7cm guns in six twin turrets 8 x 2cm guns on single mounts
Draught	7.74m	Torpedoes	12 x 53.3cm torpedo tubes in four triple mounts
Maximum displacement	18,694 tons	Aircraft	3 x Arado 196 floatplanes
Main armament	8 x 20.3cm guns in four twin turrets	Complement	50 officers and 1,500 men

Blücher's Commanders

September 1939–April 1940	Kapitän zur See Heinrich Woldag

Prinz Eugen

Widely considered the most attractive of the German warships, with a 212.5m-long hull divided into 14 compartments and a beam of 21.9 m, it was slightly longer and wider than its sisters. A single funnel was located amidships directly above the boiler rooms, of which in *Prinz Eugen* there were six, each with four boilers, and from which led massive gas trunking pipes up into the funnel. It could carry a crew of between 1,400 and 1,600 men at any one time. This class was similar in layout and design to the Bismarck class which the cruisers very closely resembled visually.
(Ian Palmer © Osprey Publishing)

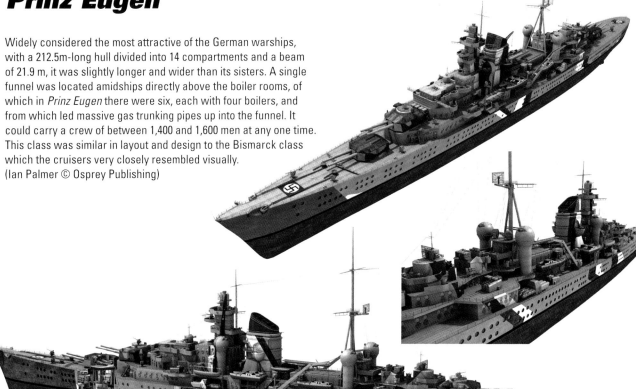

Schwere Kreuzer *Prinz Eugen*

The third vessel in the Hipper class was named for Prince Eugene of Savoy (1663–1736), a French-born statesman who departed France at the age of 20 and transferred his loyalty to Austria. As launched, *Prinz Eugen* featured a straight stem, and had its bow anchors set two to port and one to starboard, emerging from hawse pipes in the hullside. It also lacked any form of funnel cap. Before being accepted into the Kriegsmarine, it had its straight stem replaced by a clipper bow and a raked funnel cap fitted. Its anchor arrangement was also altered to bring it into line with its sisters, with just one bow anchor to port and one to starboard, sitting at an anchor cluse each side of the bow. *Prinz Eugen* also had a prominent degaussing coil running along the hull just below the lower row of portholes. Although when launched it featured its crests on shields either side of the bow, as opposed to a single shield on the straight stem as with *Admiral Hipper*, both shields were removed after commissioning but before it saw active service, as was the large metal eagle on its transom.

Prinz Eugen Specifications

Length	212.5m	**Secondary armament**	12 x 10.5cm guns in six twin turrets
Beam	21.9m	**Flak armament**	12 x 3.7cm guns in six twin turrets 8 x 2cm guns on single mounts
Draught	7.95m	**Torpedoes**	12 x 53.3cm torpedo tubes in four triple mounts
Maximum displacement	19,042 tons	**Aircraft**	3 x Arado 196 floatplanes
Main armament	8 x 20.3cm guns in four twin turrets	**Complement**	50 officers and 1,500 men

Prinz Eugen's Commanders

August 1940–August 1942	Kapitän zur See Helmuth Brinkmann
August 1942–October 1942	Korvettenkapitän Wilhelm Beck
October 1942–February 1943	Kapitän zur See Hans-Erich Voss
March 1943–January 1944	Kapitän zur See Werner Ehrhardt
January 1944–May 1945	Kapitän zur See Hansjürgen Reinicke

(1)

(2)

(3)

(4)

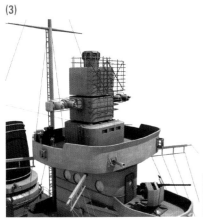

(1) *Prinz Eugen* in profile. The clipper bow and raked funnel cap are particularly distinctive. Additional flak armament, is installed on the roof of turrets 'Bruno' and 'Caesar' as well as on the foredeck and quarterdeck. (2) *Prinz Eugen* in plan view. The basic layout remains as for *Admiral Hipper* and *Blücher*. (3) *Prinz Eugen*'s foretop. Note the extensive FuMo radar array it carried in the late stages of the war. Note also the steeply raked funnel cap. (4) Turret 'Bruno' on *Prinz Eugen*. Note the flak armament mounted on the roof and on the main deck between 'Anton' and 'Bruno'. (Ian Palmer © Osprey Publishing)

ABOVE Its demise imminent, *Prinz Eugen* awaits the atomic bomb tests which will destroy it. By the end of the war it carried far more extensive radar and much heavier anti-aircraft armament. At the time this photograph was taken, it was under US Navy control and turret 'Anton' had been removed. (NHHC)

ABOVE RIGHT An extremely handsome ship, *Prinz Eugen* had its straight stem altered to a raked stem during construction and before entering service with the Kriegsmarine. Note the camouflage scheme and early radar fitting on the foretop rangefinder. One of its bronze propellers was saved from its wreck and is on display at the Laboe Naval Memorial near Kiel, Germany. (DUBM)

Schwere Kreuzer *Seydlitz*

The fourth heavy cruiser in the Hipper class was named after Friedrich Wilhelm von Seydlitz (1721–73). The *Seydlitz* was laid down at the Deschimag Yard in Bremen on 29 December 1936, five months after the contract for its manufacture was placed. Construction of the basic hull and superstructure took just over two years, the ship finally being launched on 19 January 1939. It was never commissioned into the Kriegsmarine, a decision being made in June 1942 to convert the partially completed hull into an aircraft carrier. The hull was transferred to Königsberg for completion as a carrier and work continued at a slow pace until January 1943, when it was finally halted. Never completed, *Seydlitz* was scuttled in January 1945 as the Red Army approached Königsberg.

Schwere Kreuzer *Lützow*

The final ship in the Hipper class was named for Adolf Freiherr von Lützow (1782–1843). The *Lützow* was laid down at the Deschimag Yard in Bremen on 2 August 1937, the contract for its construction having been issued at the same time as that for *Seydlitz*. Construction of the basic hull and superstructure took just under two years, the ship finally being launched on 1 July 1939. Like *Seydlitz*, it was never completed, its partially finished hull being sold to the Soviet Union in April 1940.

Armour, gunnery and radar

The Hipper-class cruisers were provided with belt armour of 7–8cm thickness, upper deck armour of 1.2–3.0cm and a main armoured deck of 2–5cm thickness. Once again, the armour on this class was little more than adequate, but as they too were intended as commerce raiders, it was probably appropriate for that purpose.

The main armament for the Hipper class comprised the 20.3cm SK L/60 C34 naval gun. Eight were carried in twin turrets. They could fire a 122kg shell to a maximum effective distance of 25km with a rate of fire of around three per minute per barrel.

Admiral Hipper

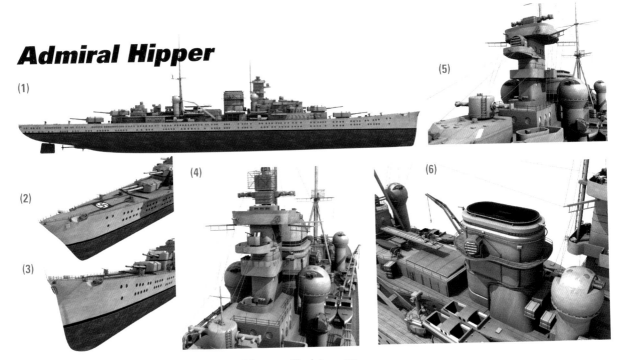

(1) (2) (3) (4) (5) (6)

(1) *Admiral Hipper* as completed with early straight stem. The later, very distinctive, raked funnel cap has not yet been fitted and its anchor is still in the hullside anchor hawse.
(2) Revised 'clipper' bow with distinct rake.
(3) Bow view, showing the ship's crest, as originally completed.
(4) The revised tower structure showing enclosed glazed bridge area and radar mounted on the foretop.
(5) The original tower structure with open-topped bridge and searchlight platform, the searchlight being replaced later by an additional flak gun position.
(6) Midships view showing the funnel as originally completed.
(Ian Palmer © Osprey Publishing)

BELOW A bomb-damaged *Admiral Hipper* in dry dock, Kiel, May 1945, following several direct hits during a raid by British bombers on 9 April. It was scuttled in dry dock but later towed out and beached in Heikendorf Bay, where it was eventually scrapped after the war. (NHHC)

Late-war camouflage schemes

(1) *Admiral Hipper* in a colour scheme dating from mid-1944.

(2) USS *Prinz Eugen* is shown in its final appearance before being used in the atomic bomb test programme at Bikini Atoll in July 1946.

(3) This view shows *Prinz Eugen* in the aftermath of being torpedoed by the British submarine *Trident* in 1942. Its ruined stern and rudder has been neatly cut away and plated over, shortening its length significantly and giving it a squared-off stern. It then had to be steered manually, using a capstan on its quarterdeck.
(Ian Palmer © Osprey Publishing)

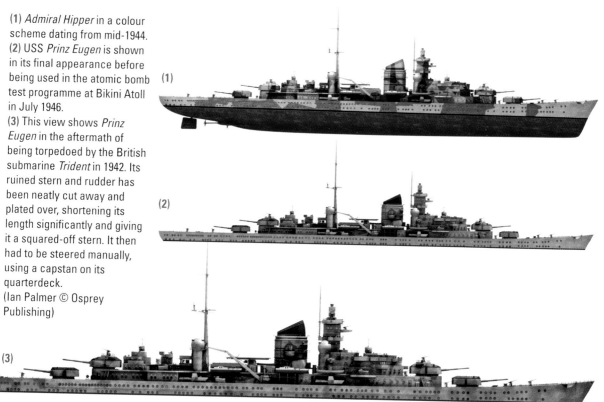

Fire control on the Hipper class was by 7m stereoscopic rangefinders for the main armament. These were fitted in turrets 'Bruno' and 'Caesar' with one on the foretop and a final set on the aft control centre. Secondary armament was controlled by 4m rangefinders in domed housings either side of the bridge and at either side of the mainmast.

No radar was installed on *Admiral Hipper* as first built, but in late 1940 FuMO 22 surface search radar was installed and in 1941/42 FuMO 27 sets with a 3m x 4m 'mattress' antenna were mounted on the fire control stations on the foretop and on the aft fire control centre. In the latter part of the war, the fittings for an additional FuMO 25 with 3m x 2m antenna were installed, but it is unclear whether this equipment was actually fitted.

Due to its extremely brief life, *Blücher* did not see much in the way of radar modifications. It had a FuMO 22 with a 2m x 6m 'mattress' antenna fitted to its foretop rangefinder housing. This was the only radar it was to carry.

Prinz Eugen was equipped with FuMO 27 radar sets with the 2m x 4m 'mattress' antenna, on the foretop rangefinder housing and on the rangefinder on the aft control centre. These were carried from 1940 to 1942. Sometime in September 1942, after its participation in the 'Channel Dash', the foretop radar was extended to include a new radar housing atop the rangefinder for a FuMO 26 set with 2m x 4m antenna whilst below this sat a *Timor* antenna for the FuMB 4 *Samos* passive radar detector system, the latter installed in mid-1944. FuMB 4 equipment was also installed on the mainmast. FuMB 1 and FuMB 10 *Borkum* equipment was carried on the foretop rail, and FuMB 9 *Cypern* on the foretop itself. FuMB 26 *Tunis* receivers were carried on the foretop radar housing.

In the final part of the war *Prinz Eugen* carried a large 3m x 6m 'mattress' antenna for the FuMO 26 set on its foretop. In addition, an antenna was fitted to the foremast for the advanced FuMO 81 Berlin 6cm wavelength reconnaissance radar and a FuMO 25 antenna mounted on a platform on its mainmast. Certainly *Prinz Eugen* was one of the best-equipped German warships as far as radar was concerned.

Light Cruisers

Kreuzer *Emden*

Emden was the sole example of its class, its design severely restricted by conditions imposed by the Allied Control Commission, and was based on the design concept for the Imperial Navy cruiser *Karlsruhe*.

The *Emden* was the first modern light cruiser to be constructed for the German Navy after World War I. The contract for its construction was placed with the Marinewerft in Wilhelmshaven on 7 April 1921 and the keel laid some eight months later. Construction took just over four years and it was launched on 7 January 1925. After fitting out and finishing work was completed, *Emden* was commissioned into the *Reichsmarine* on 15 October 1925.

Emden featured belt armour up to 5cm in thickness, with deck armour from 2cm to 4cm. It carried eight 15cm SK L/45 C16 naval guns, World War I designs, which fired a 17kg round up to 17km. Already obsolescent, it would never be involved in any direct action with enemy warships. *Emden* did not carry radar.

Emden during a courtesy visit to Honolulu, under the command of Kapitän zur See Johannes Bachmann, in February 1936. It also briefly served on non-intervention patrols off the Spanish coast during the Spanish Civil War before resuming its flag-waving cruises and serving for a short period as a fishery protection vessel. (NHHC)

Emden Specifications

Length	155.1m	**Secondary armament**	3 x 8.8cm guns in single mounts (later 3 x 10.5cm twin barrel mounts)
Beam	14.3m	**Flak armament**	4 x 3.7cm guns on single mounts 7 x 2cm guns on single mounts 2 x 2cm Flakvierling
Draught	5.93m	**Torpedoes**	4 x 50cm torpedo tubes in two twin mounts
Maximum displacement	6,990 tons	**Aircraft**	None
Maximum speed	29.5 knots	**Complement**	19 officers and 464 men
Maximum endurance	5,300 nautical miles		
Main armament	8 x 15cm guns in eight single gun turrets		

Emden's Commanders

October 1925–December 1928	Kapitän zur See Foerster
December 1928–October 1930	Fregattenkapitän Lothar Arnauld de la Periere
October 1930–March 1932	Fregattenkapitän Witthoeft-Emden
March 1932–September 1934	Fregattenkapitän Grassmann
September 1934–September 1935	Fregattenkapitän Karl Dönitz
September 1935–August 1936	Fregattenkapitän Bachmann
August 1936–July 1937	Kapitän zur See Lohmann
July 1937–June 1938	Fregattenkapitän Bürkner
June 1938–May 1939	Kapitän zur See Wever
May 1939–August 1940	Kapitän zur See Werner Lange
August 1940–July 1942	Kapitän zur See Mirow
July 1942–September 1943	Kapitän zur See Friedrich Traugott Schmidt
September 1943–March 1944	Kapitän zur See Henigst
March 1944–January 1945	Fregattenkapitän Hans-Eberhard Meissner
January 1945–May 1945	Kapitän zur See Wolfgang Kähler

The oldest of Germany's light cruisers, *Emden*'s primary purpose pre-war was as a training ship, allowing many distinguished future officers to gain invaluable command experience on flag-waving cruises around the world. *Emden*'s commander during 1934 was future Grossadmiral and Oberbefehlshaber der Kriegsmarine Karl Dönitz. (Author's collection)

Emden

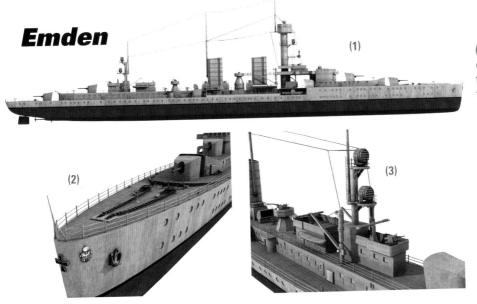

(1)

(2)

(3)

(1) *Emden* in wartime configuration, *c.*1942. Note the considerable difference in the appearance of its foretop and enlarged deckhouse structures on its after deck.
(2) Prior to the outbreak of war, *Emden* carried, as well as the usual ship's crest on the side of its bow, a large Iron Cross.
(3) *Emden*'s mainmast was redesigned and shortened to little more than a support pole for two searchlight positions. This was carried out during the refit of 1933–34.
(Ian Palmer © Osprey Publishing)

The K-Class Cruisers

This class of cruiser, of which three, the *Königsberg*, *Köln* and *Karlsruhe* were built, was classed as *Spähkreuzer*, literally reconnaissance or scouting cruiser. They were never intended to give serious battle to equivalent enemy warships, but rather to 'hit and run'. Thus, six of their nine 15cm guns were mounted in two triple turrets facing aft, to give them a better chance of fending off pursuing enemy ships. In the K class, the two aft turrets were also mounted off centre, allowing these stern turrets to traverse further round in the direction of the bow and be brought into action if the cruiser was pursuing a victim.

The severe treaty restrictions under whose terms the K-class cruisers were built, and the many weight-saving measures employed, resulted in vessels that were rather weak structurally, as would be proven by the storm damage suffered by *Karlsruhe* during its 1936 cruise to the Pacific. In addition, the effective range without refuelling was rather modest when compared with ships such as the pocket battleships and heavy cruisers that were built later. The K class were not really suitable for long-distance operational use, indeed being inferior to the older *Emden* in this respect, and in the event, after the outbreak of war, they were restricted to coastal duties.

The K class carried 5–7cm belt armour and deck armour 2–4cm thick. The main armament consisted of nine 15cm SK L/60 C25 naval guns, mounted in three triple turrets, one forward and two aft, that fired a 45.5kg shell and had a maximum range of 25.7km. A firing rate of up to eight rounds per minute could be achieved.

All of the light cruisers were equipped with three sets of 6m stereoscopic rangefinders, one on the foretop and one each in the forward and aft control centres.

Neither *Königsberg* nor *Karlsruhe* were fitted with radar. *Köln*, however, had a FuMO 21 radar set installed in place of the forward 6m rangefinder. Three 3m rangefinders were carried to control the heavy flak, one either side of the main mast and one on the aft control centre.

Kreuzer *Königsberg*

Königsberg was the first of the three K-class cruisers to be laid down. The original order for its construction was issued to the Marinewerft in Wilhelmshaven in 1925 and its keel was laid in April 1926. Basic construction took just under a year, the cruiser being launched in April 1929. Exactly eight months later, in December 1929, with the fitting out work completed, it was commissioned into the Reichsmarine. *Königsberg* was allocated as flagship of the newly created *Aufklärungs streitekräfte*, or reconnaissance forces, and took part in a series of goodwill cruises flying the flag in various Mediterranean ports.

Königsberg during Operation *Weserübung*, the invasion of Norway, under a surprise attack from British aircraft. *Königsberg*'s flak is putting up as heavy a barrage as it can. One of the 1,000lb bombs has exploded between the quay and the cruiser's hull. Another has passed clean through the ship before exploding and holing it below the waterline. Three have scored direct hits and others have exploded near the stern, ripping open the plates there too. It is developing a list to port. The damage to the cruiser was fatal but it settled relatively slowly, giving the crew time to evacuate.
(Ian Palmer © Osprey Publishing)

Königsberg

(1)

(2)   (3)

(4)

(1) *Königsberg* after its 1939–40 refit, with catapult installed and an extended pole mast fitted to the rear of its second funnel. Both funnels have caps and searchlight platforms fitted. The foretop has been remodelled and the anchor moved from a hawse hole on the hull side to a cluse on the forecastle.
(2) *Königsberg*'s aircraft catapult was installed between its funnels.

(3) The standard aircraft carried by the K-class light cruisers was the Heinkel He 60.
(4) This view shows the forward torpedo tube position on the K-class cruisers. Four sets were carried, each with three tubes (Ian Palmer © Osprey Publishing)

Königsberg received its first major modifications in 1931 when the mast at its foretop was shortened and the rear superstructure extended slightly by having a single-storey housing erected upon it. This latter modification was extended further during the following year. It underwent minor modifications during a refit in 1932, predominantly to the mast and foretop, before undertaking more goodwill trips around European ports. In 1934, its crane was replaced, and two 8.8cm flak guns installed on the roof of the aft superstructure between turret 'Bruno' and the above-mentioned housing. Modifications were also made to the bridge structure. In 1935 an aircraft catapult was added between the funnels, with an aircraft crane fitted to the port side, replacing the smaller derrick that had been located there. The derrick on the starboard side remained, however. During the following year a pole mast was fitted to the rear face of the aft funnel and a twin 8.8cm flak unit on a triaxially stabilized mount replaced the two single 8.8cm guns on the aft superstructure. Two further units were added, one to either side of the housing on the aft superstructure, which was also extended and fitted with a rangefinder/fire control housing. *Königsberg* underwent its final modifications in late 1939 when a degaussing coil was fitted around the hull just above the waterline.

Königsberg Specifications			
Length	169m	**Main armament**	9 x 15cm guns in three triple gun turrets
Beam	15.2m	**Secondary armament**	12 x 10.5cm guns in six twin turrets
Draught	5.7m	**Flak armament**	12 x 3.7cm guns in six twin turrets 8 x 2cm guns on single mounts
Maximum displacement	6,750 tons	**Torpedoes**	12 x 53.3cm torpedo tubes in four triple mounts
Maximum speed	32 knots	**Aircraft**	2 x Heinkel He 60 floatplanes
Maximum endurance	5,700 nautical miles (turbines) 8,000 nautical miles (diesels)	**Complement**	50 officers and 1,500 men

Königsberg's Commanders	
April 1929–June 1929	Kapitän zur See Wolf von Trotha
June 1929–September 1930	Fregattenkapitän Robert Witthöft-Emden
September 1930–September 1931	Fregattenkapitän Hermann Densch
September 1931–September 1934	Fregattenkapitän Otto von Schrader
September 1934–September 1935	Fregattenkapitän Hubert Schmundt
September 1935–February 1937	Fregattenkapitän Bachmann
February 1937–November 1938	Fregattenkapitän Robin Schall-Emden
November 1938–June 1939	Kapitän zur See Ernst Scheurlen
June 1939–September 1939	Kapitän zur See Kurt-Caesar Hoffmann
September 1939–May 1940	Kapitän zur See Heinrich Ruhfus

Kreuzer *Karlsruhe*

Karlsruhe was laid down at the Deutsche Werke yard in Kiel in July 1926, and launched just over a year later in August 1927. Completion and fitting-out work took a further two years, and the cruiser was finally commissioned into the *Reichsmarine* in November 1929.

Karlsruhe was first modified over the winter of 1930/31. This involved shortening the pole mast attached to its foretop and adding additional housings on the roof of its aft superstructure and on the boat deck between its funnels.

The next series of significant modifications came in 1935 when a pole mast was fitted to the rear face of the aft funnel, and an aircraft catapult added between the funnels. An aircraft crane was also fitted on the port side, replacing the smaller derrick that had been sited there. Modifications were also made to the platforms on its battlemast. In July 1936 it underwent further modifications which mirrored those made to its older sister, namely the extending of the housing on its aft superstructure roof and the provision of a rangefinder/fire control unit on this structure, plus the replacement of its elderly single-barrelled 8.8cm flak guns with the three new twin 8.8cm housing sited as on *Königsberg*. Bridge wings were

The unfortunate *Karlsruhe* was struck by enemy torpedoes during the attack on Norway in 1940. After the commander gave the order to abandon ship, it was sunk by a German torpedo boat. The wreck of *Karlsruhe*, still in remarkably good condition sitting upright on the seabed, was rediscovered in 2017. (NHHC)

also added at this point. In 1938, *Karlsruhe* underwent a major refit. The housing on its foretop was reduced to single storey and modifications made to the battlemast platforms. Raked funnel caps were fitted to both the funnels and the smaller starboard derrick was replaced by a larger crane. Searchlight platforms were added to each side of both of the funnels, its 8.8cm flak guns were replaced by heavier 10.5cm units, and a tripod mainmast fitted to the rear face of its aft funnel.

Modifications were also made to its anchor stowage. The older style hawse pipe opening on its starboard bow was deleted and an anchor cluse installed on the starboard side of its forecastle. Strangely, this modification was only carried out on the starboard side, the twin anchors to port remaining in a hawse pipe opening on the hull side. *Karlsruhe* received its final major modification in 1940 when a degaussing coil was added.

Karlsruhe Specifications			
Length	169m	**Main armament**	9 x 15cm guns in three triple gun turrets
Beam	15.2m	**Secondary armament**	12 x 10.5cm guns in six twin turrets
Draught	5.7m	**Flak armament**	12 x 3.7cm guns in six twin turrets 8 x 2cm guns on single mounts
Maximum displacement	6,750 tons	**Torpedoes**	12 x 53.3cm torpedo tubes in four triple mounts
Maximum speed	32 knots	**Aircraft**	2 x Heinkel He 60 floatplanes
Maximum endurance	5,700 nautical miles (turbines) 8,000 nautical miles (diesels)	**Complement**	50 officers and 1,500 men

Karlsruhe's Commanders	
November 1929–September 1931	Fregattenkapitän Eugen Lindau
September 1931–December 1932	Kapitän zur See Erwin Wassner
December 1932–September 1934	Fregattenkapitän Wilhelm Harsdorf von Enderndorf
September 1934–September 1935	Kapitän zur See Günther Lütjens
September 1935–September 1937	Kapitän zur See Leopold Siemens
September 1937–May 1938	Kapitän zur See Erich Förste
(Decommissioned May 1938 and recommissioned 1939)	
November 1939–April 1940	Kapitän zur See Friedrich Rieve

Karlsruhe, during a pre-war flag-flying tour of the Far East, is shown here in Calcutta in December 1933. A tripod mainmast would later be installed abaft the second funnel, and the large searchlight platforms seen here replaced with small platforms on each side of the two funnels. (Keystone/Getty Images)

Kreuzer *Köln*

The keel of the third of the K-class cruisers was laid down at the Marinewerft at Wilhelmshaven in August 1926 and the ship launched in May 1928. On completion of its fitting out, *Köln* was commissioned into the *Reichsmarine* in January 1930, after which followed the usual period of trials and working up in the Baltic. The following year saw it take part in fleet manoeuvres as well as making a short goodwill cruise in the summer.

Köln's first modifications, in 1931, followed those of its sisters. Housings were erected on the roof of its aft superstructure, between the funnels and forward of turret 'Bruno', the latter being provided with a rangefinder/fire control unit. Its original 8.8cm single flak units were replaced by twins, and signal wings added to its bridge. In 1935 modifications were made to the bridge deck and to the platform arrangement on its battlemast, an aircraft catapult added and the port derrick replaced by an aircraft crane. The aftmost housing on the rear superstructure was also extensively reworked and a raised circular platform added for a flak director position. A pole mast was also added to the rear face of the aft funnel. Further modifications were made in 1937 when the aircraft catapult was removed and replaced by another housing similar to that which had been fitted earlier. The port aircraft crane was also removed and replaced by a simple derrick. During its winter 1940/41 refit, a degaussing coil was added and a helicopter landing pad added to the roof of turret 'Bruno'. Its final major modifications came in the spring of 1942 when a FuMO 21 radar set was installed in place of the forward rangefinder unit on the forward command-centre roof. Very little in the way of augmentation to its flak armament seems to have been made to *Köln*, apart from the addition of single-barrelled 2cm flak guns on the forecastle.

Köln Specifications

Length	169m	**Main armament**	9 x 15cm guns in three triple gun turrets
Beam	15.2m	**Secondary armament**	12 x 10.5cm guns in six twin turrets
Draught	5.7m	**Flak armament**	12 x 3.7cm guns in six twin turrets 8 x 2cm guns on single mounts
Maximum displacement	6,750 tons	**Torpedoes**	12 x 53.3cm torpedo tubes in four triple mounts
Maximum speed	32 knots	**Aircraft**	2 x Heinkel He 60 floatplanes
Maximum endurance	5,700 nautical miles (turbines) 8,000 nautical miles (diesels)	**Complement**	50 officers and 1,500 men

Köln's Commanders

October 1937–January 1940	Kapitän zur See Theodor Burchardi
January 1940–May 1941	Kapitän zur See Ernst Kratzenberg
May 1941–March 1942	Kapitän zur See Friedrich Hüffmeier
March 1942–May 1942	Korvettenapitän Hellmuth Strobel
May 1942–December 1942	Kapitän zur See Martin Baltzer
December 1942–February 1943	Kapitän zur See Hans Meyer
(Decommissioned and then recommissioned.)	
April 1944–January 1945	Kapitän zur See Hellmuth Strobel

The third of the ill-fated K-class, after 1940 *Köln* saw little significant combat action and avoided any major damage through the first part of the war. Its later use was limited, due to serious reliability problems, to minor escort duties. It ended the war in Kiel harbour, where it was sunk by US bombers. (Author's collection)

Visually, *Leipzig* was superficially similar to the K class but with a single large funnel. It spent the early part of the war as an escort for heavier units and was torpedoed by the British submarine HMS *Salmon*, and after repairs was relegated to training duties. An incident on 15 October 1944 which saw it colliding with *Prinz Eugen* ensured it would see no further serious action. (Author's collection)

The Leipzig-Class Cruisers

This class, of which only two examples were built, was broadly similar in appearance to the K class, at least in original form. The principal obvious difference was that both of these vessels were somewhat larger than the K class, and had only a single funnel. *Nürnberg* featured a much more heavily developed bridge superstructure unlike any of the other light cruisers. *Leipzig's* forward superstructure resembled far more closely that of the K class. One further difference, though not immediately apparent in photos, especially those from a broadside aspect, is that the aft main armament turrets of these later cruisers were mounted on the centreline and not offset like their earlier counterparts.

These cruisers were driven by three shafts rather than the two of *Emden* and the K class. For *Nürnberg*, each of the main shafts was driven by a single high-pressure turbine and two low-pressure turbines, all manufactured by Deutsche Werke of Kiel. In *Leipzig's* case, each main shaft was driven by one high-pressure and one low-pressure turbine, all built by Krupp. In both cases, the central shaft was powered by four Maschinenfabrik Augsburg-Nürnberg (MAN) two-stroke seven-cylinder diesels. The flexibility offered by this arrangement was not without its costs. If one or the other system was in use, and it was required to bring both systems into use, all engines had to be stopped for several minutes before the systems could be double-coupled.

In both ships, the turbines were fed by six oil-fired boilers, arranged in three boiler rooms each, with one boiler to port and one to starboard. The cruisers were steered by the use of a single rudder. Electrical power was provided by two 250kW turbo generators and two 90kW diesel generators.

Apart from being mounted on the centreline, the main armament of the Leipzig class was identical to the K class. The Leipzig-class cruisers featured belt armour from 1.8cm to 5cm with deck armour 2cm thick.

Kreuzer *Leipzig*

The keel of *Leipzig* was laid in April 1928 at the Marinewerft in Wilhelmshaven and the vessel launched in October 1929. Completion and fitting out took two more years and the new cruiser was commissioned into the Reichsmarine in October 1931.

Leipzig's first major modification came in late 1934 when the housing on the superstructure roof between the funnel and the battlemast was removed and replaced by an aircraft catapult. An aircraft crane also replaced the port derrick at this time. As with the K-class cruisers, its original 8.8cm single flak gun fittings were replaced by twin units. In 1940 a degaussing cable was fitted and in 1941 its aircraft catapult and the aftmost pair of torpedo tube mounts were removed. In 1943, the forward torpedo tube mounts were also removed. At the same time, however, it was fitted with a FuMO 24/25 radar antenna on a new platform replacing the searchlight platform on its battlemast. A further platform just below the foretop now carried a FuMB 6 set. This was to be the last major modification/improvement to the cruiser. None of the planned major improvements to *Leipzig*'s flak armament appear to have come to fruition.

Leipzig Specifications			
Length	177m	Main armament	9 x 15cm guns in three triple gun turrets
Beam	16.3m	Secondary armament	12 x 10.5cm guns in six twin turrets
Draught	5.7m	Flak armament	12 x 3.7cm guns in six twin turrets 8 x 2cm guns on single mounts
Maximum displacement	8,427 tons	Torpedoes	12 x 53.3cm torpedo tubes in four triple mounts
Maximum speed	32 knots (turbines) 16.5 knots (diesels)	Aircraft	2 x Heinkel He 60 floatplanes
Maximum endurance	3,780 nautical miles	Complement	24 officers and 826 men

Leipzig's Commanders			
October 1931–September 1933	Kapitän zur See Hans-Herbert Stobwasser	September 1942–February 1943	Kapitän zur See Waldemar Winther
September 1933–September 1935	Korvettenkapitän Otto Hormel	Decommissioned February 1943 Recommissioned August 1943	
September 1935–October 1937	Fregattenkapitän Otto Schenk	October 1943–August 1944	Kapitän zur See Walter Hülsemann
October 1937–April 1939	Kapitän zur See Werner Löwisch	August 1944–November 1944	Kapitän zur See Heinrich Spörel
April 1939–February 1940	Kapitän zur See Heinz Nordmann	November 1944–January 1945	Korvettenkapitän Hagen Küster
(Decommissioned then recommissioned.)		January 1945–May 1945	Korvettenkapitän Walter Bach
December 1940–August 1942	Kapitän zur See Werner Stichling		
August 1942–September 1942	Kapitän zur See Friedrich-Traugott Schmidt		

Leipzig

(1)

(2)

(3)

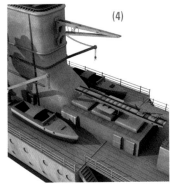

(4)

(1) and (2) *Leipzig* as constructed. Identifiable as distinct from the K class by its single rather than twin funnels. It has no provision for an aircraft and no radar equipment fitted.
(3) In the latter part of its career, *Leipzig* had FuMO 25 and FuMB radar antennae fitted to its mainmast, following the removal of the searchlight platform. (4) In 1935, *Leipzig* had the deckhouse forward of the funnel removed to facilitate the addition of a catapult for a Heinkel He 60 floatplane.
(Ian Palmer © Osprey Publishing)

Kreuzer *Nürnberg*

Nürnberg's keel was laid at the Deutsche Werft in Kiel in November 1933. Construction took just over one year, with the cruiser being launched in December 1934. On completion, it was commissioned into the Kriegsmarine in November 1935.

Not being completed until 1935, many of the improvements that were carried out to its predecessors were incorporated into *Nürnberg* during its construction. The first significant modification came in March 1941 when it had a FuMO 21 radar set installed in place of the 6m forward rangefinder. In early 1942 its aircraft catapult was removed and its radar equipment upgraded to a FuMO 25 set, but mounted on a platform on the face of the battlemast and with the forward rangefinder reinstated. In 1944, a FuMO 63 set was installed on a mount on the mainmast.

Nürnberg was the only light cruiser to have been given significant additional flak armament. *Flakvierling* were installed on the roof of turret 'Bruno' and on the roof of the navigating bridge, and the number of 2cm single-barrelled units was also increased. The *Flakvierling* on the roof of the navigating bridge was replaced in 1944 by a more powerful 4cm Flak 28, and a second example of this weapon installed on the tower, which had previously supported the aircraft catapult after the latter feature had been removed. An additional 2cm single-barrelled unit was also installed around this time, together with five twin 2cm mounts.

Nürnberg Specifications

Length	181m	**Main armament**	9 x 15cm guns in three triple gun turrets	
Beam	16.4m	**Secondary armament**	12 x 10.5cm guns in six twin turrets	
Draught	5.8m	**Flak armament**	12 x 3.7cm guns in six twin turrets 8 x 2cm guns on single mounts	
Maximum displacement	9,040 tons	**Torpedoes**	12 x 53.3cm torpedo tubes in four triple mounts	
Maximum speed	32 knots (turbines) 16.5 knots (diesels)	**Aircraft**	2 x Heinkel He 60 floatplanes	
Maximum endurance	3,780 nautical miles (turbines)	**Complement**	26 officers and 870 men	

Nürnberg's Commanders

November 1935–October 1936	Kapitän zur See Hubert Schmundt
October 1936–October 1937	Kapitän zur See Theodor-Heinrich Riedel
October 1937–November 1938	Kapitän zur See Walter Krastel
November 1938–December 1938	Kapitän zur See Heinz Degenhardt
December 1938–August 1940	Kapitän zur See Otto Klüber
August 1940–March 1941	Kapitän zur See Leo Kreisch
March 1941–June 1943	Kapitän zur See Ernst von Studnitz
June 1943–October 1944	Kapitän zur See Gerhardt Böhmig
October 1944–May 1945	Kapitän zur See Helmuth Geissler

Nürnberg served variously as a minelayer and training ship until extreme fuel shortages saw it removed from active service. It survived the war and was given to the USSR as war reparations, serving in the Soviet Navy as the *Admiral Makarov* until decommissioned in 1960. (Author's collection)

Nürnberg

As this cutaway of *Nürnberg* shows, its basic layout was fairly conventional, the greatest part of the ship's innards, from the base of the battle mast through to the stern, being taken up by the various engine-room compartments with most crew accommodation forward. *Nürnberg* is wearing the camouflage scheme it sported in 1941. It has the FuMO 21 radar set installed, which replaced the original forward 6m rangefinder. *Nürnberg*, being the last of the light cruisers to be constructed, was the best protected, featuring the latest developments in armour plating, Krupp Pz240 nickel steel protection. (Ian Palmer © Osprey Publishing)

Auxiliary Cruisers

The Kriegsmarine's use of auxiliary cruisers should not have come as any surprise to the Allies, since the *Kaiserliche Marine* had employed such *Hilfskreuzer* widely during World War I. A number of these had achieved fame, when converted merchant vessels such as the *Berlin*, *Kronprinz Wilhelm*, *Möwe*, *Prinz Eitel Friedrich* and *Wolf II* between them took a heavy toll of Allied shipping. The auxiliary cruisers of the Kaiser's navy ranged from sailing ships through merchantmen to large ocean liners, but experience proved that those which showed most promise were the converted merchantmen. Although they lacked the speed of the ocean liners, the smaller merchantmen made less obvious targets for enemy warships and had much lower fuel requirements.

Between them, nine of the auxiliary cruisers of the World War II Kriegsmarine sank or captured a total of 129 vessels, representing some 780,000 tons of shipping. This achievement, by a total of around 3,400 officers and men – the total who served aboard the auxiliary cruisers – represented incredible value. The cost of refurbishing the entire fleet of former merchantmen, generally outfitted with older, surplus weaponry, was only around 1 per cent of the cost of constructing a single major warship such as *Bismarck* or *Tirpitz*.

HSK 1 *Orion*

HSK 2 *Atlantis*

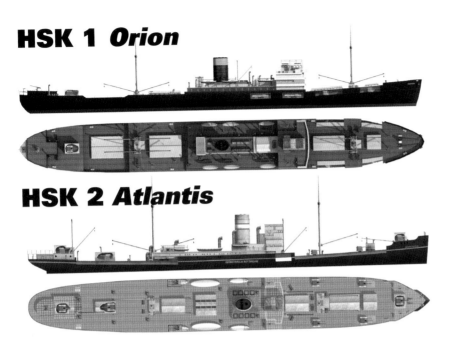

TOP HSK 1 *Orion* shown in its first wartime disguise as Dutch merchantman *Beemsterdijk*, carrying its national colours on the hull side, along with its name and port of registration – Rotterdam. *Orion*'s main armament was mounted above decks, concealed within false deckhouses. Its Arado Ar 196 floatplane was carried in the forward hold.

LEFT HSK 2 *Atlantis* in spring 1940, in the guise of Dutch merchantman *Abbekerk*. *Atlantis* occasionally carried a false second funnel. The main armament was mounted below deck level. The aftermost gun was not concealed, since many merchant ships carried a single defensive gun astern; its presence would not betray the raider's true nature. (Ian Palmer © Osprey Publishing)

None of these auxiliary cruisers could possibly be described as aesthetically attractive, but that was a positive point in their favour. They were intended to look anonymous and unthreatening until the moment when the *Reichskriegsflagge* (Reich's war flag) was run up at the mast, the guns were cleared for action and the destructive potential of a powerful warship was unleashed against the shocked victim. Despite the great successes they would achieve, the auxiliary cruisers were not initially considered as particularly important. They were crewed by volunteers who could be spared from other branches, and commanded by officers – usually from the Reserves – not considered dashing and aggressive enough to be given command of modern warships.

Although a minor degree of success was achieved by some of the larger warships in attacks on Allied merchant shipping, the auxiliary cruisers – relatively unknown when compared to famous vessels like *Admiral Graf Spee*, or indeed when compared to the most famous of all German warship types, the U-boats – proved to be, in comparative terms, immensely successful. This success could be measured not only in terms of the tonnage of Allied shipping that they sank, but also in the number of Allied warships that were diverted from other missions to try to track them down.

The Royal Navy also used 'auxiliary cruisers', but the British term tended to be applied to merchant vessels that had been openly fitted with a few medium-calibre guns in order to protect convoys from attack. The German auxiliary cruisers, though also starting life as merchantmen, were very heavily armed, usually carrying torpedo tubes as well as guns, and sometimes even their own aircraft – and their weapons were carefully concealed. Far from being tasked simply with protecting other merchantmen, these ships were aggressive predators, searching the sea-lanes for unsuspecting Allied

RIGHT The auxiliary cruiser *Orion*, which began life as the freighter *Kurmark*, looking exactly as intended – an innocent and inoffensive merchantman. Eleven enemy ships would fall victim to its guns. During evacuation operations in 1945, it was bombed by Soviet aircraft and beached near Swinemünde. (DUBM)

ABOVE Kapitän zur See Bernhard Rogge, commander of the *Atlantis*. One of the most highly respected of German naval officers he ended the war with the rank of Vizeadmiral and went on to serve in the post-war West German *Bundesmarine*. Rogge received a special diamond studded version of the Auxiliary Cruiser War Badge. (Author's collection)

vessels which would not suspect their true nature until it was too late. (It is worth noting that many of the Allied crews that fell foul of these raiders, removed from their ships before they were sunk or sent back to Germany as prizes, commented on the decent treatment they received while held prisoner.) These powerful ships were capable not only of destroying merchant ships but, in extremis, of defending themselves against well-armed enemy warships; in the most famous of such encounters, the heavy cruiser HMAS *Sydney* was sunk in battle by the *Hilfskreuzer Kormoran*.

A total of 11 ships were converted into auxiliary cruisers, usually in great secrecy; and although their designations were simply a blandly anonymous number, such as Schiff 16, they quickly became better known by their more evocative names – *Atlantis, Kormoran, Thor, Komet* and the rest.

Regarding terminology, printed sources refer to each of the auxiliary cruisers in a number of ways. Firstly, each was given an official number with the prefix HSK, running in chronological sequence. Officially this was the abbreviation for *Handelsschutzkreuzer*, 'trade protection cruiser', but the term *Hilfskreuzer*, 'auxiliary cruiser', was more common. Secondly, each was given a coded ship number (e.g. Schiff 36); each captain gave his ship a name; and finally, each was given a code letter by the Allies (e.g. Raider A). Thus, for example, HSK 2 *Atlantis* was referred to officially as Schiff 16, and was known to the Allies as Raider C. In the text that follows the 11 vessels whose conversion to this role was completed or begun are listed by name, in order of their actual or potential HSK pennant numbers.

The *Hilfskreuzer*
Orion – HSK 1; Schiff 36; Raider A

Departing port on 30 March 1940, *Orion* made one war cruise lasting 511 days during which it sank 11 enemy ships and captured one other. It returned safely but, due to its worn and unreliable engines, was not used further.

Orion Specifications			
Built	Blohm & Voss, Hamburg	**Powerplant**	2 x Blohm & Voss turbines
Launched	1930	**Top speed**	15 knots
Original name	_Kurmark_	**Endurance**	35,000 nautical miles
Length	148m	**Armament**	6 x 15cm guns, 1 x 7.5cm, 2 x 3.7cm flak, 4 x 2cm flak; 6 x torpedo tubes; up to 230 mines
Beam	18.6m	**Aircraft**	2 x Arado Ar 196 floatplanes
Displacement	7,020 tons	**Complement**	376

Orion's Commander
Kapitän zur See Kurt Weyher

Atlantis – HSK 2; Schiff 16; Raider C

Atlantis only made one war cruise, spending an incredible 622 days at sea and sinking 22 enemy ships with a further six captured. Its luck finally ran out when it was intercepted and sunk by the heavy cruiser HMS _Devonshire_. The commander was awarded the Auxiliary Cruiser War Badge with Diamonds.

Atlantis Specifications			
Built	Bremer Vulkan, Bremen	**Powerplant**	2 x MAN diesels
Launched	1937	**Top speed**	17.5 knots
Original name	_Goldenfels_	**Endurance**	60,000 nautical miles
Length	155m	**Armament**	6 x 15cm guns, 1 x 7.5cm, 2 x 3.7cm, 4 x 2cm; 4 x torpedo tubes; up to 92 mines
Beam	18.6m	**Aircraft**	2 x Heinkel He 114 floatplanes
Displacement	7,860 tons	**Complement**	347

Atlantis's Commander
Fregattenkapitän Bernhard Rogge

LEFT The most famous of all the auxiliary cruisers, _Atlantis_, seen here in one of its many disguises, as the Japanese merchant _Kasii Maru_, was originally built as the freighter _Goldenfels_. Some of its disguises were quite elaborate and included erecting a second, false, funnel. Crew members often dressed as civilians, or even women, in case they were observed through binoculars. (DUBM)

Widder – HSK 3; Schiff 21; Raider D

Widder made only one war cruise, between 6 May and 31 October 1940, during which it sank ten enemy ships. With its engines in poor condition, its life as a raider was ended and it was renamed *Neumark* and found a new position as a supply/repair ship.

Widder Specifications			
Built	Howaldtswerke, Kiel	Powerplant	2 x Blohm & Voss turbines
Launched	1929	Top speed	15 knots
Original name	*Neumark*	Endurance	34,000 nautical miles
Length	152m	Armament	6 x 15cm guns, 1 x 7.5cm, 2 x 3.7cm, 4 x 2cm; 4 x torpedo tubes
Beam	18.2m	Aircraft	2 x Heinkel He 114 floatplanes
Displacement	7,850 tons	Complement	363

Widder's Commander
Kapitän zur See Helmut von Ruckteschell

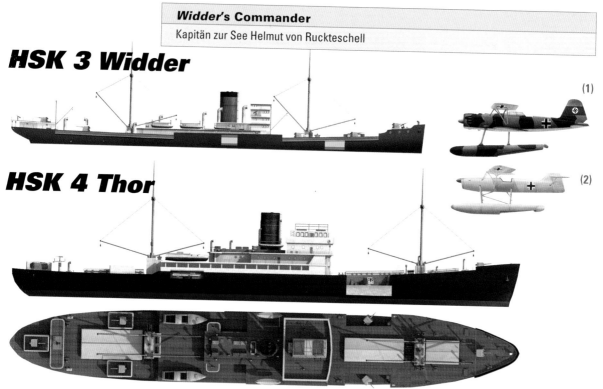

HSK 3 Widder

(1)

HSK 4 Thor

(2)

TOP *Widder* was a sister-ship to the *Orion*, and had an almost identical layout. *Widder* was the less successful of the two in terms of Allied shipping sunk.

ABOVE *Thor* had a displacement of only 3,860 tons. All of *Thor*'s main armament was mounted on deck, hidden from view by either false deckhouses or hinged plates on the hull

side. Its single torpedo tubes were mounted on the main deck just under the boat deck.

ABOVE RIGHT Auxiliary cruiser aircraft: **(1)** A Heinkel 114, as carried on *Atlantis*, *Widder* and *Pinguin*; **(2)** An Arado Ar 231, carried only on *Stier*.

(Ian Palmer © Osprey Publishing)

Thor – HSK 4; Schiff 10; Raider E

The first war cruise for *Thor* began on 6 June 1940 and lasted 328 days during which it sank 12 enemy ships before safely returning to port. Its second cruise began on 30 November 1941 and lasted 314 days, sinking a further ten enemy ships before docking at Yokahama in Japan. It was sunk on 30 November 1942 when the tanker *Uckermark* which was moored next to it exploded.

Thor Specifications			
Built	Deutsche Werft, Hamburg	**Powerplant**	2 x AEG turbines
Launched	1938	**Top speed**	18 knots
Original name	*Santa Cruz*	**Endurance**	40,000 nautical miles
Length	122m	**Armament**	6 x 15cm guns, 1 x 6cm, 2 x 3.7cm, 4 x 2cm; 4 x torpedo tubes
Beam	16.7m	**Aircraft**	1 x Arado Ar 196 floatplane
Displacement	3,860 tons	**Complement**	349

Thor's Commanders
(First cruise) Kapitän zur See Otto Kähler
(Second cruise) Kapitän zur See Günther Gumprich

Sinking 22 enemy ships over the course of two war cruises, the military career of *Thor* was ended not by the enemy but by an explosion on the tanker *Uckermark* which it was moored next to in Yokahama. *Thor* was damaged beyond repair as were two other vessels moored nearby. (DUBM)

Pinguin – HSK 5; Schiff 33; Raider F

Pinguin began its first war cruise on 15 June 1940, sinking or capturing 28 enemy ships and spending a total of 357 days at sea before being intercepted and sunk by the heavy cruiser HMS *Cornwall* on 8 May 1941.

Pinguin Specifications			
Built	AG Weser, Bremen	**Powerplant**	1 x MAN 6-cylinder diesel
Launched	1936	**Top speed**	17 knots
Original name	*Kandelfels*	**Endurance**	60,000 nautical miles
Length	155m	**Armament**	6 x 15cm guns, 1 x 7.5cm, 2 x 3.7cm, 4 x 2cm; 2 x torpedo tubes; up to 300 mines
Beam	18.7m	**Aircraft**	2 x Heinkel He 114 floatplanes, later 1 x Arado Ar 196
Displacement	7,760 tons	**Complement**	420

Pinguin's Commander
Fregattenkapitän Ernst-Felix Krüder

The auxiliary cruiser *Pinguin*, formerly the freighter *Kandelfels*, had a highly successful career, sinking or capturing 28 enemy ships, but was brought to a violent end when it was attacked and sunk by the cruiser HMS *Cornwall*. Although *Pinguin* scored hits on the cruiser it was blown apart when a shell from HMS *Cornwall* hit its mine storage, detonating well over 100 mines. (DUBM)

Stier – HSK 6; Schiff 23; Raider I

Stier began its first war cruise on 9 May 1942, sinking three enemy ships before meeting its fourth victim, the US liberty ship USS *Stephen Hopkins*, the return fire from which damaged *Stier* so badly that *Stier* itself sank.

Stier Specifications			
Built	Germaniawerft	**Powerplant**	1 x 7-cylinder diesel engine
Launched	1936	**Top speed**	14 knots
Original name	*Cairo*	**Endurance**	50,000 nautical miles
Length	134m	**Armament**	6 x 15cm guns, 1 x 7.5, 1 x 3.7cm, 4 x 2cm; 2 x torpedo tubes
Beam	17.3m	**Aircraft**	2 x Arado Ar 196
Displacement	11,000 tons	**Complement**	324

Stier's Commander
Fregattenkapitän Horst Gerlach

HSK5 *Pinguin*

HSK 6 *Stier*

HSK 7 *Komet*

TOP HSK 5 *Pinguin* in its disguise as the Greek freighter *Kassos*, the Greek colours being emblazoned in three places along its hull side, and the name KASSOS GREECE painted in large white letters amidships.
CENTRE HSK 6 *Stier* was one of the larger raiders. Its guns were concealed within false deckhouses and no special folding hull plates were used. Interestingly, *Stier*'s two torpedo tubes, one on either side, were below the waterline.
BOTTOM HSK 7 *Komet* was the smallest of the raiders. The small *Leicht-S-Boot* (midget-torpedo boat) it carried was intended for use in mine laying rather than torpedo attacks.
(Ian Palmer © Osprey Publishing)

Komet – HSK 7; Schiff 45; Raider B

The first cruise for *Komet* began on 3 July 1940 and lasted for 516 days during which the raider sank seven enemy ships before returning safely to Germany. Its second, much shorter cruise began on 8 October 1942 and ended just six days later when it was sunk by a British motor torpedo boat off Cherbourg.

Komet Specifications			
Built	Deschimag, Bremen	**Powerplant**	2 x MAN 6-cylinder diesels
Launched	1937	**Top speed**	16 knots
Original name	*Ems*	**Endurance**	35,000 nautical miles
Length	115m	**Armament**	6 x 15cm guns, 1 x 6cm, 2 x 3.7cm, 4 x 2cm; 6 x torpedo tubes; up to 30 mines
Beam	15.3m	**Aircraft/boat**	2 x Arado Ar 196 floatplanes, 1 x *Leicht-S-Boot*
Displacement	3,280 tons	**Complement**	274

Komet's Commanders
(First cruise) Kapitän zur See Robert Eyssen
(Second cruise) Kapitän sur See Ulrich Brocksien

RIGHT Formerly the merchant ship *Ems*, its first war cruise proved successful for *Komet*, resulting in the sinking of seven enemy ships. On its second cruise it was intercepted and torpedoed by a British motor torpedo boat (MTB) off the French coast and sunk. There were no survivors. (DUBM)

Kormoran – HSK 8; Schiff 41; Raider G

Kormoran was the largest and most powerful of the auxiliary cruisers. On its first cruise, after 351 days at sea and sinking 12 enemy ships, *Kormoran* was scuttled after a battle with the cruiser HMAS *Sydney* on 19 November 1941.

Kormoran Specifications

Built	Germaniawerft, Kiel	**Powerplant**	4 x Krupp-Germaniawerft 9-cylinder diesels
Launched	1938	**Top speed**	19 knots
Original name	*Steiermark*	**Endurance**	84,500 nautical miles
Length	164m	**Armament**	6 x 15cm guns, 1 x 7.5cm, 2 x 3.7cm, 5 x 2cm; 6x torpedo tubes; up to 360 mines
Beam	20.2m	**Aircraft/boat**	2 x Arado Ar 196 floatplanes, 1 x *Leicht-S-Boot*
Displacement	8,730 tons	**Complement**	400

Kormoran's Commander

Korvettenkapitän Theodor Detmers

LEFT Having spent almost a full year at sea *Kormoran,* originally the merchant *Steiermark,* was spotted and challenged by the cruiser HMAS *Sydney* in waters to the west of Australia. The battle which ensued saw the destruction of both ships. Although many of the German crew were later rescued, there were no survivors from HMAS *Sydney.* (DUBM)

HSK 8 *Kormoran*

HSK 8 *Kormoran* The upper three decks were given over to accommodation, both for the crew and any prisoners, and for storage, while the lower levels accommodated fuel bunkers and an ammunition magazine. *Kormoran*'s four large diesel engines were mounted amidships, under the main provision stores, with further fuel bunkers and storerooms ahead and astern of the engine room. Virtually all of *Kormoran*'s armament was well concealed, the only exception being small anti-aircraft guns – if these were spotted they would not give rise to any suspicion as to *Kormoran*'s true nature. (Ian Palmer © Osprey Publishing)

Michel – HSK 9; Schiff 28; Raider H

Michel left port on 9 March 1942 and spent 373 days at sea. It sank 14 enemy ships before docking at Kobe in Japan. Its second cruise lasted 149 days, during which it sank just three enemy ships before being torpedoed and sunk by the submarine USS *Tarpon*.

Michel Specifications			
Built	Danziger Werft, Danzig	**Powerplant**	2 x MAN 8-cylinder diesels
Launched	1939	**Top speed**	16 knots
Original name	*Bielsko*	**Endurance**	34,000 nautical miles
Length	133m	**Armament**	6 x 15cm guns, 1 x 10.5cm, 4 x 3.7cm, 4 x 2cm; 6 x torpedo tubes
Beam	16.8m	**Aircraft/boat**	2 x Arado Ar 196 floatplanes, 1 x *Leicht-S-Boot*
Displacement	4,740 tons	**Complement**	400

Michel's Commanders
(First cruise) Kapitän zur See Hellmuth von Ruckteschell
(Second cruise) Kapitän sur See Günther Gumprich

Having previously served as a hospital ship, *Michel*'s career as an auxiliary cruiser saw it achieve a total of 522 days at sea over two war cruises. After sinking 17 enemy ships, *Michel* was eventually intercepted by the American submarine USS *Tarpon* off the coast of Japan and sank after being torpedoed. (DUBM)

Coronel – HSK 10; Schiff 14; Raider K

After departing port on 31 January 1943 and unable to break out into the Atlantic when attacked by enemy aircraft, *Coronel* was forced to return to port after 29 days at sea and saw no further action.

Coronel Specifications

Built	Bremer-Vulkan, Bremen	**Powerplant**	1x MAN 8-cylinder diesel
Launched	1938	**Top speed**	16 knots
Original name	*Togo*	**Endurance**	36,000 nautical miles
Length	134m	**Armament**	6 x 15cm guns, 6 x 4cm, 8 x 2cm
Beam	17.9m	**Aircraft**	3 x Arado Ar 196 floatplanes
Displacement	5,040 tons	**Complement**	350

Coronel's Commander

Kapitän sur See Ernst-Ludwig Thienemann

LEFT The war badge awarded to crews of the auxiliary cruisers. Created by artist Wilhelm Ernst Peekhaus of Berlin, its design harked back to the days of the Vikings as the original sea raiders. It was earned by having taken part in a successful long-distance voyage and could also be awarded to crews of the ships which supplied the raiders at sea. (Author's collection)

Hansa – HSK 5 (II); Schiff 5

Prior to conversion into an auxiliary cruiser at the Wilton-Fijenoord yard in Rotterdam in 1942, this ship had been used as a target-training vessel for U-boats in the Baltic. Work on conversion was seriously delayed due to crippling material shortages, and when moved to Blohm & Voss in Hamburg for completion of its conversion it was badly damaged in a British air raid during July 1943. The damage was sufficient for conversion work to be abandoned.

Instead, *Hansa* was commissioned as a gunnery training ship, and fulfilled that role until February 1944. In the final stages of the war it too was used to evacuate refugees from the Eastern Front down the Baltic, and was finally put out of action when it ran onto a mine on 4 May 1945. Raised after the war, it was taken back into service by its original pre-war owners, eventually being broken up for scrap in 1971.

Hansa was not given a raider name by the Royal Navy because it did not enter active service as a commerce raider.

FAR LEFT The auxiliary cruiser career of *Coronel* was short lived indeed. Having served as a transport and then as a minelayer, after conversion to an auxiliary cruiser it was unable to break out into the Atlantic. It was eventually repurposed as the night-fighter direction ship *Togo*, and survived the war. (DUBM)

Hansa Specifications

Built	Wilton, Rotterdam/Blohm & Voss, Hamburg	Top speed	20.5 knots
Acquired	1940	Endurance	65,000 nautical miles
Original name	*Glengarry*	Armament	8 x 15cm guns, 1 x 10.5cm, 6 x 3.7cm, 36 x 2cm
Length	153m	Aircraft	1 x Arado Ar 196
Beam	20.1m	Complement	400
Displacement	19,000 tons		

Hilfskreuzer Weaponry

The principal type of main armament of the auxiliary cruisers was the 15cm SK L/45 C16 naval gun. This was a rather elderly weapon which had seen widespread use during World War I but was only used on one regular warship during World War II, the cruiser *Emden*. Though somewhat outdated it was still a perfect weapon for use on the auxiliary cruisers, considering the only enemies it was assumed they would meet would be unarmed or lightly armed merchants. The fact that the raider *Kormoran* sank the more powerful cruiser HMAS *Sydney* testifies to the effectiveness of this weapon, even if *Kormoran* itself was lost in this action.

Oberleutnant zur See Jochen Seeger is shown here wearing the Auxiliary Cruiser War badge earned aboard *Atlantis*. It is interesting to note that a number of former auxiliary cruiser crew members then went on to serve on U-boats. Having served on *Atlantis*, as a *Steuermannsmaat* (coxswain's mate), Seeger gained his commission and went on to command U-393.

All of the auxiliary cruiser commanders were high ranking, highly experienced officers, usually from the Reserves. Of the 11 who commanded auxiliary cruisers, nine held the Knights Cross of the Iron Cross and four held the Oak Leaves to the Knights Cross.

Summary of *Hilfskreuzer* Operations

Raider	Ships sunk	Approx tonnage	Days at sea
Pinguin	32	154,700	320
Atlantis	22	146,000	601
Orion	16	77,000	510
Michel	15	99,400	354
Thor	12	96,500	328
Kormoran	12	75,400	351
Widder	10	58,600	178
Komet	6	41,000	511
Stier	4	31,000	146
Coronel	0	0	29
Hansa	0	0	0

DESTROYERS
Type 34 Leberecht Maas Class

Four examples (Z1–Z4) of this type were manufactured. All were constructed at the Deutsche Werke yard in Kiel.

- Z1 Keel laid 15/10/34; launched 18/8/35; commissioned 14/1/37. This ship, the *Leberecht Maas*, ran on to a mine and was sunk whilst attempting to evade an Allied air attack, 22 February 1940, in the North Sea.
- Z2 Keel laid 25/10/34; launched 18/8/35; commissioned 27/2/37. This ship, the *Georg Thiele*, was run aground and scuttled, Narvik, 13 April 1940.
- Z3 Keel laid 2/1/35; launched 30/11/35; commissioned 6/4/37. The *Max Schultz*, with *Leberecht Maas*, ran on to a mine evading enemy air attack in the North Sea, 22 February 1940.
- Z4 Keel laid 7/1/35; launched 30/11/35; commissioned 13/5/37. *Richard Beitzen* was the only destroyer of the Leberecht Maas class to survive the war. It was allocated to Great Britain and ultimately scrapped in 1947.

A destroyer of the Leberecht Maas class in port. Only four of this class were built of which only one, the *Richard Beitzen*, survived the war. Note the large bronze eagle and swastika affixed to the face of the bridge indicating a pre-war image. (NHHC)

Type 34 Specifications			
Length	119m	**Main armament**	5 x 12.7cm guns in single turrets
Beam	11.3m	**Flak armament**	8 x 3.7cm guns in four twin mounts 6 x 2cm guns on single mounts
Draught	4m	**Torpedoes**	8 x 53.3cm torpedo tubes in two quadruple mounts
Maximum displacement	2,619 tons	**Depth charges**	4 launchers
Fuel oil carried	715 tons max	**Mines**	Up to 60 carried
Maximum speed	38 knots	**Complement**	325 officers and men
Maximum endurance	1,825 nautical miles		

Type 34 Commanders	
Z1	
January 1937–September 1937	Korvettenkapitän Schmidt
October 1937–April 1939	Korvettenkapitän Wagner
April 1939–February 1940	Korvettenkapitän Bassange
Z2	
February 1937–August 1938	Korvettenkapitän Hartmann
August 1938–October 1938	Korvettenkapitän von Pufendorf
October 1938–April 1940	Korvettenkapitän Wolff
Z3	
April 1937–October 1938	Korvettenkapitän Baltzer
October 1938–February 1940	Korvettenkapitän Trampedach
Z4	
May 1937–May 1938	Korvettenkapitän Gadow
May 1938–October 1939	Korvettenkapitän Schmidt
October 1939–January 1943	Korvettenkapitän von Davidson
January 1943–January 1944	Korvettenkapitän Dominik
January 1944–April 1944	No allocated commander
April 1944–June 1944	Korvettenkapitän Lüdde-Neurath
June 1944–September 1944	Korvettenkapitän Gade
September 1944–May 1945	Korvettenkapitän Neuss

Type 34 Leberecht Maas class

(1)

(2)

(1) Z1, Leberecht Maas. Note that as built the first three of the type had a straight stem, later modified during refit to give it a slight rake.
(2) In the plan view can be seen the mine rails which ran on the port side from the forward funnel all the way to the stern and to starboard from the aft funnel to the stern. These mines were used to good effect in the early part of the war.
(3) This detail shows the stern area which is squared off in a quite distinctive fashion. Note the rails for the mine load.
(Ian Palmer © Osprey Publishing)

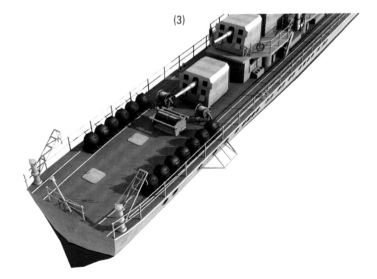
(3)

This shows Z15, *Erich Steinbrink*, one of 12 vessels of the Paul Jacobi (34A) class. Z15 was its correct title. The numeral 31 on its side is the pennant number showing it as the first ship of the third flotilla. It survived the war and subsequently served in the Soviet Navy as the *Pylkiy*. (Author's collection)

Type 34A Paul Jacobi Class

A total of 12 vessels in the 34A class were constructed. Of these 12, Z5–Z9 were built at the Deschimag in Bremen, Z10–Z13 at the Germaniawerft in Kiel and Z14–Z16 at the Blohm & Voss yard in Hamburg.

- Z5 Keel laid 15/7/35; launched 24/3/36; commissioned 29/6/37. The *Paul Jacobi* survived the war and was taken over initially by the Royal Navy and then passed to France. It was scrapped in 1951.
- Z6 Keel laid 18/6/35; launched 22/4/36; commissioned 2/7/37. *Theodor Riedel* survived the war and was taken over by the French Navy, where it served as the *Klebar*. It was finally scrapped in 1958.
- Z7 Keel laid 7/9/35; launched 16/6/36; commissioned 9/9/37. *Hermann Schoemann* was sunk on 2 May 1942 after a naval engagement with British destroyers and the cruiser HMS *Edinburgh*.
- Z8 Keel laid 14/1/36; launched 15/9/39; commissioned 9/1/38. *Bruno Heinemann* ran on to a mine in the English Channel and sank on 25 January 1942.
- Z9 Keel laid 22/3/35; launched 27/3/36; commissioned 2/7/38. *Wolfgang Zenker* was damaged beyond repair during the battle for Narvik and was run aground and scuttled on 13 April 1940.
- Z10 Keel laid 1/4/35; launched 14/5/36; commissioned 17/9/38. *Hans Lody* survived the war to be taken over by the Royal Navy. It was finally scrapped in 1949.
- Z11 Keel laid 26/4/35; launched 8/7/36; commissioned 6/12/38. *Bernd von Arnim* was run aground and scuttled after being mortally damaged in the battle for Narvik, 13 April 1940.
- Z12 Keel laid 3/5/35; launched 12/3/37; commissioned 4/3/39. *Erich Giese* was sunk during the battle for Narvik, 13 April 1940.
- Z13 Keel laid 12/10/35; launched 18/3/37; commissioned 28/8/39. *Erich Koellner* ran aground and was subsequently blown apart by heavy fire from the battleship HMS *Warspite*, Narvik, 13 April 1940.
- Z14 Keel laid 30/3/35; launched 5/11/35; commissioned 6/4/38. *Friedrich Ihn* survived the war to be handed over to the Soviet Navy.

- Z15 Keel laid 30/3/35; launched 24/9/36; commissioned 31/5/38. *Erich Steinbrink* survived the war to be handed over to the Soviet Navy.
- Z16 Keel laid 9/11/35; launched 21/3/37; commissioned 28/7/39. *Friedrich Eckoldt* was sunk in action with the cruisers HMS *Sheffield* and HMS *Glasgow*, 31 December 1942.

Type 34A

(1)

(2)

(1) Z6, *Theodor Riedel*, as it appeared *c.*1942. **(2)** Z10, *Hans Lody, c.*1942. Although the Type 34A destroyers were all broadly similar, to the rear of the forward funnel were grouped a number of steam vent pipes. Various yards used different configurations for these pipes. At right **(3)**, the configuration found on Z9 to Z13 shows three narrow pipes flanked by two large bore pipes. These destroyers were built by Germaniawerft in Kiel. Seen below **(4)**, Z5 to Z8, which were constructed by Deschimag in Bremen, had vents grouped as six small-bore pipes.
(Ian Palmer © Osprey Publishing)

(4)

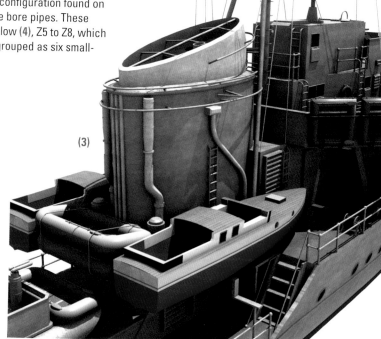

(3)

Type 34A Specifications

Length	119m	Main armament	5 x 12.7cm guns in single-barrelled turrets
Beam	11.3m	Flak armament	• 8 x 3.7cm guns in four twin turrets • 6 x 2cm guns on single mounts
Draught	4.23m	Torpedoes	8 x 53.3cm torpedo tubes in two quadruple mounts
Maximum displacement	3,510 tons	Depth charges	4 launchers
Fuel oil carried	715 tons max	Mines	Up to 60 carried
Maximum speed	38 knots	Complement	325 officers and men
Maximum endurance	1,825 nautical miles		

Type 34A Commanders

Z6
June 1937–October 1938 — Korvettenkapitän Peters
October 1938–February 1941 — Korvettenkapitän Zimmer
February 1941–July 1944 — Korvettenkapitän Schlieper
July 1944–May 1945 — Korvettenkapitän Bülter

Z7
July 1937–October 1938 — Korvettenkapitän Fechner
October 1938–November 1940 — Korvettenkapitän Böhmig
November 1940–April 1941 — No allocated commander
April 1941–September 1943 — Korvettenkapitän Riede
September 1943–January 1944 — Korvettenkapitän von Hausen
January 1944–June 1944 — Korvettenkapitän Menge
June 1944–May 1945 — Kapitänleutnant Blöse

Z8
September 1937–October 1938 — Korvettenkapitän Schulte-Mönting
October 1938–July 1940 — Korvettenkapitän Detmers
July 1940–October 1940 — Kapitänleutnant Loerke
October 1940–May 1942 — Korvettenkapitän Wittig

Z9
January 1938–December 1939 — Korvettenkapitän Berger
December 1939–May 1940 — Korvettenkapitän Langheld
May 1940–January 1942 — Korvettenkapitän Alberts

Z10
July 1938–April 1940 — Korvettenkapitän Pönitz

Z11
September 1938–August 1939 — Korvettenkapitän von Pufendorf

August 1939–October 1940 — Korvettenkapitän von Wangenheim
November 1940–August 1942 — Korvettenkapitän Pfeiffer
August 1942–March 1943 — Korvettenkapitän Zenker
March 1943–April 1943 — Kapitänleutnant Vorsteher
April 1943–November 1943 — Fregattenkapitän Marks
November 1943–May 1945 — Korvettenkapitän Haun

Z12
December 1938–April 1940 — Korvettenkapitän Rechel

Z13
March 1939–April 1940 — Korvettenkapitän Schmidt

Z14
August 1939–April 1940 — Fregattenkapitän Schulze-Hinrichs

Z15
April 1939–October 1939 — Fregattenkapitän von Pufendorf
October 1939–November 1942 — Korvettenkapitän Wachsmuth
November 1942–April 1944 — Korvettenkapitän Fromme
April 1944–May 1945 — Korvettenkapitän Richter-Oldekop

Z16
June 1938–January 1942 — Fregattenkapitän Johannesson
January 1942–December 1942 — Korvettenkapitän Freytag von Löringhoven
December 1942–November 1944 — Korvettenkapitän Teichmann
November 1944–May 1945 — Fregattenkapitän Röver

Karl Galster, one of six vessels of the Type 36 Diether von Roeder class, in a pre-war photo whilst serving as the second ship in the fourth flotilla. The pennant numbers on the hull side were painted over on the outbreak of war, and at the same time the bronze eagle on the face of its bridge was removed. (Author's collection)

Type 36 Diether von Roeder Class

A total of six vessels of this class were completed.

- Z17 Keel laid 9/9/36; launched 19/8/7; commissioned 29/8/38. *Diether von Roeder* was scuttled after being seriously damaged during the battle for Narvik, 13 April 1940.
- Z18 Keel laid 9/9/36; launched 12/12/37; commissioned 8/10/38. *Hans Lüdemann* was severely damaged during the battle for Narvik and was scuttled by a British boarding party.
- Z19 Keel laid 5/10/36; launched 22/12/37; commissioned 12/1/39. *Hermann Künne* was run aground and scuttled during the battle for Narvik, 13 April 1940.
- Z20 Keel laid 14/9/37; launched 15/7/38; commissioned 21/3/39. *Karl Galster* survived the war to be handed over to the Soviet Navy. It was scrapped in 1958.
- Z21 Keel laid 15/12/37; launched 20/8/38; commissioned 10/7/39. *Wilhelm Heidkamp* was sunk by torpedoes from a British destroyer at Narvik, 11 April 1940.
- Z22 Keel laid 3/1/38; launched 20/9/38; commissioned 24/9/39. *Anton Schmitt* was sunk by torpedoes from a British destroyer 10 April 1940.

Type 36 Specifications			
Length	123m	Main armament	5 x 12.7cm guns in single-barrelled turrets
Beam	11.7m	Flak armament	• 8 x 3.7cm guns in four twin turrets • 7 x 2cm guns on single mounts
Draught	4.5m	Torpedoes	8 x 53.3cm torpedo tubes in two quadruple mounts
Maximum displacement	3,469 tons	Depth charges	4 launchers
Fuel oil carried	750 tons max	Mines	Up to 60 carried
Maximum speed	40 knots	Complement	323 officers and men
Maximum endurance	2,020 nautical miles		

Type 36 Commanders	
Z17	
August 1938–April 1940	Korvettenkapitän Holtorf
Z18	
October 1938–April 1940	Korvettenkapitän Friedrichs
Z19	
January 1939–April 1940	Korvettenkapitän Kothe
Z20	
March 1939–August 1942	Korvettenkapitän von Mauchenheim
August 1942–January 1945	Fregattenkapitän Harmsen
January 1945–May 1945	Fregattenkapitän Schmidt
Z21	
June 1939–April 1940	Korvettenkapitän Erdmenger
Z22	
September 1939–April 1940	Korvettenkapitän Böhme

BELOW LEFT German destroyers were handsome, well-armed vessels, but were bedevilled with technical problems with their complex high-pressure steam turbines. *Anton Schmitt*, seen here, was lost at Narvik when it was hit by two torpedoes fired by a British destroyer while waiting to refuel. (DUBM)

ABOVE Z21, *Wilhelm Heidkamp*. Commissioned in September 1939, it survived for less than a year, being torpedoed and sunk by a British destroyer at Narvik on 11 April 1940. Hit by the torpedo aft, its magazine blew up killing Kommodore Bonte, the flotilla commander, and 81 crewmen. The wreck eventually sank the next day. (NHHC)

LEFT A pre-war shot of *Hans Lüdemann* in Kiel Harbour in 1938. This ship engaged the battleship HMS *Warspite* and its accompanying destroyers at Narvik as a floating battery until it had expended all its ammunition. Its commander, Korvettenkapitän Friedrichs, then ran it on to the rocks to prevent it being captured. (Sobotta/ullstein bild via Getty Images)

Type 36A Z23 Class

Eight vessels of this class were completed, all being built by Deschimag.

The *Zerstörerkriegsabzeichen* (Destroyer War Badge) was instituted in June 1940 and designed by artist Paul Casberg of Berlin. It was issued to crewmen of destroyers and torpedo boats who had seen action in three combat engagements, had served on a ship sunk in battle, were wounded in action or had performed some outstanding deed. (Author's collection)

- Z23 Keel laid 15/11/38; launched 15/12/39; commissioned 15/9/40. Decommissioned by the Germans in August 1944, it survived the war and was taken into the French Navy in 1946, where it served as the *Leopard*. It was scrapped in 1951.
- Z24 Keel laid 2/1/39; launched 7/3/40; commissioned 26/10/40. Sunk by Allied aircraft on 25 August 1944.
- Z25 Keel laid 15/2/39; launched 3/3/40; commissioned 30/11/40. Survived the war and was taken over by the Royal Navy until given to France in 1946, serving as the *Hoche*, until finally scrapped in 1959.
- Z26 Keel laid 1/4/39; launched 2/4/40; commissioned 11/1/41. Sunk in action against British warships in the Barents Sea, March 1942.
- Z27 Keel laid 27/12/39; launched 1/8/40; commissioned 26/2/41. Sunk in action against British warships in the Bay of Biscay, 28 December 1943.
- Z28 Keel laid 30/11/39; launched 20/8/40; commissioned 9/8/41. Sunk by British aircraft, 6 March 1945.
- Z29 Keel laid 21/3/40; launched 15/10/40; commissioned 25/7/41. Survived the war and was taken over briefly by the Royal Navy before being passed to the USA. Sunk in target practice, December 1946.
- Z30 Keel laid 15/4/40; launched 8/12/40; commissioned 15/11/41. Survived the war. Taken over by the Royal Navy, and used as a target hulk, before being scrapped in 1949.

A wartime shot of Z28 at Kiel. Note that the pennant numbers usually painted on the hull side would soon be removed for security reasons. It had a fairly active service life including shore bombardment of Soviet positions and rescue of refugees towards the end of the war. On 4 March 1945 however it was hit by bombs from enemy aircraft and sank. (Sobotta/ullstein bild via Getty Images)

Bow view of a German destroyer in a heavy swell showing the forward 15cm turret. These turrets were not fully enclosed, being open to the rear, so that serving this weapon in winter or in heavy seas was no pleasant task. These destroyers were relatively 'wet' ships. (NHHC)

Type 36A Specifications

Length	127m	Main armament	4 x 15cm guns in single-barrelled turrets
Beam	12m	Flak armament	• 8 x 3.7cm guns in four twin turrets • 5 x 2cm guns on single mounts
Draught	4.5m	Torpedoes	8 x 53.3cm torpedo tubes in two quadruple mounts
Maximum displacement	3,691 tons	Depth charges	4 launchers
Fuel oil carried	825 tons max	Mines	Up to 70 carried
Maximum speed	38 knots	Complement	332 officers and men
Maximum endurance	2,500 nautical miles		

Type 36A Commanders

Z23

September 1940–May 1942	Fregattenkapitän Böhme
May 1942–March 1944	Fregattenkapitän Wittig
March 1944–August 1944	Korvettenkapitän von Mantey

Z24

October 1940–August 1943	Korvettenkapitän Saltzwedel
August 1943–September 1943	Kapitänleutnant Burkart
September 1943–August 1944	Korvettenkapitän Birnbacher

Z25

November 1940–July 1941	Korvettenkapitän Gerlach
July 1941–August 1943	Fregattenkapitän Peters
August 1943–September 1943	Korvettenkapitän Birnbacher
September 1943–May 1945	Fregattenkapitän Gohrbandt

Z26

January 1941–March 1942	Korvettenkapitän Ritter von Berger

Z27

February 1941–August 1942	Fregattenkapitän Schmidt
August 1942–December 1943	Korvettenkapitän Schultz

Z28

August 1941–February 1943	Fregattenkapitän Erdmenger
February 1943–March 1943	Fregattenkapitän Reinicke
March 1943–January 1944	Korvettenkapitän Zenker
January 1944–October 1944	Fregattenkapitän Gerlach
January 1945–March 1945	Fregattenkapitän Lampe

Z29

June 1941–March 1943	Fregattenkapitän Rechel
April 1943–May 1945	Korvettenkapitän von Multius

Z30

November 1941–March 1943	Fregattenkapitän Kaiser
March 1943–December 1944	Fregattenkapitän Lampe
December 1944–April 1945	Korvettenkapitän Hoffmann
April 1945–May 1945	Korvettenkapitän Erdmann

Type 36A (Mob) Z31 Class

A total of seven vessels of this type were completed. Z31–Z34 were built by Deschimag of Bremen, and Z37–Z39 by Germaniawerft in Kiel.

- Z31 Keel laid 1/9/40; launched 15/5/41; commissioned 11/4/42. Survived the war and passed to the Royal Navy before being given to France in 1946. It served in the French Navy as the *Marceau* before being scrapped in 1951.
- Z32 Keel laid 1/11/40; launched 15/8/40; commissioned 15/9/42. Sunk in battle with Allied warships off Normandy, 9 July 1944.
- Z33 Keel laid 22/12/40; launched 15/9/41; commissioned 6/2/43. Survived the war and passed to the Soviet Navy. Scrapped in 1959.
- Z34 Keel laid 15/1/41; launched 5/5/42; commissioned 5/6/43. Survived the war to be passed to the US Navy. Scuttled March 1946.
- Z37 Keel laid 1940; launched 24/2/41; commissioned 16/7/42. Decommissioned and disarmed, August 1944. Hulk survived the war and was scrapped in 1949.
- Z38 Keel laid 1940; launched 5/8/41; commissioned 20/3/43. Survived the war to be passed to the Royal Navy where it served as a trials ship, HMS *Nonsuch*, until scrapped in 1949.
- Z39 Keel laid 1940; launched 5/8/41; commissioned 21/8/43. Survived the war and passed to the US Navy where it served as a trials ship, the DD939, until passed to the French, who used it for spare parts before it was scrapped in 1964.

Z23 – Type 36A destroyer

(1)

(2)

The side profile (1) and plan view (2) show a Type 36A destroyer, Z23, as built. Note it features only one forward main armament turret. The position of the second turret on earlier types is now occupied by a single 2cm flak gun. Two platforms are provided either side of the superstructure, and are mounted symmetrically, one each side carrying a 3.7cm twin flak gun and one a single 2cm flak gun. After a major refit, this class sported a twin 15cm gun turret forward and had the forward 2cm flak gun replaced by a *Flakvierling*, shown in (3).
(Ian Palmer © Osprey Publishing)

(3)

Type 36A (Mob) Specifications

Length	127m	Main armament	5 x 15cm guns, three in single-barrelled turrets, plus one twin mount
Beam	12m	Flak armament	• 8 x 3.7cm guns in four twin turrets • 5 x 2cm guns on single mounts
Draught	4.5m	Torpedoes	8 x 53.3cm torpedo tubes in two quadruple mounts
Maximum displacement	3,690 tons	Depth charges	4 launchers
Fuel oil carried	825 tons max	Mines	Up to 70 carried
Maximum speed	38.5 knots	Complement	332 officers and men
Maximum endurance	2,087 nautical miles		

Type 36A (Mob) Commanders

Z31

February 1941–August 1942	Fregattenkapitän Schmidt
August 1942–December 1943	Korvettenkapitän Schultz

Z32

September 1941–February 1943	Fregattenkapitän Erdmenger
February 1943–March 1943	Fregattenkapitän Reinicke
March 1943–January 1944	Korvettenkapitän Zenker
January 1944–October 1944	Fregattenkapitän Gerlach
January 1945–March 1945	Fregattenkapitän Lampe

Z33

June 1941–March 1943	Fregattenkapitän Reichel
April 1943–May 1945	Korvettenkapitän von Multius

Z34

November 1941–March 1943	Kapitän zur See Kaiser
March 1943–December 1944	Fregattenkapitän Lampe

December 1944–April 1945	Korvettenkapitän Hoffmann
April 1945–May 1945	Korvettenkapitän Erdmann

Z37

May 1942–October 1943	Fregattenkapitän Langheld
October 1943–March 1944	Korvettenkapitän von Mantey
March 1944–July 1944	Korvettenkapitän Ulrich
July 1944–August 1944	Fregattenkapitän Heppe

Z38

March 1943–September 1944	Korvettenkapitän Brutzer
September 1944–May 1945	Korvettenkapitän von Lyncker

Z39

August 1943–May 1945	Korvettenkapitän Loerke

FAR LEFT The radar array on Type 36A (Mob) destroyer Z39 was extensive: a FuMO21 on the bridge, four FuMB4 on the searchlight platform, one FuMB3 and one FuMB81 at the masthead. (NHHC)

LEFT The later twin turret fitted to German destroyers was fully enclosed. Standard on the Type 36A (Mob), it was also retrofitted to several Type 36A vessels, though the extra weight adversely affected handling. (NHHC)

Type 36B (Mob) Z35 Class

Eight ships of this design were ordered, but the orders for three ships were cancelled before construction began. All were to be built by Deschimag of Bremen.

- Z35 Keel laid 6/6/41; launched 2/10/42; commissioned 22/9/43. Sunk by mines in the Baltic, 12 December 1944.
- Z36 Keel laid 15/9/41; launched 15/5/43; commissioned 9/2/44. Sunk by mines in the Baltic, 12 December 1944.
- Z43 Keel laid 1/5/42; launched 15/9/43; commissioned 20/3/44. Scuttled May 1945 after being severely damaged by mines.
- Z44 and Z45 were cancelled and scrapped before launch.

Z39 – Type 36A (Mob)

The Type 36A (Mob) was the most modern and streamlined looking of the destroyer designs. A huge twin 15cm gun turret gave a substantial level of firepower for a destroyer. Each bridge wing was home to a single 2cm flak gun. Two quadruple torpedo tube sets were carried. Either side of the funnel were platforms to take twin 3.7cm and single 2cm flak guns. On the forward part of the rear superstructure roof was a single turret facing forward, and on the after end was a second turret facing the stern. On the rear deck, facing astern, was the fourth turret. (Ian Palmer © Osprey Publishing)

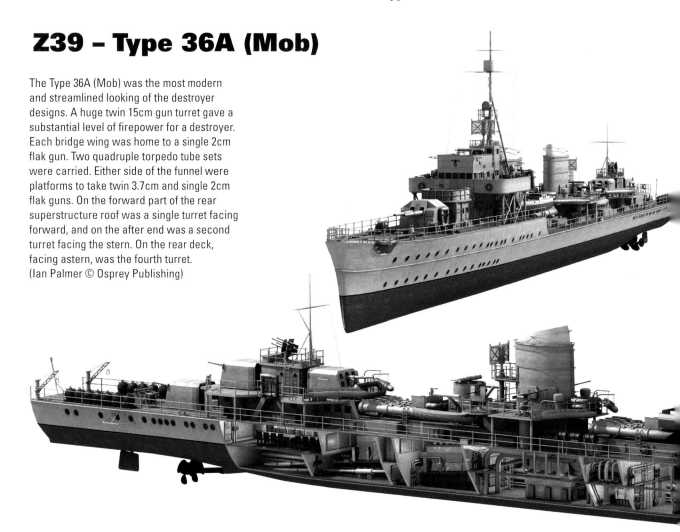

Type 36B (Mob) Specifications

Length	127m	Main armament	5 x 12.7cm guns, in single-barrelled turrets
Beam	12m	Flak armament	• 8 x 3.7cm guns in four twin turrets • 15 x 2cm guns, three quadruple and three single mounts
Draught	4.5m	Torpedoes	8 x 53.3cm torpedo tubes in two quadruple mounts
Maximum displacement	3,542 tons	Depth charges	4 launchers
Fuel oil carried	825 tons max	Mines	Up to 76 carried
Maximum speed	37 knots	Complement	332 officers and men
Maximum endurance	2,900 nautical miles		

Type 36B (Mob) Commanders

Z35
September 1943–December 1944   Korvettenkapitän Bätge
Z36
February 1944–December 1944   Korvettenkapitän Freiherr von Hausen
Z43
August 1943–May 1945   Korvettenkapitän Loerke

This shot of Z39 after being handed over to the US Navy at the end of the war shows the extreme elevation the forward twin 15cm guns were capable of. The new twin turrets weighed more than three times the weight of the single units. They were used to provide shore-bombardment support to Wehrmacht units on the Eastern Front towards the end of the war. (NHHC)

Armour, gunnery and radar

The standard main armament for German destroyers in World War II was the 12.7cm C/34 naval gun, mounted in five single turrets. The gun fired a 28kg shell for a distance of up to 17.4km.

With the Type 36A (Z23) class, main armament was changed to four single turrets each holding a 15cm TK C/36, the TK designation representing *Torpedobootskanone* (torpedo boat canons). In German terms of course the *Torpedoboot* was a small destroyer escort. The gun fired a 45.3kg shell for a range of up to 21.9km.

Type 36A (Mob) destroyer

(1)

(2)

(3)

Here we see Z37 (**1** and **2**), one of the last destroyers to be built, with pronounced clipper bow and large twin 15cm turret as part of its initial design. Note the single 2cm flak gun at the bow and aft of the forward turret. The aft deckhouse roof bears a *Flakvierling*. This class also had a distinctive searchlight platform fitted to the foremast, and a FuMO radar antenna on the bridge structure. (**3**) shows detail of the bridge area of the Type 36A (Mob), with so-called 'Barbara'-style radar array with large 'mattress'-type antenna.
(Ian Palmer © Osprey Publishing)

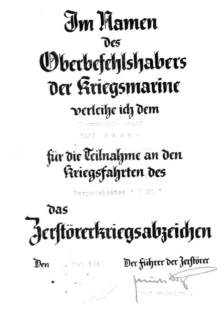

A further change came with the Type 36A (Mob) when a twin turret was fitted forward with three single turrets aft, all bearing the 15cm TK C/36. With this level of armament the destroyer was coming close to having the firepower equivalent of a light cruiser.

Fire control was typically by means of a 4m rangefinder on the bridge and another aft of the second funnel.

Z1 through to Z3, having been destroyed early in the war, were never fitted with radar. Thereafter the principal radar types installed were the FuMO 24/25 on the bridge and a FuMO 63 to the rear of the second funnel. As the war progressed, however, some destroyers received additional radar fittings.

AIRCRAFT CARRIERS

Unfortunately for the Kriegsmarine, Germany's efforts in creating a naval air arm were doomed to failure. It had been intended for two carriers to be constructed, and the keel of the first, and ultimately only, example was laid on 28 December 1936. The ship was launched at the Deutsche Werft in Kiel, and named *Graf Zeppelin*, after the famous airship designer. Work on it continued until after the outbreak of war.

Following the invasion of Norway and then France and the Low Countries, it was decided it would not be needed, and other projects would be given priority for the massive amount of war materials required to finish it. *Graf Zeppelin* was subsequently used as a storage hulk.

ABOVE LEFT View from the bow looking aft, on Z39. Taken over by the US Navy in 1945, it served as DD939, the DD prefix indicating that it was a war prize. After service with the US Navy, it was handed to France where it was designated with the name *Leopard*. It was eventually scrapped in 1964. (NHHC)

ABOVE Award document for the *Zerstörerkriegsabzeichen* (Destroyer War Badge). As can be seen here, the badge was also awarded to crews of the *Torpedoboote*. These large vessels however were equivalent to destroyer escorts in the Allied navies. The vessel in question, T23, survived the war to be taken first into the Royal Navy and then the French Navy where it served as *L'Alsacien*. (Author's collection)

Shown here shortly after its launch, *Graf Zeppelin* was Germany's only aircraft carrier. Work was halted in 1943 and it was never fully completed. It retained a skeleton crew for the duration of the war and was scuttled in March 1945 just outside Stettin as Soviet forces approached. Although it was subsequently raised, it sank during tests in 1947. (NHHC)

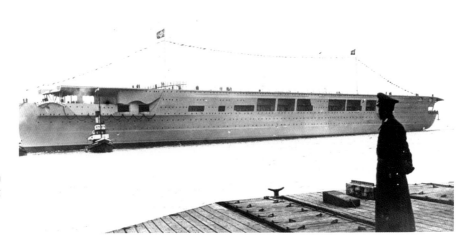

By May 1942 the important part played by the aircraft carriers of other nations and the lack of ability to provide air cover for Kriegsmarine warships other than close to coastal areas forced a re-think and construction work began again. In January 1943 however, Hitler was so annoyed at the lack of successes by his surface fleet that he cancelled all work on new construction. *Graf Zeppelin* then lay at a remote wharf near Stettin with a skeleton maintenance crew until April 1945 when, as Soviet forces approached, it was scuttled.

Raised by the Soviets in 1946, its exact fate is a matter of dispute at to whether it was deliberately sunk by the Soviets or struck a mine whilst under tow. The remains were discovered in 2006 near Władysławowo in Poland.

Graf Zeppelin Specifications			
Length	263m	Maximum endurance	8,000 nautical miles
Beam	36m	Main armament	6 x 15cm guns, in single-barrelled turrets
Draught	8.5m	Flak armament	12 x 10.5cm guns, 22 x 3.7cm guns, 28 x 2cm guns
Maximum displacement	33,550 tons	Aircraft (intended)	30 fighters, 12 dive-bombers
Maximum speed	33.8 knots	Complement	1,720 officers and men

Special versions of the Messerschmitt Bf 109, designated Bf 109T, were to be fitted with an arrestor hook at the tail, and test flights were made with only limited success. The remainder of the 'fighter' element was to be made up from Fieseler Fi 167 torpedo-carrying biplanes which had short take-off and landing capabilities. In the event, due to lack of need, they were sold to Croatia.

The bomber element would be made up of Junkers Ju 87 Stukas. Designated the Ju 87C-1, they were fitted with an arrestor hook and folding wings. Only a small number had been produced by the time the project was cancelled.

Given Hermann Göring's insistence that 'everything that flies belongs to me', it would have been interesting to see how much interference the Luftwaffe would have exerted over the operational use of these aircraft from a Kriegsmarine aircraft carrier.

U-BOATS

In terms of operational success and impact on the war effort, the U-boats were certainly the most successful element of the Kriegsmarine, at least in the first half of the war. Ultimately, improvements in Allied anti-submarine measures reduced their effectiveness, but it is safe to say no other nation in history has made such effective use of submarines during wartime.

Early Kriegsmarine U-boats.

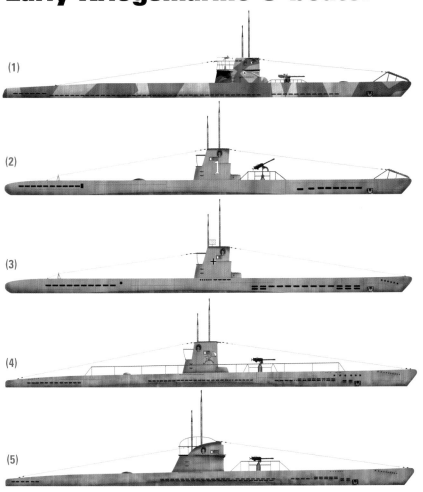

(1) Type IA. U-25, was one of only two Type IA boats built. Both saw combat service and were sunk in the summer of 1940. (2) Type IIA. The first of the Type II boats, U-1 as shown here is in its pre-war livery of pale grey with the boat's number painted on the side of the tower. (3) Type IIB. U-9, the 'Iron Cross Boat', was similar in appearance to the Type IIA, but marginally longer. (4) Type IIC. This type was slightly longer and was identifiable by the additional draining ports for the free-flooding area.(5) Type IID. This type had a distinctive conning tower shape. (Ian Palmer © Osprey Publishing)

Type I

One of the least successful U-boat designs, only two Type IAs were ever built. Constructed by the Deschimag yard, U-25 and U-26 were to be the only boats of their type, though this model was a direct forebear of the later, much more successful Type IX.

Type I Specifications				
Length	72.4m	Endurance	6,700 nautical miles surfaced 78 nautical miles submerged	
Beam	6.2m	Powerplant	2 x 1,540bhp MAN diesels coupled with 2 x 500bhp electric motors	
Draft	4.3m	Armament	• 6 torpedo tubes (4 bow, 2 stern), 14 torpedoes • 1 x 10.5cm gun • 1 x 2cm gun	
Displacement	862 tons surfaced 983 tons submerged	Complement	43	
Speed	17.8 knots surfaced 8.3 knots submerged			

U-26 was one of only two examples of the Type IA to be built. Moderately successful, it sank 11 enemy ships before being so badly damaged by depth charges from a Royal Navy corvette supported by a Sunderland flying boat on 1 July 1940 that it had to be scuttled. (Author's collection)

U-25 was commissioned on 6 April 1936 and had a brief, but successful combat career, sinking eight ships and damaging one. However, it came to grief on 3 August 1940 when it ran into a British mine off Norway, and was lost with all hands.

U-26 carried out eight war cruises. On its first cruise, it was employed on minelaying duties, and was rewarded by the sinking of three merchant ships and the damaging of one British warship by mines laid by it. On its second cruise it became the first U-boat of the war to enter the Mediterranean, though the remainder of the cruise was uneventful. Its third cruise saw it add a further three merchant ships to its score in a brief sortie into the Atlantic. The fourth cruise saw it being used for transport duties during the Norwegian Campaign, though it sank a 5,200-ton merchantman during its return trip from one of its transport sorties. After three more uneventful patrols, U-26 set off on its eighth war cruise on 20 June 1940. Three merchantmen were sunk on 30 June, and on the next day an attack damaged a further merchant ship. The attack was followed by a severe depth-charging from two British warships that forced U-26 to the surface where it was bombed by a Sunderland flying boat. The crew were forced to scuttle it, the majority being rescued by their attackers.

Despite both boats having relatively successful, if short, combat careers, they were technically not particularly good sea boats, especially when considering that they were intended as oceangoing rather than coastal vessels. Their stability was poor, their diving speed slow, and their manoeuvrability under water not impressive. Nevertheless, with 13 war cruises and 18 ships sunk between them, the Type IAs had acquitted themselves well.

Type II

The Type II was a natural enough progression from the U-boat coastal types of the *Kaiserliche Marine* in World War I. Small, cheap and easy to build, they could be produced in a remarkably short time. Based on the CV-707 export design produced for Finland between the wars, the Type II made excellent training vessels, but due to their small size and tendency to roll heavily when on the surface they were rather contemptuously referred to as *Einbäume* or 'canoes' by the Germans. Nevertheless, several of this type acquitted themselves well in combat operations as well as in training, and a number of variant types were produced. All carried just three bow torpedo tubes in an unusual, inverted triangle arrangement, with one each to port and starboard and a third below them on the boat's centre line.

Ideally, all of the Type II vessels would have been relegated to training duties by the outbreak of war in September 1939. However, as Germany was nowhere near its intended submarine strength by this point, the need for *Frontboote* (operational submarines) meant that many Type IIs had to be pressed into combat service. As the number of available Type VII and Type IX vessels increased, so Type IIs were released from combat service, once again for use with the training flotillas. By mid-1941, all Type IIAs and Type IIBs had been returned to training duty. Almost all of the Type IICs were used during the invasion of Norway before they too were gradually released back to the training flotillas.

U-2, one of the first of the Type IIA boats at far left. Only four such vessels were built before the improved Type IIB was introduced. After serving with the U-boat training school it was allocated to *21.Unterseebootsflottille* (Submarine Flotilla). It was sunk on 8 April 1944 after a collision with a trawler. (DUBM)

Type IIA

A total of just six Type IIAs were built. Of these, U-1 was sunk by a mine, and all of the others took part in support operations in the invasion of Norway with U-2, U-5 and U-6 returning thereafter to training duties. U-3 had a slightly more eventful career, carrying out five war cruises and sinking two enemy ships before being relegated to training duties. U-4 took part in four war cruises, sinking three enemy ships and a British submarine, HMS *Thistle*, before joining the training flotilla.

Type IIA Specifications			
Length	40.9m	Endurance	2,000 nautical miles surfaced 71 nautical miles submerged
Beam	4.1m	Powerplant	2 x 350bhp MWM diesels coupled with 2 x 180bhp electric motors
Draft	3.8m	Armament	• 3 bow torpedo tubes, 6 torpedoes carried • 1 x 2cm flak gun
Displacement	254 tons surfaced 301 tons submerged	Complement	25
Speed	13 knots surfaced 6.9 knots submerged		

Type IIB

The Type IIB was basically a lengthened version of the Type IIA, the additional hull capacity allowing a greater fuel load to be carried, thus enhancing the boat's endurance. Five seconds were also shaved off the critical time taken to dive the boat – a reduction from 35 down to 30 seconds. A total of 20 Type IIBs were built, the largest number of any sub-type.

Many of the Type IIB boats returned to training duties after the invasion of Norway. A total of 150 war cruises were carried out by these small coastal boats,

The most famous of the Type IIB boats was undoubtedly U-9, carrying the Iron Cross emblem on its tower in commemoration of the original U-9 from the Imperial Navy. It spent the war alternating between service as a training boat and active service, and was eventually sunk during a bombing raid on its base on 20 August 1944. (DUBM)

however, with 97 enemy merchant ships and nine enemy warships being sunk. Though small, they served their purpose well.

Six of the Type IIB vessels (U-9, U-18, U-19, U-20, U-22 and U-23) were dispatched to the Eastern Front for service in the Black Sea against Soviet shipping. The diminutive size of these boats allowed them to be partially dismantled and loaded onto barges to be transferred as far as possible along inland waterways, then loaded onto large flatbed trailers and transported by road. These obsolescent boats succeeded in sinking a number of Soviet ships. As fortunes on the Eastern Front went into reverse, it became impossible to consider taking them back to Germany by the same route. They were offered to Turkey and, on this being refused, were scuttled to prevent them falling into Soviet hands.

Just forward of the tower on the Type IIB was a large pedestal base onto which a 2cm flak gun could be mounted. In this exposed position it was of little use as a defensive weapon, but could be useful when stopping and searching enemy merchants. Even such a light weapon could inflict damage on a smaller merchant ship. (DUBM)

Type IIB Specifications				
Length	42.7m	**Endurance**	3,900 nautical miles surfaced 71 nautical miles submerged	
Beam	4.1m	**Powerplant**	2 x 350bhp MWM diesels coupled with 2 x 180bhp electric motors	
Draft	3.9m	**Armament**	• 3 bow torpedo tubes, 6 torpedoes carried • 1 x 2cm flak gun	
Displacement	279 tons surfaced 329 tons submerged	**Complement**	25	
Speed	13 knots surfaced 7 knots submerged			

Type IIC

Once again, this boat was simply a lengthened version of its immediate predecessor, with increased bunkerage. The Type IIC also had a lengthened control room and a second periscope. The Type IIC can easily be identified on photographs by the flush front to the tower, rather than the stepped front found on the IIA and IIB.

Of the eight Type IIC boats that were built, only one (U-63) was lost to enemy action. All of the others eventually returned to training duties after the type had completed a total of 56 war cruises and sunk 57 enemy ships, including three warships.

Type IIC Specifications			
Length	43.9m	Endurance	4,200 nautical miles surfaced 71 nautical miles submerged
Beam	4.1m	Powerplant	2 x 350bhp MWM diesels coupled with 2 x 205bhp electric motors
Draft	3.8m	Armament	• 3 bow torpedo tubes, 6 torpedoes carried • 1 x 2cm flak gun
Displacement	291 tons surfaced 341 tons submerged	Complement	25
Speed	12 knots surfaced 7 knots submerged		

TOP RIGHT A typical Type IIC, U-61 was slightly longer and had a larger tower than its predecessors. The eagle on the face of the tower would later be removed, and its boat number on the side of the tower painted over. (DUBM)

BELOW RIGHT Seen here is the tower of U-139, a Type IID. This type had an even larger tower with a position for the 2cm flak gun. The Type IID had a much greater range than earlier Type IIs. U-139 spent most of its career as a training vessel after sinking 5 enemy ships during the first year of the war. (DUBM)

FAR RIGHT U-147 shows the typical appearance of an active service Type IID in wartime, with camouflage scheme applied. The boat's emblem, a flying fish, was chosen by its then commander Kapitänleutnant Reinhard Hardegen, who would go on to be one of the top U-boat aces. (DUBM)

Type IID

The Type IID, but for its small size, might almost pass for the Type VII with its enlarged conning tower with rear flak platform, and its distinctive saddle tanks. It had greatly increased range, and more up-to-date self-compensating fuel bunkers.

A total of 16 Type IIDs were produced, many of which went directly into the training flotillas and saw no action whatsoever. Those that did participate in combat sorties completed a total of 36 war cruises, resulting in 27 enemy ships being sunk, including three warships. One was lost to a depth-charge attack by enemy destroyers, and one was sunk by an enemy submarine. The others all served out the war in the various training flotillas.

Type IID Specifications			
Length	44.0m	**Endurance**	5,680 nautical miles surfaced 71 nautical miles submerged
Beam	5.0m	**Powerplant**	2 x 350bhp MWM diesels coupled with 2 x 205bhp electric motors
Draft	3.9m	**Armament**	• 3 bow torpedo tubes, 6 torpedoes carried • 1 x 2cm flak gun
Displacement	314 tons surfaced 364 tons submerged	**Complement**	25
Speed	12.7 knots surfaced 7.4 knots submerged		

Type VII

The Type VII was a single-hulled boat, the pressure hull in places forming the outer hull of the boat. It differed principally from earlier designs in that its bunkerage was contained within the pressure hull rather than in saddle tanks, giving additional protection to the precious fuel. A single central ballast tank was provided, together with bow and stern ballast tanks out with the pressure hull, and two large saddle tanks on either side of the hull. Outside the pressure hull was a streamlined external casing, the area between the two being free flooding. Between the deck and the top of the pressure hull a considerable amount of ducting and trunking was fitted, as well as the mounting for the deck gun, ready-ammunition locker for the deck gun, a small dinghy and, ultimately, storage for spare torpedoes. All could be accessed via hatches or by removal of deck plating. An 8.8cm naval gun was fitted on the foredeck just in front of the conning tower and a 2cm flak gun just aft.

The first variant to be produced was the Type VIIA, of which ten were completed. These were allocated the numbers U-27 through to U-36. Four were built by Germaniawerft and six by AG Weser. Construction began in February 1935 with the first boat (U-33) of the type launched on 11 June 1936. One of the most instantly recognizable visual characteristics of the Type VIIA was the hump of the external stern torpedo tube, clearly visible on the aft decking.

The *U-Boot-Kriegsabzeichen* (U-boat War Badge), issued to men who had undertaken at least two war cruises. This actual example was awarded to U-boat commander Oberleutnant zur See Heinrich Niemeyer. The badge was based on the original submarine badge of the Kaiserliche Marine which had been designed by the famous sculptor Walter Schott. (Author's collection)

Type VIIA Specifications			
Length	64.5m	**Endurance**	4,300 nautical miles surfaced 90 nautical miles submerged
Beam	5.8m	**Powerplant**	2 x 1,160bhp diesels coupled with 2 x 375bhp electric motors
Draft	4.4m	**Armament**	• 5 torpedo tubes (4 bow, 1 stern) • 1 x 8.8cm gun • 1 x 2cm gun
Displacement	626 tons surfaced 745 tons submerged	**Complement**	44
Speed	16 knots surfaced 8 knots submerged		

ABOVE One of the most obvious distinguishing features of the early Type VIIA was the stern torpedo tube being mounted above the waterline as can be seen here. Only ten of this type were built. The drawback to this feature was that it could only be reloaded when the vessel was on the surface. (DUBM)

The Type VIIB was a marked improvement over the initial variant. It was given twin rather than single rudders to improve its turning circle, and the external stern torpedo tube of the VIIA was brought inside the pressure hull, firing out between the two rudders. The boat was given an increase in length of 2m to provide additional bunkerage, and additional fuel was now also carried in special fuel cells within the saddle tanks. These cells were self-compensating – as fuel was drawn from the top of the tank, sea water entered at the bottom, compensating for the loss in weight. Compensating tanks were also installed to help prevent the boat rolling when on the surface. Finally, turbochargers were fitted to the diesel engines to provide a modest increase in speed. All of these changes increased the size and weight of the boat significantly.

TOP FAR LEFT The conning tower of U-35, a Type IIA. Note the practice pre-war of marking the life preserver on the side of the tower with the boat number and flotilla name (in this case *Unterseebootsflottille Saltzwedel*). It was sunk on 2 August 1940 when it ran into a British minefield and was lost with all hands. (DUBM)

ABOVE LEFT With the Type VIIB, the stern torpedo tube was now internal, firing between the twin rudders. The boat was also slightly longer, giving it more fuel carrying capacity. Shown here is U-101, which sank 22 merchants and one warship during its combat career. It almost survived the war, but met its fate on 3 May 1945 when it was sunk by rocket-firing aircraft. (DUBM)

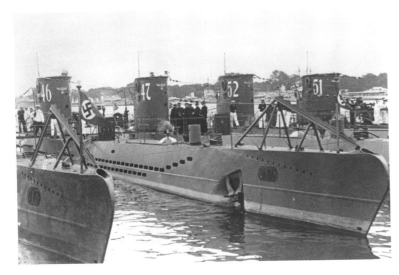

LEFT A number of Type VIIBs in port pre-war. All carry the boat number on the tower and on a small plate at the bow. The bronze eagle is also featured on the front of the tower. Second from left is U-47, the boat which would infiltrate Scapa Flow and sink the battleship HMS *Royal Oak*. (Central Press/Hulton Archive/Getty Images)

A total of 24 Type VIIBs were built: the first seven (U-45 to U-51) by Germaniawerft, a second tranche of four, also from Germaniawerft, and a third tranche consisting of four boats each from Germaniawerft and Vulcan, with five from Flenderwerft.

Type VIIB Specifications			
Length	66.5m	**Endurance**	6,500 nautical miles surfaced 90 nautical miles submerged
Beam	6.2m	**Powerplant**	2 x 1,400bhp diesels coupled with 2 x 375bhp electric motors
Draft	4.7m	**Armament**	• 5 torpedo tubes (4 bow, 1 stern) • 1 x 8.8cm gun • 1 x 2cm gun • 15 mines
Displacement	753 tons surfaced 857 tons submerged	**Complement**	44
Speed	17.2 knots surfaced 8 knots submerged		

The early Type VIIC was externally very similar to the Type VIIB. As the war progressed, however, many Type VIIC were heavily modified. Amongst the many modifications, the net cutter at the bow would be removed and later the 8.8cm deck gun also removed as these were no longer often used and merely created drag when submerged. (Author's collection)

The third and most significant variant of this class was the Type VIIC. It was originally proposed as a vessel for the new sonar search equipment known as the *Such-Gerät* (S-Gerät), with an increase in length to both the control room and the conning tower to accommodate the necessary equipment. Other smaller, but nevertheless welcome, modifications were also incorporated. A small buoyancy tank was fitted within the saddle tanks, which could also be flooded to improve diving time. A new filtration system for the diesel engines, a new diesel rather than electric-powered compressor for the air tanks – to ease demands on the electrical system – and more modern electrical switching systems were all added to this model.

Type VIIC Specifications			
Length	67.1m	**Endurance**	6,500 nautical miles surfaced 80 nautical miles submerged
Beam	6.2m	**Powerplant**	2 x 1,400bhp diesels coupled with 2 x 375bhp electric motors
Draft	4.8m	**Armament**	• 5 torpedo tubes (4 bow, 1 stern) • 1 x 8.8cm gun • 1 x 2cm gun
Displacement	761 tons surfaced 865 tons submerged	**Complement**	44
Speed	17 knots surfaced 7.6 knots submerged		

U-251, a Type VIIC, entering port at Narvik in 1942. The boat's emblem, shown on the conning tower, is of a chimney sweep carrying a ladder. Serving with a training flotilla in the late part of the war, it was attacked on the surface and sunk by rocket-firing aircraft on 19 April 1945. (NHHC)

The first major sub-variant of this type was the Type VIIC/41. This variant featured extensive replacement of existing electrical equipment by newer, more compact models. The weight thus saved (some 11 tons overall) was utilized in thickening the steel plate used for the pressure hull by a further 2.5mm, thus allowing an increase in diving capabilities from a maximum depth of 250m to 300m. The bow was also lengthened slightly to increase seaworthiness.

Type VIIC/41 Specifications				
Length	67.2m	**Endurance**	6,500 nautical miles surfaced 80 nautical miles submerged	
Beam	6.2m	**Powerplant**	2 x 1,400bhp diesels coupled with 2 x 375bhp electric motors	
Draft	4.8m	**Armament**	• 5 torpedo tubes (4 bow, 1 stern) • 1 x 8.8cm gun • 1 x 2cm gun	
Displacement	759 tons surfaced 860 tons submerged	**Complement**	44	
Speed	17 knots surfaced 7.6 knots submerged			

The Type VIIC/42 projected sub-variant was an attempt to improve speed further by adding additional turbochargers, coupled with an increase in length to give greater fuel storage capabilities. Armour-plate was to be used rather than normal steel for the pressure hull, taking the maximum depth possible up to 500m. No examples of the Type VIIC/42 were ever completed.

Another design that got no further than the drawing board was the Type VIIC/43 – essentially a Type VIIC/42 with armament upgraded to provide six rather than four bow torpedo tubes.

The Type VIID version of the versatile Type VII design was a minelayer. The hull of the basic Type VII was extended by almost 10m, just aft of the control room, to provide five vertical mine shafts. Additional benefits of the extension in hull length included space for additional fuel and extra trim tanks. These boats also had the luxury of refrigerated food storage. The full torpedo and gun armament of the standard Type VII was retained. On the downside, the additional weight and length, to say nothing of the raised decking required for the mine shafts, reduced overall speed and handling qualities, though overall endurance was increased.

A Type VIID minelayer. Based on the Type VIIC, its hull was lengthened by almost 10m, and a number of vertical mine tubes were fitted. These can be seen immediately aft of the conning tower. (DUBM)

Type VIID Minelayer Specifications			
Length	76.9m	**Endurance**	8,100 nautical miles surfaced 69 nautical miles submerged
Beam	6.4m	**Powerplant**	2 x 1,400bhp diesels coupled with 2 x 375bhp electric motors
Draft	5.0m	**Armament**	• 5 torpedo tubes (4 bow, 1 stern) • 1 x 8.8cm gun • 1 x 2cm gun • 15 mines
Displacement	965 tons surfaced 1,080 tons submerged	**Complement**	44
Speed	16 knots surfaced 7.3 knots submerged		

Type VII variants

(1) Type VIIA recognizable by its prominent stern torpedo tube, mounted outside the pressure hull.
(2) Type VIIB with the later style of bridge for this model, with prominent air ducting up the side of the tower.
(3) Type VIIC, U-995, a typical Type VIIC in late-war configuration. It has a 3.7cm flak gun on the lower 'Wintergarden' platform, and two twin 2cm flak guns on the upper platform.
(4) Type VIIC/42, the ultimate Type VII, has a quadruple 2cm *Flakvierling*, with two twin 2cm flak guns on the upper platform.
(Ian Palmer © Osprey Publishing)

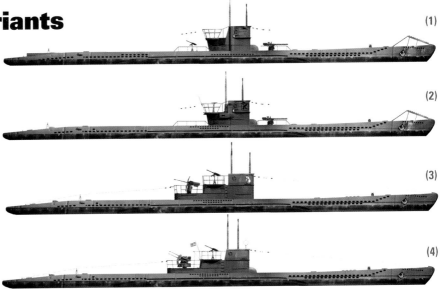

(1)

(2)

(3)

(4)

The Type VIIE was a design project only, which was to have been fitted with a new type of two-stroke V12 lightweight diesel engine made by the Deutz firm. The project was abandoned before any could be built.

The Type VIIF was a modification of the basic Type VII design similar to that of the Type VIID, in that a 10.5m additional length of hull was inserted just abaft the control room. This allowed an extra 24 torpedoes to be carried, as well as additional refrigerated food storage and two extra crew members. The Type VIIF was to act as a resupply boat, carrying additional torpedoes to frontline boats that had expended their ammunition. Only four of this type were eventually built (U-1059 to U-1062), all produced by Germaniawerft.

Type VIIF Specifications				
Length	77.6m	**Endurance**	9,500 nautical miles surfaced 75 nautical miles submerged	
Beam	7.3m	**Powerplant**	2 x 1,400bhp diesels coupled with 2 x 375bhp electric motors	
Draft	4.9m	**Armament**	• 5 torpedo tubes (4 bow, 1 stern) • 1 x 8.8cm gun • 1 x 2cm gun	
Displacement	1,084 tons surfaced 1,181 tons submerged	**Complement**	46	
Speed	16.9 knots surfaced 7.9 knots submerged			

Type VIIC Variants

Of all of the Type VII models, none saw as much modification and improvement to the basic design as did the most common model of all, the Type VIIC. The variants mentioned above relate principally to internal modifications, which would not be obvious from photographs of the boats themselves. However, one major series of modifications that became necessary during the course of the war, and which drastically altered the appearance of each type, was made to the conning tower.

As Allied anti-submarine measures improved, the use of aircraft against U-boats took on a considerable significance and it quickly became apparent that the single 2cm anti-aircraft gun carried on the basic Type VII was woefully inadequate. In fact, no matter how much the flak armament was beefed up, few U-boats would risk taking on enemy aircraft (although in several recorded cases, when left with no option but to remain on the surface, U-boats did take on enemy aircraft, and succeeded in shooting them down).

The various conning tower configurations, beginning with the basic circular platform to the rear of the tower, with its single 2cm flak gun, were given numeric codes, the basic configuration being known as *Turm 0*.

The first major attempt to beef up flak defences was to widen the platform somewhat, and replace the single 2cm flak gun with two twin 2cm machine-gun mounts.

- *Turm 1*: This design was to see a second, lower, platform fitted to the rear of the conning tower (generally known to U-boat men as the '*Wintergarden*') on which would be fitted a twin 2cm flak. This design was approved in June 1942.
- *Turm 2*: Due to problems with the supply of the new weapons required for the *Turm 1* design, a second new tower configuration was introduced in which the original round upper platform was joined by a similar lower platform, both of

which were fitted with a single 2cm flak gun. Installation of this type commenced in December 1942.

- *Turm 3*: This little-used configuration saw two single 2cm flak guns mounted side by side on the upper platform and was used only on the Type VIID.
- *Turm 4*: This configuration, destined to become the most common, had two twin 2cm guns fitted on a widened upper platform, and a single four-barrelled 2cm flak gun, the *Flakvierling*, on the lower. The *Flakvierling* was gradually replaced by a single-barrelled 3.7cm flak gun.

The heavily modified tower of a late-war Type VIIC. Note the extensive armour protection to the side of the tower, the extended flak platforms and the armament increased from a single 2cm flak to two twin 2cm flak and one 3.7cm flak. This was a typical mid- to late-war armament. (DUBM)

Interior of a Type VII U-boat

The interior layout of the Type VIIC/42, shown here, was typical of German submarine design. At the bow was the forward torpedo room, with four tubes and accommodation for junior ratings, and a roof hatchway for loading fresh torpedoes.In the centre of the boat was the control room, containing the main helm, diving controls, navigator's table and auxiliary bilge pumps. In the centre were the tubes into which the periscopes retracted.Above was the conning tower, containing the commander's attack station.The engine room contained the boat's two diesel engines. In the motor room aft were located the boat's two electric motors, and the stern torpedo tube. (Ian Palmer © Osprey Publishing)

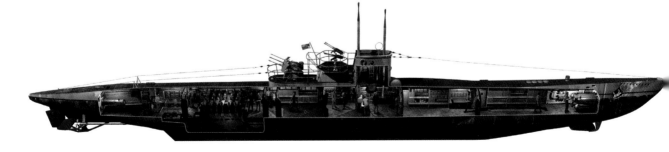

- *Turm 5*: An experimental model, fitted to only one U-boat (U-362), this configuration had two twin 2cm flak guns on the upper platform, a single twin 2cm flak gun on the lower, and a fourth twin 2cm gun on a platform built on to the front of the tower.

- *Turm 6*: Another little-used model, only two boats received this modification. This configuration had a single-barrelled 3.7cm flak gun on the lower platform, two twin 2cm flak guns on the upper, and a single twin 2cm in front of the tower on a separate pedestal. Only U-673 and U-973 were so converted.

- *Turm 7*: A 'concept' only and never actually built, this tower would have seen twin 3.7cm flak guns on platforms both to the rear and in front of the tower.

- *Flakboote* (flak boats): A small number of boats (seven only) were ordered to be converted into *Flakboote*, and given heavy anti-aircraft armament to allow them to take on enemy aircraft on relatively even terms. U-441 was given a *Flakvierling* on a mount in front of the tower and another on the upper platform at the rear of the tower, as well as a 3.7cm flak gun on the rear lower platform. Although U-441 succeeded in shooting down a Sunderland flying boat, the adverse effect of the new bridge structure combined with the heavy armament, saw the order cancelled with all *Flakboote* reconverted back to *Turm 4* configuration.

The 'core' of any submarine is, of course, its pressure hull. In the case of the Type VII this was of circular section, tubular in the centre section, and then tapering slightly towards the bow and stern. The pressure hull was made from welded rolled steel up to 2.2cm thick. The whole consisted of six sections, plus a bow and stern end cap. Around this pressure hull was built the external casing, an area which was free flooding and was used to accommodate ventilation trunking and for storage.

Starting from the bow, the first compartment was the forward torpedo room, into which the four bow torpedo tubes penetrated by some 4m. To the ceiling was attached a hoist used for manoeuvring the torpedoes into the tubes, and the angled torpedo loading hatch. To the rear of the compartment were located three sets of two-tier bunks on each side. Compressed air cylinders were located below the bottom bunk, as were collapsible tables for the use of the junior ratings who occupied this compartment. Under the decking there was storage space for two additional torpedoes and under these, the bow trim tanks.

After passing through the first bulkhead, the next compartment in line was the senior non-commissioned ranks' accommodation, comprising two sets of two-tier bunks each side.

A further bulkhead followed before reaching the officer accommodation. Again, two sets of two-tier bunks were provided but as only three officers were normally carried, one of these was usually stowed. A small table was provided on the port side.

Then came the commander's bunk. He was the only man on board afforded a modicum of privacy, provided by a simple curtain at the entry to his 'quarters'. Directly across the walkway were located the radio room and sound detector room, giving the operators of these essential pieces of equipment instant access to the commanding officer. Under the decking of this area were stored the forward batteries as well as ammunition for the deck gun.

Exterior of a Type VII U-boat

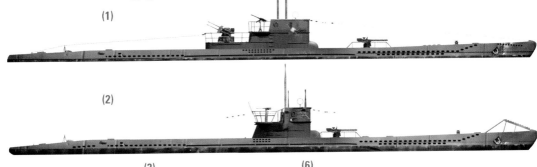

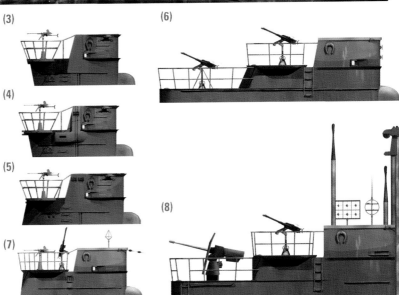

Deck armament configurations on the Type VII U-boat. (1) Type VIIF with a 10.5m 'plug' inserted into the hull abaft the conning tower, allowing this version to carry 24 additional torpedoes. (2) Early Type VIIC with 8.8cm deck gun still fitted and a single 2cm flak gun on the tower platform. (3) The Type VIIA bridge. (4) The Type VIIB bridge. (5) The standard early Type VIIC bridge. (6) A few Type VIIC had the width of the platform between the rear 2cm flak gun mount and the bridge widened to allow the fitting of two twin 2cm flak guns. (7) Type VIIC *Turm 2* conversion. (8) The Type VIIC *Turm 4*.
(Ian Palmer © Osprey Publishing)

Reaching the central portion of the boat, the hub of activity was the control room, or *Zentral*, with a heavy pressurised bulkhead at either end. On the starboard side from the bow end, were located the boat's main helm, the diving planes, the navigator's table and the auxiliary bilge pumps. On the port side were the periscope motor, the main vent controls, the main bilge pump and a drinking water tank. In the centre of the compartment were the periscope tubes, the main optics for the sky, or navigation, periscope being located in the control room.

Above the control room was the conning tower. In it was a tiny space, the commander's attack station. Within this tiny compartment were the optics for the attack periscope, the attack computer, the compass and the exit hatch to the exterior of the conning tower. Under the decking of the *Zentral* were fitted ballast tanks and fuel bunkers.

Passing through the rear control room bulkhead, the next compartment was the junior non-commissioned ranks' accommodation, consisting of two pairs of twin bunks each side. Towards the rear of this compartment, on one side was the boat's tiny galley and on the other the aft WC and food storage pantry. The aft batteries were stored under the deck plates of this area.

The next bulkhead led through to the engine room. Within this small space were located the boat's two diesel engines on their massive founds, with only a narrow passageway in between. A further bulkhead allowed passage into the motor room in which were located the boat's two electric motors, coupled to the same shafts as the diesels. Also contained in this compartment were a compressor for the boat's modest refrigerated storage, the main electrical control panels and the stern torpedo tube, which fired out between the boat's twin rudders. Beneath the deck plating in this area were the stern trim tanks.

The U-boat's external decking was covered in wood planking, with a 1cm gap between planks to allow for drainage. Wood was used to avoid the degree of icing up in winter conditions that would have been encountered with metal decking.

The area between the outer casing and pressure hull was free flooding, and along the side of the outer casing of any Type VII will be seen numerous draining slots. The exact number and positioning of these varied from manufacturer to manufacturer. In the area between pressure hull and outer casing, in the forward portion of the boat, was located a storage tube for a spare torpedo. On some boats this was replaced by a series of watertight containers for life rafts.

Moving away from the bow, there was an angled torpedo loading hatch leading from the outer deck to the pressure hull. This allowed the torpedo to be taken into the boat nose first, facing the tube into which it would be loaded. Beyond the torpedo loading hatch was a watertight storage container with a small amount of ammunition for the deck gun. This allowed the gun to be brought into action swiftly, while the remainder of the ammunition was brought up through the boat from the ammunition storage under the deck plating on the *Zentral*.

On the outer decking itself, at the forward point, some early boats still had the serrated net cutter fitted to World War I boats, but by the outbreak of World War II most of these had been removed. Retractable bollards were fitted near the bow and stern, with additional pairs, port and starboard approximately midway between the bow/stern and the conning tower. A retractable capstan winch and retractable hydrophone array were also mounted on the foredeck.

The conning tower, as has already been noted, was one of the areas in which considerable differences may be found from boat to boat and at different stages throughout the war. In general, the front and sides of the tower were screened up to a height of some 1.5m to give the crew some measure of protection against the elements. The rear of the bridge was open, leading onto the aft platform which was surrounded by a safety railing. On the bridge itself were the mounts that supported the periscopes, a pedestal mount for the UZO (*Uberwasserzieloptik*) torpedo aiming device, a binnacle and, on the starboard wall of the tower, a slot to house the retractable direction-finding loop. Later examples of the Type VII had the snorkel fitting mounted on the port side of the tower.

Type VII Construction Details

The below list represents the only boats that were completed. Others were laid down, but never completed, or were broken up, or had the order for their manufacture cancelled.

Germaniawerft, Kiel
- VIIA U-33 to U-36 4 boats
- VIIB U-45 to U-55 11 boats
- VIIB U-99 to U-102 4 boats
- VIIC U-69 to U-72 4 boats
- VIIC U-93 to U-98 6 boats
- VIIC U-201 to U-212 12 boats
- VIIC U-221 to U-232 12 boats
- VIIC U-235 to U-250 16 boats
- VIIC U-1051 to U-1058 8 boats
- VIIC U-1063 to U-1065 3 boats
- Total 80 boats

Bremer Vulcan, Vegesack
- VIIB U-73 to U-76 4 boats
- VIIC U-77 to U-82 6 boats
- VIIC U-132 to U-136 5 boats
- VIIC U-251 to U-300 50 boats
- VIIC U-1271 to U-1279 9 boats
- Total 74 boats

Deschimag, Bremen
- VIIA U-27 to U-32 6 boats
- (This firm concentrated on the Type IX.)

Flenderwerft, Lubeck
- VIIB U-83 to U-87 5 boats
- VIIC U-88 to U-92 5 boats
- VIIC U-301 to U-330 30 boats
- VIIC U-903 to U-904 2 boats
- Total 42 boats

Nordsee Werke, Emden
- VIIC U-331 to U-350 20 boats
- VIIC U-1101 to U-1110 10 boats
- Total 30 boats

Flensburger Schiffsbau, Flensburg
- VIIC U-351 to U-370 20 boats
- VIIC U-1301 to U-1308 8 boats
- Total 28 boats

Howaldts Werke, Kiel
- VIIC U-371 to U-400 30 boats
- VIIC U-651 to U-683 33 boats
- VIIC U-1131 to U-1132 2 boats
- Total 65 boats

Danzigerwerft, Danzig
- VIIC U-401 to U-430 30 boats
- VIIC U-1161 to U-1172 12 boats
- Total 42 boats

Stülcken Sohn, Hamburg
- VIIC U-701 to U-722 22 boats
- VIIC U-905 to U-908 4 boats
- Total 26 boats

Schichauwerft, Danzig
- VIIC U-431 to U-450 20 boats
- VIIC U-731 to U-750 20 boats
- VIIC U-825 to U-828 4 boats
- VIIC U-1191 to U-1210 20 boats
- Total 64 boats

Deutsche Werke, Kiel
- VIIC U-451 to U-458 8 boats
- VIIC U-465 to U-486 22 boats
- Total 30 boats

Blohm & Voss, Hamburg
- VIIC U-551 to U-650 100 boats
- VIIC U-951 to U-1031 81 boats
- Total 181 boats

Kriegsmarinewerft, Wilhelmshaven
- VIIC U-751 to U-779 29 boats

Oder Werke, Stettin
- VIIC U-821 to U-822 2 boats

Vulcan, Stettin
- VIIC U-901 1 boat

Neptunwerft, Rostock
- âVIIC U-921 to U-930 10 boats

The afterdeck was relatively featureless. Apart from the small stern torpedo loading hatch, the space under the rear decking was devoted almost entirely to trunking. The trunking, which passed through the free-flooding area under the afterdeck, led up through the conning tower casing to the rear outer tower wall. Types VIIA and VIIB had large trunking running up the outside face of the tower, but by the VIIC model this was contained within the tower casing.

A single, thick antenna cable ran from the most forward point of the bow to just before the conning tower, where it split, one fork running to a locating point either side of the top of the tower wall. From here, one antenna cable ran down to an anchor point on each side near the stern.

Type VII Operational Use

With just over 700 examples built, the Type VII was by far the most successful of all the U-boat types. It fitted well with the decision taken that Germany would build a large fleet of small- to medium-sized boats rather than a small fleet of large boats. Despite its modest size, and relative ease of construction, it proved itself a reliable design, capable of operating throughout the Atlantic, its capabilities restricted only by the amount of fuel/munitions it could carry.

The Type VII had a faster diving speed than the larger Type IX (see below), a critical factor that endeared it to its crews, as did its capability of diving, on occasion, much deeper than its recommended safe maximum depth without mishap. The biggest 'downside' for the crews was the extremely cramped interior. Space was at an absolute premium and conditions within these boats could become extremely uncomfortable very quickly. However, to many U-boat men, even though the Type IX was more spacious and thus more comfortable, its slow diving speed and thus greater vulnerability when caught on the surface made the Type VII a relatively 'safer' boat.

Without doubt, the Type VII in its many guises was by far the most influential submarine in the U-boat war. Through the course of the war, over 2,600 war cruises were undertaken in the Type VII boats. During the course of these cruises, around 1,365 enemy ships were sunk, that total including 190 warships. From the total of just over 700 Type VIIs that were built, over 400 were sunk by enemy action. In the great majority of these cases, the boats were lost with all hands. Of the total of approximately

---

Type VII Flotillas

Many operational flotillas used a variety of different U-boat types through the course of the war, while others seemed to use a specific type predominantly, if not exclusively. The following flotillas are those in which use of the Type VII predominated:

1.Unterseebootsflottille	Types VIIB, VIIC and VIID
3.Unterseebootsflottille	Types VIIB and VIIC
6.Unterseebootsflottille	Types VIIB and VIIC
7.Unterseebootsflottille	Various Type VIIs
9.Unterseebootsflottille	Types VIIC and VIID
11.Unterseebootsflottille	Type VIIC
13.Unterseebootsflottille	Type VIIC
14.Unterseebootsflottille	Type VIIC

30,000 U-boat men who lost their lives in World War II, around 22,000, or 73 per cent, were serving on the Type VII.

The capabilities of the Type VII boat in the hands of an expert commander are easily established by a quick review of some of the most successful U-boat commanders of World War II, and the types of boats in which they operated.

On 17 September 1939, the Type VIIA U-29 under the command of Kapitänleutnant Otto Schuhart struck the first major blow against the Royal Navy when the aircraft carrier HMS *Courageous* was intercepted and sunk in the waters off the west coast of Ireland. Schuhart went on to accumulate of total of 12 enemy ships totalling some 83,700 tons before being given a shore command. He was decorated with the Knight's Cross and survived the war to serve in the West German *Bundesmarine*.

The first truly spectacular U-boat success of World War II, however, came on 14 October 1939 when Kapitänleutnant Günther Prien succeeded in penetrating the fleet anchorage at Scapa Flow, and torpedoed and sank the battleship HMS *Royal Oak*. Although this warship was obsolete and its loss to the Royal Navy would have no major effect on the combat capabilities of the British fleet, the mere fact that a U-boat had penetrated what was considered to be a safe anchorage and sunk a major surface warship with considerable loss of life, and had then escaped unscathed, was a major progadanda disaster for Britain, and one which Germany exploited to the full. Coming hard on the heels of the sinking of the *Courageous*, it was a serious blow to the morale of the Royal Navy. Prien's entire crew was decorated with the Iron Cross and Prien himself with the Knight's Cross of the Iron Cross.

Prien's boat, the U-47, was an early Type VIIB that continued to serve him well. Prien quickly established that his success at Scapa Flow was no fluke as his score of tonnage sunk rapidly rose. Prien sank a total of 31 ships, some 192,000 tons, before U-47 was attacked and sunk by the destroyer HMS *Wolverine* on 8 March 1941. There were no survivors. Prien had added the Oak Leaves to his Knight's Cross on 20 October 1940.

A contemporary of Prien, Kapitänleutnant Joachim Schepke, also commanded a Type VIIB, the U-100. Unlike Prien, there were no spectacular warship sinkings in his tally, but rather a steady and remorseless list of merchantmen sent to the bottom. He was decorated with the Knight's Cross of the Iron Cross on 24 September 1940, to which were added the Oak Leaves on 20 December 1941. His boat was finally forced to the surface and rammed by the destroyer HMS *Vanoc* on 17 March 1941. Schepke was on the bridge at the time and was crushed against the periscope mount by the impact and dragged down with the sinking U-boat. At the time of his death, he had sunk 37 ships totalling over 145,000 tons.

The third and by far the most successful of the Type VIIB 'aces' was Fregattenkapitän Otto Kretschmer. Kretschmer's quiet, serious demeanour earned him the nickname 'Silent Otto'. In command of U-99, however, his combat career was anything but 'quiet'. On his very first war cruise, Kretschmer sank 11 enemy ships. He was awarded the Knight's Cross on 4 August 1940 and added the Oak Leaves on 4 November that same year. His score continued to rise, reaching 56 ships for a total of 313,600 tons sunk. Kretschmer finally met his match when he succumbed to a joint attack by the destroyers *Vanoc* and *Walker* on 17 March 1941, in the same convoy battle in which Schepke was killed. Fortunately, the majority of U-99's crew, including Kretschmer himself, were able to abandon their stricken U-boat safely and spent the remainder of the war in a POW camp. Whilst in captivity Kretschmer learned that he had been decorated with the Swords to his Knight's Cross with Oak Leaves on 26 December 1941. Kretschmer's total tonnage sunk, which was never surpassed, made him the highest-scoring U-boat ace of World War II. This highly respected sailor survived the war and, when the German Navy was re-formed, returned to the service and eventually retired with the rank of *Flottillenadmiral.*

Amongst those who achieved great success with the Type VIIC, there are two main types of ace: the tonnage aces and the warship killers. One of the most famed Type VIICs is undoubtedly U-96, the subject of the acclaimed movie *Das Boot* (*The Boat*). Whilst the film is based on a real boat, the account is fictionalized and not altogether accurate. In the film, the boat's commander dies, but in reality the factual commander, Fregattenkapitän Heinrich Lehmann-Willenbrock, went on to even greater success and survived the war. Like the fictional captain, Lehmann-Willenbrock was decorated with the Knight's Cross of the Iron Cross, receiving his award on 26 February 1941.

Lehmann-Willenbrock also received the Oak Leaves, on 31 December 1941, and went on to sink a total of 25 enemy ships, for a total tonnage of 183,000 before moving to a shore posting, in command of first 9.Unterseebootsflottille then 11.Unterseebootsflottille.

The list of highly successful tonnage aces included Korvettenkapitän Adalbert Schnee, who sank a total of 24 enemy ships totalling 88,995 tons with his Type VIIC U-boat U-201. Schnee was awarded the Knight's Cross on 30 August 1941 and the Oak Leaves on 15 July 1942. Schnee (whose name in German means 'snow') was known for the emblem of a snowman on the conning tower of his boat. He was one of the first to be given command of one of the new Type XXI U-boats (U-2511). Although he only put to sea on his first operational cruise in the closing days of the war, and was unable to achieve any contact with the enemy before the order to cease hostilities was transmitted, he did carry out a successful dummy attack run on a group of British warships and escaped totally undetected.

Another of the great Type VIIC tonnage aces was Fregattenkapitän Erich Topp, whose conning tower emblem of a prancing devil painted in red earned U-552 the nickname of the 'Red Devil Boat'. Topp was decorated with the Knight's Cross on 20 June 1941, the Oak Leaves on 11 April 1942 and the Swords on 17 August 1942. His eventual total of enemy ships sunk was 35, for a total of 192,600 tons. Amongst his kills was the destroyer USS *Reuben James*. Like Schnee, Erich Topp was given command of one of the latest Type XXI boats in the closing stages of the war. Schnee also joined the re-formed Bundesmarine after the war and eventually retired with the rank of

Kapitänleutnant Hans Günther Lange, commander of U-711, a Type VIIC. U-711 took part in 12 patrols during the war and was sunk on 4 May 1945 by British aircraft. (Author's collection)

Konteradmiral. In 2000, this highly respected sailor, who over the years had made innumerable historians and researchers welcome to his home, was dismayed to discover that one 'guest' had stolen many of his decorations as well as his bejewelled naval Honour Dagger.

Several of the great Type VIIC aces earned their Knight's Cross, not by sinking huge tonnages of enemy merchant ships, but by spectacular sinkings of major enemy warships. Amongst these was Kapitänleutnant Hans Diedrich von Tiesenhausen, commander of U-331. Although this commander, operating in the Mediterranean, sank but two ships, his total tonnage score was 40,435. The reason for the high tonnage with just two ships was that one of these was the battleship HMS *Barham*, torpedoed and sunk by von Tiesenhausen on 25 November 1941. His other sinking was a 9,000-ton freighter, the *Leedstown*. He was awarded the Knight's Cross for his sinking of the *Barham* on 25 January 1942. On 17 November 1942, U-331 was attacked and sunk by Swordfish torpedo bombers from the aircraft carrier HMS *Formidable*. Von Tiesenhausen and 15 of his crew were rescued and spent the remainder of the war in captivity.

Other warship killers included Kapitänleutnant Klaus Bargsten, commander of U-521, whose sinkings, though totalling only six ships, included the famous Tribal-class destroyer HMS *Cossack* and the US sub-chaser *Bredon*, and Korvettenkapitän Helmut Rosenbaum, commander of U-753, whose similar total of six ships sunk included the aircraft carrier HMS *Eagle*.

A Type VII U-boat was also responsible for sinking one of the Royal Navy's most famous ships, the aircraft carrier HMS *Ark Royal*. On 13 November 1941, the 26-year-old Kapitänleutnant Friedrich Guggenberger, having just reached the Mediterranean in command of U-81, torpedoed the *Ark Royal* just 25 miles from Gibraltar. It was a propaganda triumph for Germany, which had in fact been prematurely claiming the sinking of the *Ark Royal* for some time, and a disaster for the Royal Navy, especially in light of the result of subsequent enquiries, which established that *Ark Royal* might have been saved had it not been prematurely abandoned.

One of the most interesting of U-boat commanders was Korvettenkapitän Peter Erich 'Ali' Cremer. Cremer was decorated with the Knight's Cross of the Iron Cross on 5 June 1942 as commander of the Type VII U-333, the boat's first commander having served previously on the destroyer *Theodor Riedel*. Cremer sank a modest seven enemy ships totalling some 36,000 tons, and was eventually given a shore posting where he commanded the 'Wachbattailon Dönitz'. Thrown into combat around Hamburg in the last few days of the war, Cremer led a highly successful 'tank-hunting' unit that knocked out a significant number of British tanks during the defensive battles around the port.

Not all of the most highly decorated Type VII aces were tonnage or warship killers. Only two men in the entire Kriegsmarine were decorated with the coveted Oak Leaves, Swords and Diamonds to the Knight's Cross. One, Wolfgang Lüth, was a Type IX commander, and the other, Albrecht Brandi, commanded a Type VII.

Albrecht Brandi had begun his naval career with the minesweeping branch and only came to the *U-Bootwaffe* in April 1941. Having completed his conversion training, he took command of U-617 in September 1942. On his first war cruise he sank four ships totalling 15,163 tons. On his next war cruise, Brandi entered the Mediterranean, where he made attacks on a destroyer, a cruiser and a battleship, but without success. His next cruise saw him sink a seagoing naval tug and damage a destroyer before sinking two medium-sized freighters. On 21 January 1943, he was decorated with the Knight's Cross of the Iron Cross. On Brandi's fourth war cruise, he sank the minelayer HMS *Welshman* and two merchant ships. His fifth cruise saw U-617 attacking a British cruiser and two destroyers. Hits were claimed, but it has not been possible to verify these. Brandi was awarded the Oak Leaves on 11 April 1943. On his eighth war cruise, Brandi attacked and sank the destroyer *Puckeridge* and also claimed the sinking of two unidentified warships. U-617 was itself attacked on 11 August 1943 and severely damaged by British aircraft. Pursued by British warships, it entered Spanish territorial waters and beached itself near Sidi Amar in Spanish Morocco. The crew was initially interned but eventually repatriated to Germany.

Brandi was given command of another Type VIIC, U-967, in March 1944. This boat operated briefly in the North Atlantic before being transferred to the Mediterranean in January 1944. Here, Brandi once again attacked a number of warships, sinking the destroyer escort USS *Fechteler* on 4 May 1944. Brandi was decorated with the Swords on 9 May 1944. Whilst still in command of U-967, Brandi received the Oak Leaves, Swords and Diamonds on 24 November 1944. He was subsequently posted to command the *Kleinkampfverbände* (midget submarines, one-man torpedoes and other special weapons) and survived the war. He did not re-enter the post-war navy and died in retirement in Dortmund in 1966.

Brandi is a prime example of a U-boat captain whose actual, verified sinkings are rather modest in terms of tonnage sunk, yet who received the highest military decorations. What becomes rapidly apparent about Brandi's record is his fearless aggression in attacking enemy warships. The substantial British Navy presence in the Mediterranean, the tight control exercised over the Straits of Gibraltar and the relatively shallow nature of these waters, giving the U-boats less chance to manoeuvre, made operating here much more dangerous than in any other waters. Despite this, Brandi rarely let the opportunity to attack enemy warships pass, and in a time when U-boat losses were escalating rapidly such determination to take the battle to the enemy was highly valued by Grossadmiral Dönitz.

Several of the great U-boat aces of World War II survived the conflict and many of those have committed their memoirs to print. In the case of those who did not survive, many have had scholarly biographical studies written about them. For those who wish to read further into what life was like on the Type VII U-boat during this momentous period in history, there is a rich vein of material available.

Kapitänleutnant Klaus Korth sank over 34,000 tons of enemy shipping in command of a Type IIC, U-57, before being given command of U-93, a Type VIIC in which he sank a further 43,000 tons of enemy shipping, bringing him the award of the Knight's Cross of the Iron Cross on 29 May 1941. He survived the war. (Author's collection)

Specialized U-boat variants

(1) Type XIV U-boat tanker.
(2) Type VIID minelayer was instantly recognizable by the raised decking abaft the conning tower, which contained the openings to the mine storage tubes. (3) *Flakboot*: seven basic Type VIIC vessels were converted for use as flak 'traps', with the concentrated fire of eight 2cm flak guns (two quadruple *Flakvierlinge*) and one 3.7cm flak gun. (Ian Palmer © Osprey Publishing)

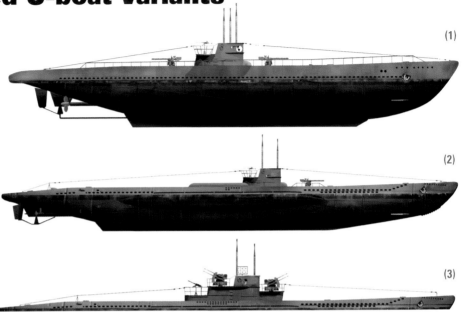

(1)

(2)

(3)

Type XIV

With the opening of the U-boat campaign in US waters, and into the South Atlantic, the need for a special resupply U-boat became more and more marked. A U-boat returning from a war patrol in far-off waters would occasionally rendezvous with another whose fuel or torpedo load was running out, and would transfer whatever it could of its remaining stock before heading for its home port, an extremely difficult and hazardous task in anything but the calmest of waters. Whilst this certainly helped, the amount of supplies which could be transferred would be extremely limited.

The solution to this problem was seen to be the construction of large supply boats capable of transporting significant amounts of fuel and other essentials to those boats operating on extended patrols in distant waters. The result, designated the Type XIV, was known to the Germans as the *Milchkühe*, or Milk Cows. A total of ten such boats were constructed, six by Deutsche Werke in Kiel (U-459, U-460, U-461, U-462, U-463 and U-464) and four by Germaniawerft (U-487, U-488, U-489 and U-490).

Initially, these boats were highly successful and played a significant role

A Type XIV U-boat. These submarine tankers could carry an extra 600 tons of fuel and 13 tons of motor oil to resupply other long-range U-boats at sea and enable them to remain in the patrol areas for extended periods. Only ten were built, all of which were either sunk by enemy action or scuttled. (DUBM)

in keeping more boats than would otherwise have been possible on station in the western and south-western Atlantic. Gradually, however, Allied intercepts of German signals, thanks to the cracking of the Enigma codes, allowed the Allies to set up ambushes in many of the designated rendezvous points, and thus, one by one, the vulnerable *Milchkühe* were attacked and sunk.

The first to be sunk, U-464, was attacked on 21 August 1942 just seven days into its first cruise when it was attacked on the surface by a US Catalina flying boat. Although the boat was lost, its crew was rescued by an Icelandic fishing boat. U-490 was next to be lost when, also on its first cruise, it was attacked en route to the Indian Ocean by a combination of US aircraft and warships. Fortunately, all but one of its crew was rescued by its attackers. U-463 succeeded in carrying out four war cruises before being attacked by a British Halifax bomber and sunk with all hands on 10 May 1943 during its fifth cruise.

Whilst running on the surface to charge its batteries, U-489 was attacked by an aircraft. It was spotted by a Sunderland flying boat and, although the flying boat was shot down, the submarine was so badly damaged that it had to be abandoned. Most of the crew was rescued. Disaster struck the U-tanker programme in July 1943 when four boats, U-459, U-461, U-462 and U-487, were all attacked on the surface and sunk by Allied aircraft. Between them, however, they had carried out 21 war cruises, replenishing combat U-boats at sea. Of Germany's two remaining U-tankers, U-460 was sunk on 4 October 1943 when it was caught by enemy aircraft on the surface along with three U-boats it was refuelling. U-488 was detected whilst submerged and attacked by enemy warships west of the Cape Verde Islands on 26 April 1944 and was never seen again.

The Type XIV could carry up to 400 tons of additional fuel as well as four torpedoes, substantial amounts of fresh food, and even had its own bakery so that boats being supplied could be treated to the luxury of freshly baked bread.

Type XIV Specifications				
Length	67.1m	**Endurance**	9,300 nautical miles surfaced 67 nautical miles submerged	
Beam	7.3m	**Powerplant**	2 x 1,400bhp diesel coupled with 2 x 375bhp electric motors	
Draft	4.9m	**Armament**	no torpedo tubes 2 x 3.7cm guns, one forward and one aft of the tower 1 x 2cm gun on the conning tower platform.	
Displacement	1,688 tons surfaced 1,930 tons submerged	**Complement**	53	
Speed	14.4 knots surfaced 6.2 knots submerged			

Early Type IX models

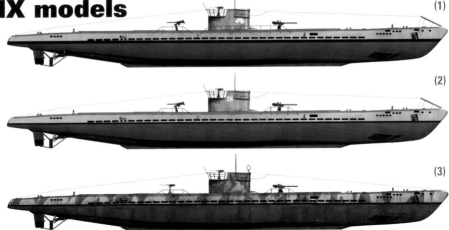

(1)

(2)

(3)

(1) U-107, an early Type IXB. The emblem adopted by U-107 was the four ace playing cards. (2) U-40, a Type IXA, shown in its pre-war livery of pale grey, with the boat number painted in white on the side of the tower. It also still retains the bow net cutter, which was removed from most (but not all) boats before the outbreak of war.
(2A) U-40's emblem. (3) U-38, another Type IXA. Its net cutter has been removed and it has had the spray deflector added to its conning tower. (Ian Palmer © Osprey Publishing)

(2A)

Type IX

The Type IX U-boat was a direct development of the unsuccessful Type IA (of which only two, U-25 and U-26, were built). Although the bulk of U-boat construction for the Kriegsmarine concentrated on the medium, sea-going Type VII, there was still a need for a larger ocean-going boat capable of operating in distant waters. The Type VII, of course, was perfectly capable of operating all the way across the Atlantic and into American waters, but larger submarines with far greater range were required if Germany was to be capable of operating further afield, far into the South Atlantic and even into the Indian Ocean. The result was the Type IX.

As with the Type VII, the design reached its optimum with the 'C' variant, which represented 141 out of the total number of 194 Type IXs built. The Type IX design was not without its drawbacks, but it was an excellent sea boat, capable of operating at great distances from its base, and was far more spacious and comfortable than the cramped Type VII.

Although, with the exception of the lack of saddle tanks as fitted to the Type VII, the Type IX resembled its smaller cousin, particularly after both types had received the *Turm 4* conning tower conversions, the Type IX was significantly different in its internal layout. The engine room was much larger and the junior NCO accommodation was moved to the forward part of the boat. Without the bulky external saddle tanks typical of the Type VII, the Type IX was a much sleeker looking boat and had greater fore and aft deck space. Its bigger size, however, meant that its diving speed was rather slower than the Type VII.

Beginning at the bow, the first compartment was the forward torpedo room with its four torpedo tubes. Along each side of the compartment were three upper and three lower bunks, which could be folded up to give more space when not in use. Folding tables were also provided. Due to the 'hot bunking' system used, these 12 bunks effectively were home to 24 sailors. Under the decking plates was storage for additional

Interior layout of a Type IX

torpedoes, and at the rear of the compartment a hatch through the pressure hull onto the upper decking allowed fresh torpedoes to be taken on board.

Through the first bulkhead was the main accommodation area. Forwardmost was the junior non-commissioned ranks area. On the port side was a WC compartment and two sets of bunks, whilst on the starboard were three sets of bunks, giving accommodation for ten men. Next followed the senior non-commissioned ranks area containing accommodation for six senior ranks. Under the deck plates of the accommodation area were stored the boat's batteries. Just beyond this accommodation area, separating the non-commissioned ranks from the officers, were the refrigerated storage lockers on the port and starboard side of the small galley. The boat's ammunition magazine was located under the deck plates of this area.

Through the next bulkhead was one officer's bunk on the port side, separated from the commander's 'compartment' by the sound room. To starboard were two officer's bunks and the radio room, directly opposite the commander. The commander's 'compartment' was a simple bunk area with a curtain that could be drawn to afford a modicum of privacy.

The commander's bunk area was slightly more spacious than any other and also had the benefit of a small washstand with a folding lid to convert it into a table. As with the Type VII, the sound and radio rooms were deliberately placed next to the commander's area to allow immediate access to him should important messages be received or enemy ships detected. Further battery storage was located under the deck plates of this area. The hub of the boat was the control room or *Zentral*. Here were the ship's helm, the diving planes, navigator's table, main ballast pump controls and periscope tubes. A ladder led up into the conning tower, which contained the commander's attack position, and on up to the main exit hatch to the bridge.

Aft of the *Zentral* was the Type IX's large engine room. First came the two large generator engines for recharging the ship's batteries. Then came the two massive diesel engines, with only a small passageway between. Aft of the main engines were the electric motors used for powering the boat under water. On the starboard side was the large compressor used to recharge the boat's compressed air supply.

The aftermost compartment was the stern torpedo room. This contained the aft WC, followed by two sets of upper and lower bunks each side, accommodating up to 16 men, as well as the two stern torpedo tubes and the emergency helm.

This sectional view shows the interior of a typical Type IX. Roomier than the Type VII, the interior layout was broadly similar to its smaller cousin. As with all boats, the nerve centre of the vessel was the control room or *Zentral*. Here were the periscope controls, dive planes, main pumps, electrical switchboard, navigator's table etc., and ladder leading up into the conning tower and commander's battle station with its attack periscope and attack computer. The aftermost compartment was the stern torpedo room, with two torpedo tubes, a small workshop area with a lathe, stern WC and the emergency helm. (Ian Palmer © Osprey Publishing)

A Type IXA, U-38, was a successful boat which carried out 11 war patrols and sank 35 enemy ships. It survived the war until 5 May 1945 when its commander, Korvettenkapitän Peters, ordered it to be scuttled near Wesermünde to avoid capture. It was raised and broken up in 1948. (DUBM)

Type IXA

The basic Type IXA was a well-armed, long-range boat, but only eight were constructed (U-37 to U-44) before the next, improved model was introduced.

Type IXA Specifications			
Length	76.5m	**Endurance**	8,100 nautical miles surfaced 65 nautical miles submerged
Beam	6.5m	**Powerplant**	2 x MAN 2,200bhp diesels 2 x SSW 500bhp electric motors
Draft	4.7m	**Armament**	• 1 x 10.5cm deck gun forward • 1 x 3.7cm deck gun aft • 1 x 2cm flak gun on conning tower platform • 6 torpedo tubes (4 bow, 2 stern) • 22 torpedoes carried
Displacement	1,032 tons surfaced 1,153 tons submerged	**Complement**	48
Top Speed	18.2 knots surfaced 7.7 knots submerged		

U-108 was a Type IXB, which carried out 11 patrols sinking 25 merchants and one warship, only to be sunk in harbour during a bombing raid on Stettin. It was raised, but decommissioned and finally scuttled to prevent capture at the end of the war. Note the 3.7cm flak gun on the aft deck. (DUBM)

Type IXB

The Type IXB was almost identical to its predecessor, with a small increase in fuel bunkerage giving it a slightly increased operational range, with its additional weight only causing a very slight reduction in its submerged top speed. The forward deck gun was also relocated to a position slightly nearer to the conning tower. Fourteen Type IXBs were constructed.

Type IX variants and the XB minelayer

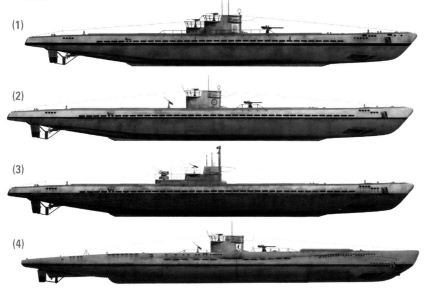

(1)

(2)

(3)

(4)

(1) Type IXC, U-511. After serving with the Kriegsmarine, this boat was sold to Japan and commissioned into the Japanese Navy as *RO500*. (2) U-180, a Type IXD1, fitted with high-speed diesel engines normally installed on E-boats. The most noticeable feature of the Type IXD was the extreme length of the boat when compared to earlier variants. (3) Type IX/D2, complete with its late-war bridge configuration. The boat is snorkel-equipped and has the *Hohentweil* radar mast. (4) Type XB minelayer. This was also extremely wide, having mine shafts set into its saddle tanks as well as on the foredeck.
(Ian Palmer © Osprey Publishing)

Type IXB Specifications			
Length	76.5m	**Powerplant**	2 x MAN 2,200bhp diesels 2 x SSW 500bhp electric motors
Beam	6.8m	**Armament**	• 1 x 10.5cm deck gun forward • 1 x 3.7cm deck gun aft • 1 x 2cm flak gun on conning tower platform • 6 torpedo tubes (4 bow, 2 stern) • 22 torpedoes carried
Draft	4.7m	**Complement**	48
Displacement	1,061 tons surfaced 1,178 tons submerged		
Top Speed	18.2 knots surfaced 7.3 knots submerged		
Endurance	8,700 nautical miles surfaced 64 nautical miles submerged		

Type IXC

The Type IXC was very slightly longer than the previous models, the principal improvement in the type being the provision of additional fuel bunkerage giving greatly extended operational range. Fifty-four Type IXCs were commissioned.

Type IXC Specifications			
Length	76.8m	**Powerplant**	2 x MAN 2,200bhp diesels 2 x SSW 500bhp electric motors
Beam	6.8m	**Armament**	• 1 x 10.5cm deck gun forward • 1 x 3.7cm deck gun aft • 1 x 2cm flak gun on conning tower platform • 6 torpedo tubes (4 bow, 2 stern) • 22 torpedoes carried
Draft	4.7m	**Complement**	48
Displacement	1,120 tons surfaced 1,232 tons submerged		
Top Speed	18.3 knots surfaced 7.3 knots submerged		
Endurance	11,000 nautical miles surfaced 63 nautical miles submerged		

Type IXC/40

The Type IXC reached its zenith in the Type IXC/40 sub-type. Once again, minor tweaking of the design allowed a marginally increased fuel bunkerage, giving a further modest extension to the operational range. Eighty-seven boats of this model were produced, more than any other Type IX variant.

Type IXC/40 Specifications			
Length	76.8m	**Powerplant**	2 x MAN 2,200bhp diesels 2 x SSW 500bhp electric motors
Beam	6.9m	**Armament**	• 1 x 10.5cm deck gun forward • 1 x 3.7cm deck gun aft • 1 x 2cm flak gun on conning tower platform • 6 torpedo tubes (4 bow, 2 stern) • 22 torpedoes carried
Draft	4.7m	**Complement**	48
Displacement	1,144 tons surfaced 1,257 tons submerged		
Top Speed	18.3 knots surfaced 7.3 knots submerged		
Endurance	11,400 nautical miles surfaced 63 nautical miles submerged		

U-889 seen here surrendering to Canadian naval forces at the end of the war. A Type IXC, it is a fine example of the extended flak platforms fitted to many U-boats of both Type VII and Type IX as the war progressed. The pipe shown alongside the tower is part of the *Schnorchel* (Snorkel) system. (Library and Archives of Canada)

Type IXD1

The Type IXD was a considerably enlarged variant, fully 11m longer than the original design. Though the operational range was reduced somewhat, this variant could achieve a highly respectable top speed in excess of 20 knots. This was achieved by substituting six Daimler Benz MB501 diesels, of the type used on the Kriegsmarine's E-boats, for the standard MAN diesels. Three of the MB501s were coupled to each shaft. Though fine in theory, in practice the experiment was not a success. Only two of this variant were completed, U-180 and U-195, and both experienced considerable technical problems with the engine arrangement, including overheating and the production of excessive exhaust smoke, which made the boat so much easier for the enemy to spot when running on the surface. Both boats were reconverted to produce the next, cargo-carrying sub-variant.

Type IXD1 Specifications			
Length	87.6m	**Endurance**	9,900 nautical miles surfaced 115 nautical miles submerged
Beam	7.5m	**Powerplant**	2 x Daimler Benz MB501 1,500bhp diesels 2 x SSW 500bhp electric motors
Draft	5.4m	**Armament**	1 x 3.7cm deck gun aft 2 x 2cm flak gun on conning tower platform
Displacement	1,610 tons surfaced 1,799 tons submerged	**Complement**	55
Top Speed	15.8 knots surfaced 6.9 knots submerged		

Type IXD1 (Cargo)

Converted from the original Type IXD1 specification, U-180 and U-195 had their Daimler Benz fast diesel motors replaced by conventional Germaniawerft submarine diesels. Also, the torpedo tubes were removed to provide additional cargo-carrying capability.

Type IXD1 (Cargo) Specifications			
Length	87.6 m	**Powerplant**	6 x Germaniawerftbhp diesels 2 x SSW 500bhp electric motors
Beam	7.5 m	**Armament**	• 1 x 10.5cm deck gun forward • 1 x 3.7cm deck gun aft • 1 x 2cm flak gun on conning tower platform • 6 torpedo tubes (4 bow, 2 stern) • 24 torpedoes carried
Draft	5.4 m		
Displacement	1,610 tons surfaced 1,799 tons submerged	**Complement**	55
Top Speed	20.8 knots surfaced 6.9 knots submerged		
Endurance	9,900 nautical miles surfaced 57 nautical miles submerged		

Type IXD2

This interesting and relatively successful variant, the penultimate Type IX, used a twin-powerplant system. As well as its powerful supercharged MAN diesels, its lengthened hull allowed it to carry two additional diesel engines that could be used for cruising on the surface whilst the supercharged diesels were switched on to freespinning mode to recharge the boat's batteries rapidly. A total of 28 of this variant were produced.

Type IXD2 Specifications			
Length	87.6m	**Powerplant**	2 x MAN supercharged 9-cylinder 2,200bhp diesels 2 x MWM 6-cylinder 500bhp diesels 2 SSW 580bhp electric motors
Beam	7.5m	**Armament**	2 x 2cm flak guns on upper conning tower platform 1 x 3.7cm or 2cm *Flakvierling* on lower platform 6 torpedo tubes (4 bow, 2 stern) 24 torpedoes carried
Draft	5.4m		
Displacement	1,616 tons surfaced 1,804 tons submerged	**Complement**	57
Top Speed	19.2 knots surfaced 6.9 knots submerged		
Endurance	23,700 nautical miles surfaced 57 nautical miles submerged		

Type IXD2/42

The flip side of the Type IXD1 concept, where the emphasis was on high speed, was the Type IXD2/42. Here, the focus was on extending operational range to the maximum possible. Only one of this variant was produced.

Type IXD2/42 Specifications			
Length	87.6m	**Powerplant**	2 x MAN supercharged 9-cylinder 2,200bhp diesels 2 x MWM 580bhp electric motors
Beam	7.5m	**Armament**	1 x 10.5cm deck gun forward 1 x 3.7cm deck gun aft 1 x 2cm flak gun on conning tower platform 6 torpedo tubes (4 bow, 2 stern) 22 torpedoes carried
Draft	5.4m		
Displacement	1,616 tons surfaced 1,804 tons submerged		
Top Speed	19.2 knots surfaced 6.9 knots submerged	**Complement**	57
Endurance	23,700 nautical miles surfaced 57 nautical miles submerged		

Type IX Flotillas and Construction

Although most U-boat flotillas contained a number of different U-boat types over the course of the war, there were certain flotillas in which a particular type predominated. The following flotillas are those that made heavy use of Type IX vessels:

- 2.Unterseebootsflottille
- 10.Unterseebootsflottille
- 12.Unterseebootsflottille
- 33.Unterseebootsflottille

Type IX Commanders and Deployment

The Type IX as we have already seen, was an excellent sea boat, larger and roomier than the Type VII. Its crew suffered somewhat less from overcrowding than their Type VII comrades. There were drawbacks, however, to serving on such a large, relatively spacious boat, not the least of which were the fact that a larger boat makes a larger target for the enemy, and that once spotted by the enemy, the Type IX had a significantly slower diving time than its smaller cousin. Lookouts on a Type IX therefore had to be

Type IX Construction Details

Type IXA

| Deschimag, Bremen | U-37 to U-44 8 boats |
| | Total for type 8 boats |

Type IXB

Deschimag, Bremen	U-64 to U-65 2 boats
	U-103 to U-111 9 boats
	U-122 to U-124 3 boats
	Total for type 14 boats

Type IXC

Deschimag, Bremen	U-66 to U-68 3 boats
	U-125 to U-131 7 boats
	U-153 to U-160 8 boats
	U-171 to U-176 6 boats
	U-841 to U-846 6 boats
	U-853 to U-858 6 boats
	U-877 to U-881 5 boats
	U-889 to U-891 3 boats
	Total 44 boats
Seebeck, Wesermünde	U-161 to U-166 6 boats
	Total 6 boats
Deutsche Werke, Hamburg	U-501 to U-524 24 boats
	U-1221 to U-1238 18 boats
	Total 42 boats
	Total for type 92 boats

Type IXC/40

Seebeck, Wesermünde	U-167 to U-170 4 boats
	U-801 to U-806 6 boats
	Total 10 boats
Deschimag, Bremen	U-183 to U-194 12 boats
	Total 12 boats
Deutsche Werke, Hamburg	U-525 to U-550 26 boats
	Total 26 boats
	Total for type 48 boats

Type IXD1

Deschimag, Bremen	U-180
	U-195
	Total for type 2 boats

Type IXD2

Deschimag, Bremen	U-181 to U-182 2 boats
	U-196 to U-200 5 boats
	U-847 to U-852 6 boats
	U-859 to U-864 6 boats
	U-871 to U-876 6 boats
	U-883 to U-886 4 boats
	Total for type 29 boats

particularly alert and watchful. A number of surviving U-boat veterans confirmed that, when an opportunity was available, they elected to serve on a Type VII, knowing that its faster diving time might well mean the difference between life and death in a combat situation.

Of the 194 built, only 24 survived to the end of the war, a loss rate of 88 per cent. Nevertheless, many top aces achieved particularly impressive results using this large boat. The small sample given here may illustrate just how effective a weapon the Type IX was in the hands of an accomplished commander. Those top Type IX aces who survived the war were generally (though there are exceptions) those who gained their successes in the early part of the war and were then posted to a shore command. Few U-boat commanders who gained their first command in the second half of the war survived long enough to become an ace.

Heinrich Liebe was one of the most experienced of the U-boat commanders, having taken command of his first boat in 1936. In October 1938, he took command of U-38, a Type IXA. Liebe was at sea when war broke out and on his first war cruise opened his score card when he sank two large British freighters. These were to be the first of many. He was decorated with the Knight's Cross on 14 August 1940 and added the Oak Leaves on 10 June 1941. Those most successful U-boat commanders, specifically the ones who had been decorated with the Oak Leaves, also qualified for a special diamond-studded version of the U-boat Badge. Though this was a personal gift from the *Oberbefehlshaber der Kriegsmarine* rather than a formal award, it became the mark of the top aces. In total, before being transferred to a shore command, Liebe accounted for 32 enemy ships totalling 168,500 tons before being posted ashore to a position on the staff of the *Oberkommando der Marine* (Naval High Command). His boat, U-38, also survived the war at sea to be scuttled in Wesermünde on 5 May 1945. It was raised and broken up in 1948.

The first command of Kapitänleutnant Harald Gelhaus was U-143, one of the early Type IID boats. His first sinking, after taking over command from its previous commander, came on 23 August 1941. Shortly thereafter, he was given command of U-107, a Type IXB, with which he continued to run up a steady score of sinkings. Decorated with the Knight's Cross on 26 March 1943, Gelhaus ultimately reached a total of 18 enemy ships totalling 100,347 tons sunk. He was eventually transferred to a shore posting with *Oberkommando der Marine* and ultimately *Marineoberkommando Nord* (Naval High Command North). Unfortunately, his boat, under its new commander, was bombed and sunk on 18 August 1944 off the French coast. There were no survivors.

One of the best-known and most respected U-boat aces was Korvettenkapitän Reinhard Hardegen. Hardegen's first command was U-147, a Type IID. Hardegen had originally served as a flier before transferring to submarines, gaining his first command in December 1940. Hardegen sank one enemy ship before being given a new command, U-123, a Type IXB. With this new boat, Hardegen was to achieve major successes. His first war cruise with U-123 resulted in five enemy ships being sunk. On the entry of the USA into the war, Hardegen operated off the US coast during Operation *Drum Beat* (*Paukenschlag*), sinking nine ships in his first operation there. His second cruise into US waters saw a further nine ships sunk, including one US Navy sub-chaser.

Hardegen received the Knight's Cross on 23 January 1942, followed by the Oak Leaves on 23 April of the same year. He was also a recipient of the U-boat Badge with Diamonds. In total, 24 ships representing some 138,200 tons fell victim to this accomplished airman turned U-boat ace. His career took another change of direction in the closing stages of the war when he was given command of a battalion in 2.Marine-Infanterie-Division, ending the war as a combat infantry soldier.

U-123 was taken out of commission in June 1944 at Lorient and its engines used as generators. This highly successful boat was refitted by the French after the war and used by the French Navy as the *Blaison* until finally being decommissioned in 1959.

Korvettenkapitän Carl Emmerman, born in Hamburg in 1915, scored his first success as a U-boat commander at the end of May 1942 when he sank a 9,000-ton tanker. It was to be the first of many for this skilled commander. His boat, U-172, was a Type IXC. Emmermann was decorated with the Knight's Cross on 27 November

One of Germany's finest U-boat commanders, Reinhard Hardegen was decorated with the Knight's Cross and the Oak Leaves to the Knight's Cross as commander of U-123. He survived the war and went on to become close friends with many Allied naval veterans who had been his former enemies. He died in 2018, at the ripe old age of 105. (Author's collection)

This illustration shows a number of the events which would be taking place during active service on a U-boat.

(1) The sound detector operator in his tiny radio room. He wears headphones that allow him to hear the sound of approaching enemy propellers. The sound detection gear is extremely sensitive and will pick up the slightest noise.

(2) Two diving planes operators sit in the control room guided by the *Leitender Ingenieur* (chief engineer). The hand wheels will alter the angle of the diving planes.

(3) At the periscope sits the commander, searching for the enemy. **(4)** In *Zentral*, the *Obersteuermann* (navigator) plots each change in course ordered by the commander.

(Darko Pavlovic © Osprey Publishing)

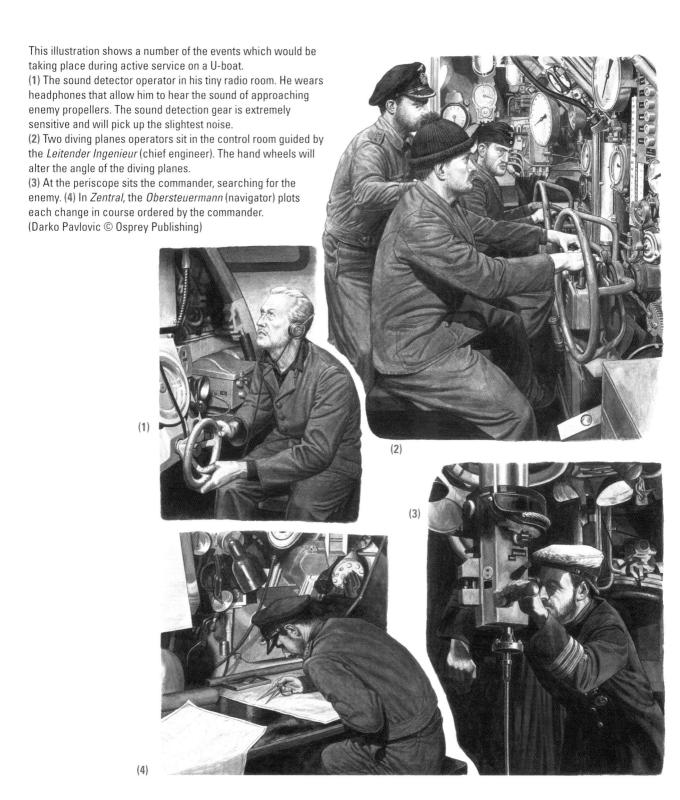

(1)

(2)

(3)

(4)

1942 and went on to achieve a total of 27 ships sunk, totalling some 152,904 tons, including the huge 27,000-ton troopship *Orcades*. He was awarded the Oak Leaves on 4 July 1943 and was also one of only a small number of recipients of the U-boat War Badge with Diamonds. In the closing stages of the war, he was given command of a Type XXI before transferring first to take command of 31.Unterseebootsflottille, then leading a Marine-Infanterie battalion in the defence of Hamburg. U-172 was sunk on 17 December 1943 but its new commander and 45 of its crew were rescued.

Günther Hessler took command of U-107, a Type IXB, in October 1940 after having served with the surface fleet on both capital ships and torpedo boats. He commanded U-107 until late 1941 and in that brief time sank 21 enemy ships totalling some 118,800 tons. He was awarded the Knight's Cross on 24 June 1941. On giving up his command, he was transferred to the staff of the *Befehlshaber der Unterseeboote* , his father-in-law, Grossadmiral Dönitz.

Johann Mohr was already serving as *Wachoffizier* (first watch officer) aboard U-124, a Type IXB, when its captain was posted to another boat and Mohr given command. On his first cruise as commander, he sank six enemy ships, two on the second cruise and seven on the third, amongst the last total being five large oil tankers. Ultimately, Mohr was to sink a total of 29 enemy ships representing some 135,000 tons and including a cruiser and a corvette. He was awarded the Knight's Cross on 27 March 1942 and the Oak Leaves on 13 January 1943. Mohr's luck finally ran out in March 1943 when his boat was attacked and sunk by the frigate *Stonecroft* and corvette *Black Swan*. The boat was lost with all hands.

One of the older U-boat captains, Victor 'Papa' Schutze, was already 33 years old when war broke out. As captain of U-25, a Type IA, he scored his first victory in October 1939 and was already a holder of the Knight's Cross by December 1940. After the award of the Knight's Cross, he was given command of a new boat, U-103, a Type IXB. Schutze was one of the true *Experten*, running up a final total of 35 enemy ships sunk, for a total of 180,000 tons. Amongst his many achievements, Schutze succeeded in sinking over 65,000 tons of shipping – some 13 ships – within a space of just six weeks. He was decorated with the Oak Leaves on 14 July 1941 and was also a holder of the U-boat Badge with Diamonds. U-103 had several other commanders after Schutze and survived intact until being taken out of service in March 1944. In February 1945, it was moved to Hamburg where it was moored and its engines used as power generators before it was finally scuttled in May 1945.

U-156, a Type IXC boat under the command of Kapitänleutnant Werner Hartenstein, was involved in one of the war's most controversial incidents. Hartenstein was an acknowledged ace and holder of the Knight's Cross with a total of 19 enemy ships, representing some 97,100 tons, to his credit. On 12 September 1942, Hartenstein encountered and sank the 17,000-ton *Laconia*. Unknown to him, the boat was also carrying a significant number of Italian POWs as well as a number of women and children. When he realized the scale of the disaster he surfaced, took some of the

injured on board, and took several of the lifeboats in tow. Hartenstein then sent a message in clear offering safe passage to any ship that would come and rescue the survivors. The response was that a Liberator bomber flew over and bombed the boat despite the extreme risk to the survivors. It had clearly been decided that the sinking of a U-boat was more important than the rescue of the survivors. In desperation, Hartenstein was forced to abandon the survivors and dive his boat to avoid it being sunk. Fate caught up with Hartenstein when U-156 was caught on the surface by US aircraft and sunk with all hands on 8 March 1943. Subsequent to the *Laconia* incident, Dönitz ordered that in future no captain should put his own boat and crew at risk by trying to rescue survivors. This, the so-called 'Laconia Order', saw him charged with war crimes at the Nuremberg Trials.

Korvettenkapitän Werner Hartenstein of U-156 represented the best of the Kriegsmarine, putting his own boat and men at great risk to save survivors of the *Laconia*, a ship he had sunk on 12 September 1942, despite being bombed by Allied aircraft during the rescue attempts. He died when U-156 was bombed and sunk on 8 March 1943. (DUBM)

Karl-Friedrich Merten was another of the 'old-guard' of U-boat commanders, already 34 years old with 13 years service in the navy when war broke out. He had served first with the surface fleet, on battleships, cruisers, escort ships and torpedo boats, before joining the *U-Bootwaffe* at the beginning of 1940. In February 1941, he took command of U-68, a Type IXC, and carried out several successful war cruises, ranging into the South Atlantic where he operated off the coast of Africa as well as into the Caribbean. Merten sank a total of 29 enemy ships, earning himself the Knight's Cross in June 1942 and adding the Oak Leaves in November of the same year. Like many senior U-boat veterans, Merten was given a shore command, first with 26.Unterseebootsflottille then with 24.Unterseebootsflottille in the Baltic port of Memel. From here, at the end of the war, he was instrumental in evacuating over 56,000 refugees from the advance of the Red Army. U-68 served on under two other commanders until 8 April 1944 when it was caught on the surface at night by US aircraft and sunk. Only one crew member survived.

Another veteran of the early days of the U-Bootwaffe who earned ace status with the Type IX was Werner Hartmann. He had commanded U-26 in pre-war days, with a young Günther Prien as his Wachoffizier. His first wartime cruise was as commander of U-37, a Type IXA, during which he sank eight enemy ships. His second war cruise netted eight more enemy ships, earning him the Knight's Cross on 9 April 1940 along with a shore posting to the staff of U-boat command. He later took command of 2.Unterseebootslehrdivisionen (U-boat Training Division) and other posts in the

The U-boat Front Clasp, introduced on 15 May 1944 in bronze and on 24 November 1944 in silver, was to recognize extended meritorious service after gaining the basic U-boat Badge. There were no laid down criteria, the award being made on the recommendation of the commander based on number of patrols undertaken, danger of the mission, gallantry shown and so on. (Author's collection)

A Focke-Achgelis Fa330 manned rotary wing kite ready to be launched from a Type IX. A rather precarious machine, in the event of an enemy warship being spotted it would be cut adrift and left to ditch in the sea in the hope the pilot could be picked up when the coast was clear. (DUBM)

training branch before returning to sea in command of U-198, a Type IXD2, in November 1942, at the age of 40 years. He proceeded to take his boat on a 200-day war cruise during which he sank a further seven enemy ships. His final tally reached 25 ships, totalling some 111,600 tons, bringing him the Oak Leaves to his Knight's Cross on 5 November 1944.

On 14 February 1945, Hartmann was given command of Marine-Grenadier-Regiment 2, part of 2.Marine-Infanterie-Division, as so many of Germany's 'sailors without ships' were thrown into action in the war on land. U-37 survived the war at sea to be scuttled in May 1945. U-198 was less fortunate and after being attacked by enemy aircraft was finally sunk by a combined attack from the sloop *Godavari* and frigate *Findhorn* off the Seychelles on 12 August 1944. There were no survivors.

Of all Germany's great U-boat aces, few can compare with Wolfgang Lüth. An ace of aces, Lüth had commanded U-138, U-43 and U-181, boats of the IXB, IXA and IXD2 types, respectively. His first boat, however, was a diminutive Type IIB, the U-9.

Lüth had already signalled his great potential by sinking a French submarine, the *Doris*, with his tiny coastal 'Canoe' in one of the war's rare submarine vs submarine encounters. Moving on to the bigger Type IX boats, he quickly began running up an impressive score. He was awarded the Knight's Cross on 24 October 1940 with a score of 49,000 tons. By the time the Oak Leaves were added to his Knight's Cross in November 1942, his score had reached 81,950 tons. His score continued to rise, and on 15 April 1943 when the Swords were added to his Oak Leaves, his score had reached 103,712 tons. In the end, Lüth accumulated a score of 47 enemy ships representing over 221,000 tons, and on 9 August 1943 he became one of only two naval officers to be decorated with the Oak Leaves, Swords and Diamonds clasp to

The extremely large size of the Schnorchel tube can be clearly seen on this shot of a Type IXC/40, U-889. Only launched in August 1944 it had a short service career, being at sea on its first patrol when the war ended and it was forced to surrender. (NHHC)

the Knight's Cross. The other, Brandi, was mentioned earlier. Of Lüth's boats, U-43 was sunk with all 55 hands (Lüth had by now left to commission U-181) by US aircraft off the Azores on 30 July 1943, U-138 was sunk after depth-charge attacks by a combined force of five Royal Navy destroyers, but the entire crew was saved, and U-181 was taken over by the Japanese at its base in Penang, Malaysia, after the German surrender.

Lüth stood head and shoulders above almost all other U-boat aces. In one spell of 192 days, Lüth carried out three war cruises and sank 11 ships. On another single, extended war cruise of 129 days, Lüth added 12 more ships to his list of victims. One amazing cruise saw Lüth at sea for 206 days in U-181, adding ten more enemy ships to his score.

Lüth was eventually transferred to a shore posting and given the position of commander of the German Naval Academy at Flensburg-Mürwick. Tragically, having survived the Battle of the Atlantic where so many of his comrades had lost their lives, Lüth was shot dead by one of his own sentries on 14 May 1945, after the end of the war. This was in the immediate post-war period when numerous German units had been permitted to retain some small arms and post sentries for their own security. Lüth had been challenged by a young sentry and had either not heard, or ignored, the challenge. He was buried two days later with full military honours.

The U-Bootwaffe rewarded not only its ace submarine commanders but those other crew members who had made a significant contribution to the success of their boat. In this respect, both Leitender Ingenieur (chief engineer) Oberleutnant zur See Karl-August Landfehrmann and Wachoffizier Oberleutnant zur See Johannes Limbach, both serving on U-181 with Wolfgang Lüth, shared in his recognition when they were decorated with the Knight's Cross on 27 October 1943 and 6 February 1945 respectively, though Lüth had already long since moved to other duties by the time of the latter award.

Type X

Broadly analogous to the large ocean-going UE (U-117) class minelayers of the *Kaiserliche Marine*, the Type X was produced specifically to handle the newly developed Sonderminen A or SMA, anchored mine. The initial design, the Type X, was to provide dry storage for its complement of SMA mines, which required the detonators to be individually, manually adjusted prior to launch, so that wet storage was impossible. This boat was projected to have displaced up to 2,500 tons, therefore a very large vessel indeed. A further variant, the Type XA, was projected, in which the main mine chamber would be supplemented by additional mine shafts in the saddle tanks. In the event, neither type was ever produced.

Type XB

A total of eight boats of the Type XB class were produced, the mine chamber of the Type XIXA projected designs being replaced by six vertical wet storage shafts in the forward part of the hull. The boat could carry up to 18 mines in these shafts (three per shaft) plus an additional 48 mines (two per shaft) in a series of 12 shafts set into the saddle tanks on each side – six just forward and six aft of the conning tower position. The Type XBs were large boats, with a very distinctive narrowing of the foredeck between the bow and conning tower area, designed to help speed up the boat's diving time.

Type XB Specifications				
Length	89.8m	**Powerplant**	• 2 x Germaniawerft 9-cylinder supercharged 2,100bhp diesels • 2 x AEG 550bhp electric motors	
Beam	9.2m	**Armament**	• 2 x 2cm flak guns on upper conning tower platform • 1 x 3.7cm flak gun on lower platform • 66 mines carried • 2 stern torpedo tubes • 5 torpedoes carried	
Draft	4.7m	**Complement**	52	
Displacement	1,763 tons surfaced 2,177 tons submerged			
Top Speed	16.4 knots surfaced 7 knots submerged			
Endurance	14,450 nautical miles surfaced 188 nautical miles submerged			

Type XB Construction Details	
Germaniawerft, Kiel	U-116 to U-119 4 boats U-219 to U-220 2 boats U-233 to U-234 2 boats Total for type 8 boats

ABOVE One of the Kriegsmarine's biggest submarines, the Type XB long-distance minelayer/supply boat displaced over 2,000 tons submerged. Shown here is U-117. It was sunk by enemy aircraft on 7 August 1943 on its fifth war patrol whilst providing resupply to U-66. The latter boat escaped. (DUBM)

Of the eight boats produced, six (U-116, U-117, U-118, U-119, U-220 and U-233) were sunk by enemy action. Of the 312 crewmen this represents, 45 survived the sinkings.

U-219 was docked in Jakarta, Malaysia, when Germany surrendered and was subsequently seized and used by the Imperial Japanese Navy.

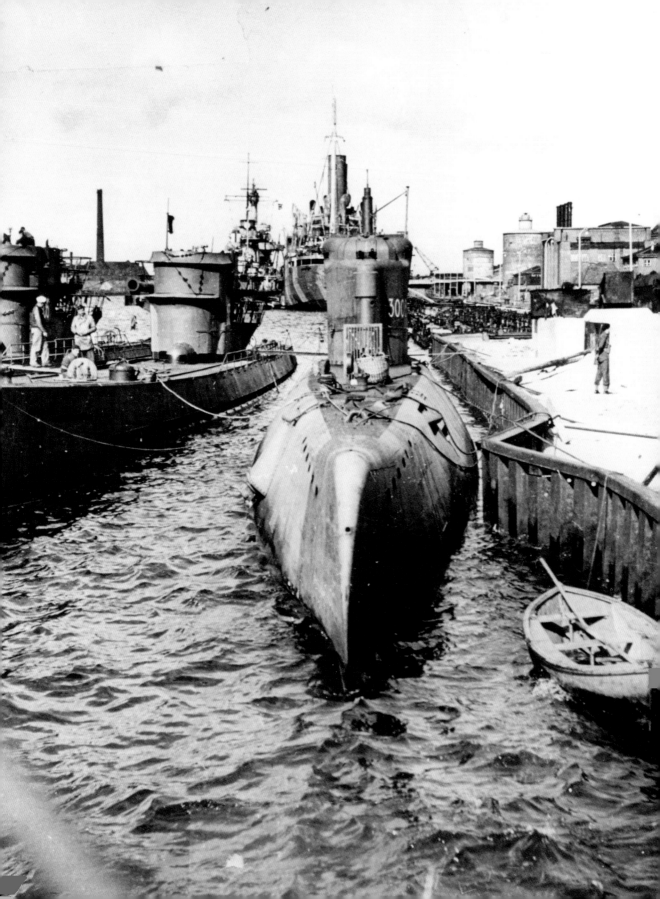

The most interesting Type XB of all, and one of the most interesting of all the U-boats, was U-234. This boat was en route to Japan at the war's end, carrying a number of high-ranking military and scientific staff, two Japanese officers, 260 tons of cargo, secret blueprints for advanced weapons, and containers of uranium oxide probably for use in atomic research. On hearing of the German surrender and orders for U-boats to give themselves up to the Allies, the Japanese officers committed suicide. U-234 was snatched by the Americans, who spirited away the uranium oxide in considerable secrecy. Much of the information regarding this boat and its fascinating final journey is still shrouded in mystery.

Given the large number of U-boats which never sank a single enemy ship, the Type XB was not unsuccessful as a class, and many of the class did achieve some successes sinking or damaging enemy ships with both torpedoes and mines.

Type XXI

With the advent of the Type XXI, the Germans made a quantum leap in submarine design and manufacture. This amazing vessel was the first to be mass-produced in modular form. In order to take advantage of manufacturing capacity throughout the Reich, actual manufacture of components and of these components into sub-assemblies was carried out in various parts of Germany, often well inland rather than at traditional coastal shipbuilding locations. Sections of hull were fabricated, had internal components fitted and were even painted, before being transported to assembly yards at Blohm & Voss, Hamburg, AG Weser, Bremen and Schichau at Danzig. At these yards, the various hull sections were carefully aligned and welded together. The theoretical total build-time for a Type XXI was estimated at 176 days.

The Type XXI was fully streamlined, with no extraneous external fittings to produce unwanted drag. All periscopes, snorkel pipes, radar masts etc. were fully retractable, and even the flak guns were built into streamlined rotating turrets and the forward and rear edges of the tower.

The design had originally been intended to accept a revolutionary new hydrogen peroxide powered propulsion system designed by Dr Helmuth Walter, but it was decided that the new boat could equally well be adapted to use diesel engines. The large, roomy hull, which had all of its six torpedo tubes mounted in the bows, could take a much larger complement of batteries to power its vastly improved electric motors, greatly improving its underwater endurance. As well as new and extremely powerful turbo-supercharged diesel engines, the Type XXI was provided with a special 'creep' motor to allow silent running, and a whole host of improved electrical gear.

The Type XXI could achieve a top speed of 17 knots submerged, more than double that of the Type IX, and could run under water on its batteries for up to 75 hours, around 50 per cent longer than the Type IX. The streamlined shape and silent running capability also made it a much harder target for the enemy to detect.

OPPOSITE U-3008, a Type XXI, is at right on this shot, which clearly illustrates the extremely streamlined shape of the boat compared to the Type IX boats at left. The war ended while it was on its first patrol in the Baltic and it surrendered at sea. Taken over by the USA it was used for testing until taken out of service in 1948. (NHHC).

The Type XXI was the first submarine to have a faster speed submerged than when running on the surface.

Type XXI Specifications			
Length	76.7m	**Powerplant**	• 2 x MAN turbo-supercharged 2,200bhp diesels • 2 x SSW 2,500bhp electric motors • 2 x SSW 320bhp 'creep' motors
Beam	6.6m	**Armament**	• 2 x twin 2cm turret-mounted flak guns on conning tower • 6 bow torpedo tubes • 23 torpedoes carried
Draft	6.3m	**Complement**	57
Displacement	1,621 tons surfaced 1,819 tons submerged		
Top Speed	15.6 knots surfaced 17 knots submerged		
Endurance	11,150 nautical miles surfaced 285 nautical miles submerged		

Type XXI Construction Details	
Blohm & Voss, Hamburg	U-2501 to U-2552 52 boats
Deschimag, Bremen	U-3001 to U-3051 51 boats
Schichauwerft, Danzig	U-3501 to U-3530 30 boats
	Total 133 boats

Interior of a Type XXI

There were several significant differences in the internal layout of the Type XXI as compared to the Type IX, not the least of which was the greater amount of space. The hull of the Type XXI was, as stated, of modular construction, made up of nine separate units: the stern section containing the WC and workshop, the electric motor room, the diesel motor room, the aft crew accommodation, the control room, the forward accommodation, the torpedo storage area, the bow cap with torpedo tubes and the conning tower unit.

Beginning at the bow end, the bow cap was pierced by six torpedo tubes rather than the four common to most previous types. Immediately abaft of this was the torpedo storage area containing the boat's payload of torpedoes. Then followed the forward crew accommodation area. This was much roomier than on previous types. On most other models, a central walkway separated two rows of bunks attached to the interior hull side. On the Type XXI, however, a double row of bunks separated by a further narrow walkway was set up on the port side, whilst to starboard was the forward WC and to the rear of this, accommodation for the three ship's officers. Moving aft, the second part of this section had, once again to port, a double row of bunks separated by a narrow walkway, accommodating the senior non-commissioned ranks, whilst to starboard was the chief engineer's quarters – a fairly spacious sleeping accommodation/office.

Moving aft again, on the port side was the commander's cabin, which was much more spacious than on earlier boats. Directly across the central walkway was the radio/sound room. The heart of the boat was the control room or *Zentral* that, as on most boats, contained the diving plane controls, main switchboard, navigator's table, periscope controls and so on.

Aft of the control room was the food preparation area. To port was the galley itself with its electric cooker, whilst on the starboard was the pantry, which boasted a freezer compartment to keep fresh foods from rotting in the damp, humid atmosphere.

The Type XXI was built using modular construction. Here, the second diesel engine is being inserted into the engine room section at the Deschimag Yard in Bremen. Although modular construction was fine in principle, it suffered from poor quality control partly due to the use of forced labour in its construction. (NHHC)

Abaft this area was the main crew accommodation. To both port and starboard of the main walkway were double rows of bunks, each separated by a further narrow walkway. The 12 bunks provided on each side could accommodate a maximum of 48 men, using the 'hot-bunking' system, where two men shared a bunk, one occupying it whilst the other was on watch.

Next came the main diesel motor room with one of the huge MAN turbo-charged diesels either side of the central walkway. This was followed by the electric motor room with, on each side, a 2,500bhp electric motor and 320bhp 'creep' motor coupled to each shaft. There were no stern torpedo tubes on the Type XXI. The stern compartment featured the stern WC to starboard and, to port, a small workshop area provided with a lathe to allow repair work to be undertaken.

Most of the space available under the floor plates of the Type XXI was taken up with storage for the boat's large complement of batteries. The Type XXI, externally, was highly streamlined with no bulging saddle tanks, no deck armament and all bridge works contained in a single hydrodynamic tower to reduce drag. On both forward and aft ends of the tower were located twin 2cm flak guns, in streamlined turrets. Periscopes, snorkel and *Hohentweil* radar array could be retracted into special housings. Everything possible was done to reduce drag and thus increase underwater speed.

On the underside of the bow, the Type XXI was equipped with a sonar array known as GHG or *Gruppenhörchgerät*. This provided a basic all-round listening device. On the front face of the tower a further active sonar array was installed, the Nibelung

Type XXI and Type XXIII U-boats

(1) The Type XXI could move faster under water than many ships on the surface. The Type XXI was provided with two twin 2cm flak mounts in turrets set into the conning tower. This illustration shows U-2511.
(2) The Type XXIII, sacrificed external fittings for streamlining, with no outer deck casing apart from a narrow walkway down the foredeck. A tubular housing in the face of the tower held a life raft. These were excellent boats, though somewhat limited in having only two torpedoes and no reloads.
(3) The experimental Wa201, a Type XVII powered by the revolutionary Walter turbine. (Ian Palmer © Osprey Publishing)

SU(R), which provided direction/range-finding capabilities. The combination of this equipment allowed the Type XXI commander to detect enemy ships, estimate their range and course and launch his torpedoes all without recourse to the use of the periscope and the risk of the betrayal of his position that periscope use entailed.

Type XXI Deployment

Although the Type XXI concept was excellent, and far ahead of its time, as with all new technology, there were teething troubles, and not everything ran smoothly. Build quality of some of the sub-assemblies was not always good and many problems did not come to light until the boats were tested after final assembly. Then many had to have remedial work carried out to make them fit for service. In addition, the constant attention given to the assembly area by Allied bombing raids caused considerable disruption.

With the Type XXI being entirely new, even experienced U-boat crews had to be trained almost from scratch. A total of 133 Type XXIs were built, of which only two were deployed on war patrols. In both cases, the order to cease hostilities came before either of them engaged the enemy. U-2511, under the command of experienced U-boat ace Korvettenkapitän Adalbert Schnee, was able to escape the attentions of a number of British escort vessels when they encountered his boat off the British coast in April 1945. A combination of the U-boat's high speed and excellent sound detection equipment allowed him to follow their changes in course and shake them off with relative ease. Four days later, Schnee encountered a group of British warships including a heavy cruiser and carried out a completely successful dummy attack, escaping without detection of the U-boat. Clearly, if the Type XXI had entered service earlier it could have altered the course of the Battle of the Atlantic.

After the end of the war, the victorious Allies showed enormous interest in the Type XXI. Most of the existing boats had been scuttled by the Germans at the close of the war, but a few survived. The US Navy took over U-2513 and U-3008, the Royal Navy took U-3017, the Soviet Navy U-2529, U-3035, U-3041 and U-3515 and the French Navy U-2518. The latter served on with the French until 1967 when it was retired, and finally scrapped in 1969.

Mention should also be made of U-2540. This boat was sunk during a bombing raid of Flensburg in 1945. The boat, although sunk, was not excessively damaged, and in 1957 the wreck was raised and taken into the Howaldts Werke yard where it was fully restored and refurbished with a redesigned bridge/conning tower structure. On 1 September 1960, it was commissioned into the new West German *Bundesmarine* as *U-Wilhelm Bauer*, commemorating the 'father' of the German U-boat. It served not as a front-line boat, but purely as a test bed before being retired in 1983. Thereafter, the boat was restored to its wartime configuration (externally at least – many of the internal fittings are modern) by Lloydwerft in Bremen and passed over to the German Maritime Museum in Bremerhaven, where it is on display to this day.

Two Type XXIII U-boats are seen here in a floating drydock at the Deschimag Werft AG in Hamburg. The bridge is accessed by means of the rungs which can be seen mounted on the face of the tower. The vessel at right is U-2321 which saw actual active service and sank a British merchant steamer on 5 April 1945 off the Scottish coast. (NHHC)

Type XXIII

Probably the least well-known of the operational U-boat types in World War II, the Type XXIII was, ironically, one of the best. Developed in 1943, this type was intended to provide a modern replacement for the obsolete Type II for operations in coastal waters and also, at the insistence of Grossadmiral Dönitz, for use in the relatively shallow waters of the Mediterranean and Black Sea.

As with its larger relative, the Type XXI, it was intended that the boat be constructed in sections, with various modules being manufactured by subcontractors. In the event, Germany's battlefield reverses, shortages of steel and Allied bombing of construction facilities meant that construction was severely delayed and was ultimately concentrated at Germaniawerft in Kiel and Deutsche Werke in Hamburg.

The boat was kept as simple as possible. It had a simple, single hull of all-welded construction, with the small conning tower as its only external structure above the waterline. The Type XXIII featured a single propeller and single rudder. Only two torpedo tubes were fitted and, due to the small size of the boat, no reloads were carried. The torpedoes were loaded into the boat in a rather ingenious fashion. Floated out to the boat on a barge or raft, they were inserted into the tubes manually, from the exterior, tail first. In order to facilitate this, the boat had to be ballasted so that it became stern heavy, lifting the bow tubes clear of the water.

Intended for operation on patrols of relatively short duration (with only two torpedoes available) in coastal waters and with a snorkel breathing device fitted, it was assumed that these boats would spend most of their time submerged. No exterior decking was therefore provided, and this in turn assisted in the streamlining of the boat and a substantial reduction in drag. Set into the forward face of the conning tower was a small watertight container that held an inflatable life raft.

This illustration shows U-2336, under the command of Kapitänleutnant Emil Klusmeier, returning from its last mission of the war on 14 May 1945. Its final victim was the freighter *Avondale Park,* the last boat to be sunk by submarine action in World War II. (Ian Palmer © Osprey Publishing)

Only a modest single 630bhp diesel was fitted but, like its larger cousin the Type XXI, this boat had a significantly better battery capacity than earlier boats. This, coupled with its snorkel facility, enabled it to remain submerged for extended periods.

The Type XXIII had a particularly fine standard of seaworthiness, being fast for its size and extremely manoeuvrable. It also had a very fast crash-dive time, of just nine seconds. This brought its own problems, however, and any ingress of water into the boat could cause disaster. Both U-2365 and U-2331 were lost to accidents when water entered the boats and caused rapid sinking. It was also discovered that the assumed maximum depth before hull failure could be expected had been grossly overestimated at some 250m. In fact, the maximum safe operating depth was eventually established at just 80m.

For the first time ever on an operational U-boat, the torpedoes left the tubes under their own power rather than being ejected solely by compressed air.

The Type XXIII was constructed from just four basic hull modules. The bow compartment contained just two torpedo tubes, with no provision for reloads. Aft of this was the crew accommodation. To port were two sets of bunks followed by a tiny galley and to starboard were three sets of bunks, allowing a total crew accommodation for 20 men.

Abaft the main crew accommodation was the *Zentral* with the commander's space followed by the sound room and radio room, all to port, and the diving planes, main electrical and pump controls to starboard. Further astern was the diesel motor room with its single MWN diesel, followed by the electric motor room. With no stern torpedo tubes, the aftermost compartment contained the boat's tiny WC. Only a single periscope was fitted to the Type XXIII, along with a snorkel mast.

The first Type XXIII, U-2321, was launched at Deutsche Werke on 17 April 1944. A total of 62 Type XXIIIs entered service before the end of hostilities, of which only about six actually had the opportunity to carry out operational war cruises. During these, however, four enemy ships were sunk, and no U-boats lost. The first Type XXIII to carry out an operational war patrol was U-2324, which set off from Kiel on 18 January 1945. Although it survived the war, no sinkings were achieved. The first Type XXIII to achieve combat success was U-2322, under the command of Oberleutnant zur See Fridtjof-Heckel. Setting off from its Norwegian base on 6 February 1945 it encountered a convoy near Berwick on the Scottish coast and sank the small coaster *Egholm* on 25 February. U-2321, also operating from the same Norwegian base as U-2322, sank the coaster *Gasray* on 5 April 1945 off St Abbs head. More successful was U-2336, under Kapitänleutnant Emil Klusmeier, which sank two ships, the 1,790-ton *Sneland* and the 2,880-ton *Avondale Park*, also off the Scottish coast, on 7 May 1945.

U-2322, one of the few Type XXIII boats to see action. Under the command of Oberleutnant zur See Fridtjof -Heckel, it sank the steamer SS *Egholm* off the English coast on 25 February 1945. The white band around the tower indicates this shot was taken whilst the boat was still in training. (DUBM)

These were the last two ships to be sunk by U-boat action during World War II. After the end of the war, two scuttled Type XXIIIs (U-2365 and U-2367) were raised and restored. These boats, commissioned into the West German Bundesmarine as the *Hai* (Shark) and *Hecht* (Pike), respectively, provided the nucleus of the second rebirth of the U-Bootwaffe.

Type XXIII Specifications			
Length	34.7m	**Endurance**	4,450 nautical miles surfaced 285 nautical miles submerged
Beam	3.0m	**Powerplant**	1 x MWN 6-cylinder 630bhp diesel, 1 x AEG 35bhp electric motor 1 x BBC electric manoeuvring motor
Draft	3.7m	**Armament**	2 bow torpedo tubes
Displacement	234 tons surfaced 275 tons submerged	**Complement**	14
Top Speed	9.7 knots surfaced 12.5 knots submerged		

Type XXIII Construction Details	
Deutsche Werke, Hamburg	U-2321 to U-2331 11 boats
	U-2334 to U-2371 38 boats
	Total 49 boats
Germaniawerft, Kiel	U-2332 to U-2333 2 boats
	Total for type 51 boats

Type XVIIA (Wa 201/Wk 202)

This was an experimental design intended to utilise the revolutionary new propulsion system developed by Dr Helmuth Walter. Hydrogen peroxide was broken down using a catalyst to provide steam and oxygen, which were then mixed with water and diesel fuel, and the mixture combusted. The resultant products were very high temperature steam and pressurised carbon dioxide, which drove a turbine. The waste products were expelled, and remaining water recirculated. The system worked superbly. An earlier experimental boat, although having poor handling characteristics when on the surface, achieved underwater speeds of up to 26 knots.

The Wa 201 (the Wa prefix identifying the designer, Walter) was produced by the Blohm & Voss yard in direct association with Dr Walter, whilst Germaniawerft produced a second variant, the Wk 202.

One of the most advanced submarines designs was the Type XVIIA, powered by a hydrogen peroxide engine giving it an underwater speed of 22 knots. Shown here is U-793, one of only four built, all of which were scuttled at the end of the war. This boat, however, was raised and used for testing by the Royal Navy, eventually being scrapped in 1947. (DUBM)

Four Type XXVIIA boats were completed, and were taken into service as U-792 and U-793 (Blohm & Voss), and U-794 and U-795 (Germaniawerft), respectively. All were used solely as test boats, and the build quality and efficiency of the Blohm & Voss boats was found to be superior.

All four had numerous teething problems, always associated with revolutionary new designs, and were eventually laid up and finally scuttled in 1945.

Type XVIIB

The Type XVIIB was a direct successor to the Type XVIIA, but larger and outfitted with two bow torpedo tubes as well as a snorkel system. Only three (U-1405, U-1406 and U-1407) were eventually commissioned, all being built by Blohm & Voss. The three were scuttled in 1945, but U-1407 was raised, repaired and taken into service in the Royal Navy as HMS *Meteorite*.

Standard U-boat equipment

The Powerplant

The typical powerplant of the U-boat was the diesel motor, with additional electric motors coupled onto the same propeller shafts as the diesels. Diesels were used for surface running, and electric motors for running submerged.

Not until the advent of the snorkel was it possible for a U-boat to charge its electric motors by running its diesels whilst still at periscope depth. The snorkel was a simple 'breathing' tube that allowed air to be drawn into the boat whilst submerged. Its head contained a simple flap mechanism with a flotation ball. The rise of a wave against the head would lift the ball, sealing the tube and preventing the ingress of water.

The main problem with the snorkel arose when the boat's depth was not correctly monitored and it slipped below periscope depth, or in heavy seas when the flap remained closed more often than open. When no air was being taken into the boat, the engines would draw their air from the boat's interior, creating a partial vacuum and debilitating the crew.

The diesel engines driving each propeller shaft were mounted on extremely robust foundations. Almost completely filling the engine room space, only a narrow access passage between the two allowed movement through the compartment. Serving in the confines of the engine room was hot, smelly and unpleasant. Many mechanical breakdowns were extremely difficult to work on due to the cramped space.

The Type VIIA was outfitted with two six-cylinder MAN or Germaniawerft diesels, each developing 1,160bhp. Coupled onto the same shafts were two 375hp electric motors that, when the clutch was disengaged and they were rotating freely whilst the diesels drove the boat, acted as generators to recharge the batteries. Principal suppliers of electric motors for U-boats were Siemens, AEG and Brown-Boveri. Later Type VIIs (B–F) used two 1,400bhp diesels paired with two 375bhp electric motors. The biggest change of course came with the Type XXI and Type XXIII *Elektroboote* with turbo-supercharged diesels and electric motors so powerful that they could drive the boat faster underwater than the diesels could on the surface.

Radios

The standard method of communication between a U-boat and its shore-based command was the short-wave radio, operating on the 3–30 MHz range. Most U-boats were fitted with a combination of a Telefunken receiver, and a 200 watt Telefunken transmitter with a smaller 40 watt Lorenz transmitter as back-up. Once at sea, communication between U-boats utilised medium-wave radio on the 1.5–3 MHz range. Once again, the equipment was manufactured predominantly by Telefunken. Finally, signals sent to U-boats whilst submerged required the use of very long wave signals on the 15–20 MHz range. These required an enormously powerful transmitter on land, but were the only sure way of making contact with a submerged boat. These signals were also received on the same Telefunken equipment as the medium-wave signals.

Radar

Basic radar equipment began to be installed on U-boats in 1940. The earliest operational type was the FuMO 29. This was predominantly used on the Type IX, but a few Type VIIs were also fitted with this equipment, easily detected on photographs because of the twin horizontal rows of eight dipoles on the upper front part of the conning tower. The top row were transmitters and the lower row receivers. An improved version, FuMO 30, was introduced in 1942 in which the tower-mounted dipoles were replaced by a so-called retractable 'mattress' antenna which was housed in a slot in the tower wall. This equipment was only partially successful in detecting other ships due to the very low position of its mounting in respect to the ocean surface (on surface ships, the radar is usually mounted high up on the mainmast or bridge top). Interference with the radar signal by the ocean surface in heavy weather meant that enemy ships might be detected visually before being picked up on radar. An improved version, the FuMO 61, was little better in this respect but did provide good aircraft detection results.

The FuMB 1 also known as *Metox,* was introduced in July 1942. This equipment was used in conjunction with an extremely crude wooden cross-shaped antenna strung with wire and known as the 'Biscay Cross'. This antenna had to be rotated by hand. Unfortunately, the *Metox*'s own emissions were detectable by Allied radar detection equipment, leading them straight to the U-boat. A later, improved version, the FuMB 9 *Zypern*, was also found to be detectable by the British H2S radar detection system. Not until the FuMB 10 *Borkum* set did the U-boat have a radar detection system that was not itself detectable.

This still left the problem of the existing equipment not covering the full radar spectrum, a problem eventually solved in November 1943 by the FuMB 7 *Naxos*. *Naxos* and *Metox* used together finally gave the U-boats excellent all-round radar detection capabilities. The range of capabilities of *Naxos* and *Metox* were finally combined in a single system with the introduction of the FuMB 24 *Fliege* and FuMB 25 *Mücke* systems in April 1944.

Sound Detection

The earliest form of sound detection equipment used on U-boats was the *Gruppenhorchgerät* (GHG) installed in early vessels. The sound detectors were installed in the hull on either side of the bow, so that sound detection was only truly accurate when the boat was abeam of the vessel being detected. Improved sound detection came with the *Kristalldrehbasisgerät* (KDB) in which the sound detection array was contained in a rotating, retractable mount set into the foredeck. This was the system carried on most Type VII vessels. A number of Type VIIs were also equipped with the so-called *Balcongerät* (Balcony Apparatus) set into a 'balcony'-shaped faring in the lower part of the bow. This gave a far better effective field than either the GHG or KDB systems.

CHAPTER THREE

COASTAL AND OTHER VESSELS

E-BOATS

Without doubt the most successful of the Kriegsmarine's craft operating in coastal waters was the *S-Boot* or *Schnellboot*, generally known to the Allies as the 'E-boat'. In what follows, these terms will be used interchangeably.

Development of the E-boats

Germany had been involved in the construction of high-quality and extremely fast motorboats since before the end of the 19th century, with one of the most influential manufacturers being the firm of Otto Lürssen. In 1908, a boat built by this firm, and powered by a Daimler engine, had reached speeds of 50 knots. Being built purely for speed, however, such boats

Leading this patrol line of E-boats is S-11, one of the batch of low forecastle types S-7 to S-13. Following it is S-22, almost identical but with more powerful engines. Boat numbers would be painted out for security reasons on the outbreak of war. These early boats would soon be superseded by faster more powerfully armed types. (Bettmann via Getty Images)

were far too fragile for combat use. The first fast motorboats built for the Kaiserliche Marine were unable to be fitted out as torpedo boats due to a general shortage of torpedoes and were used instead as sub-chasers (UZ or *U-Boot Zerstörer*).

By the outbreak of World War I, the German Navy had also experimented with remote-controlled boats. These were termed FL-boats (*Fernlenkboote*) and were effectively remote-controlled bombs, their bows packed with high explosives, intended to be steered directly at their targets – initially British 'Monitors' operating off the Flanders coast. A similar idea was resurrected in World War II with the appearance of the Linsen motorboats used by the *Kleinkampfverbände* (small battle unit). These boats had their bows packed with explosives and were driven straight at their targets, the operator diving overboard at the last moment, to be picked up later by a control boat.

True motor torpedo boats made their appearance with the L-boats, later renamed LM-boats (*Luftschiffmotorenboote* literally 'airship boats'), so-called because they were powered by the same engines used in the Zeppelin airships. The manufacture of these boats was once again pioneered by the firm of Otto Lürssen in Vegesack, though other firms were soon involved in their manufacture, particularly the Naglo firm in Zeuthen near Berlin, Oertz of Hamburg and Roland of Hemelingen. The first four boats, LM-1 to LM-4, were armed with only a 3.7cm gun. From LM-5 to LM-20, each boat was fitted with a single bow torpedo tube, backed up with machine-gun armament. LM-21 to LM-33 were planned but not completed.

The designations of the last boats planned to appear in World War I were based on a combination of the name of the shipyard wherein they were built and the type of powerplant. Thus, Lüsi 1 and 2 were to be built by Lürssen and have motors built by Siemens/Deutz, Köro 1 and 2 were to have Körting engines and were to be built by Roland, and Juno 1 to 4 were to have had Junkers engines and be built by Oertz. They were all intended to be much more powerful boats, with twin bow torpedo tubes as well as a 2cm cannon. In the event none were ever completed.

The fast motor torpedo boats were used principally in the Baltic and off the coast of Flanders. Although no major successes against enemy shipping are recorded, these boats had at least shown that such small, fast, torpedo-armed craft had considerable potential.

After World War I, the terms of the Versailles Treaty totally banned Germany from possessing submarines and severely restricted possession of surface vessels. Though Germany was left with a small fleet of torpedo boats, these were not fast motor torpedo boats, but larger, slower, steam-driven boats displacing around 900 tons and were almost the size of a small destroyer.

The new German Navy that was reborn from the ashes of the old Kaiserliche Marine was small. However, due to the loss of almost its entire navy with the scuttling of the High Seas Fleet at Scapa Flow and the dismantling of its U-boat fleet, Germany was forced to start anew, and the ships that the new Reichsmarine and its successor, the Kriegsmarine, built, were fast, modern ships that had been developed to take full advantage of the latest technologies.

As an Oberleutnant zur See, Kurt Fimmen was awarded the Knight's Cross on 14 August 1940 for his command of S-26 in actions in the English Channel. As Kapitänleutnant later, he commanded 1. Schnellbootflottille. He can be seen to be wearing the first type E-boat War Badge. Fimmen survived the war. (Author's collection)

Despite this, the Kriegsmarine, even at its most powerful, could never have hoped to match long-established and numerically superior fleets such as the British. Major surface units such as the *Bismarck* and *Tirpitz* may well have been more than a match for any single equivalent ship in any enemy navy at the time they were launched, but as they would inevitably be met with an overwhelming superiority of numbers when they did put to sea (as happened to the *Bismarck*, for example) their moment of glory would be fleeting before they inevitably succumbed. For many in Germany, it seemed that the only way of countering the might of the Royal Navy was to build substantial numbers of small, torpedo-bearing craft. In submarines, this was to result in a large number of the small Type II being constructed, and for the surface fleet, the concept found its outlet in the development of the fast motor torpedo boat.

Once again it was to be the smaller vessels of the navy (and predominantly the U-boats) that would come nearest to inflicting defeat on Germany's enemies. The E-boat fleet may have been relatively small, but its achievements were significant, ranking it amongst the most successful and cost-effective elements of the Kriegsmarine in World War II.

One of the main questions taxing the minds of those intent on perfecting the design of the ideal fast motor torpedo boat was the delivery of the main weapon – the torpedo. Three main methods of discharging the torpedo were considered: Bow Launch, Stern Launch–Tail First, and Stern Launch–Nose First.

Not surprisingly, the method selected was the bow-mounted tube. The highly experienced Lürssen firm became involved again in the manufacture of motor torpedo boats for the Reichsmarine on an official basis in 1930, with the 52-ton UZ(s)-16 (eventually to be renumbered as S-1). The boat soon proved itself in tests and was the basis for all future E-boat development.

The first type *Schnellbootkriegsabzeichen* (E-boat War Badge) was instituted on 30 May 1941 and awarded to crews of fast attack or patrol boats after completing 12 patrols, taking part in a particularly successful action, being wounded in action or performing some particularly meritorious deed. The badge was designed by Wilhelm Ernst Peekhaus of Berlin. (Author's collection)

An early model E-boat at speed. Note how high the bows rise out of the water. The boat's number has been painted out for security reasons. Note the eagle and swatika carried on the side shield just aft of the torpedo tube. (Author's collection)

E-boat Types

The basic E-boat design changed little over the course of its development. In all, there were 13 identifiable models, which could reasonably be considered under three main categories: early-, mid- and late-war types. Many of the changes were subtle and are not immediately apparent even when studying photographs of the vessels.

Early-War Low Forecastle Types

S-1 was the first true E-boat. This vessel started its life under the designation UZ(s)-16. Built by the Lürssen firm, it was a 52-ton boat with a length of 26.9m and a beam of 4.37m. It was driven by three Daimler Benz 800bhp V12 diesels with a 100bhp Maybach engine coupled to the central propeller shaft for use when manoeuvring at low speed. S-1 had a top speed of 34 knots and a crew of 12. Commissioned in August 1930, it was used for testing until December 1936, and then sold to Spain.

S-2 to S-5 were the first operational E-boats of the German Navy. These four vessels were also ordered from Lürssen. Slightly larger than their predecessor, at 27.9m, and with a beam of 4.5m, these boats weighed in at 58 tons. These boats, like S-1, were powered by three Daimler Benz 800bhp V12 diesel engines, and a supplementary Maybach engine was coupled to the centre shaft for manoeuvring. Top speed was 32 knots. This class carried 7,500 litres of fuel, giving an operational range of 350 nautical miles at top speed, extending to 2,000 nautical miles at an economic 7 knots. Armed with two bow torpedo tubes and carrying four torpedoes, supplementary armament was provided by a 2cm MG C/30 amidship and a 7.92mm MG08 at the bow.

S-6 was the only boat of this class produced. Displacing 85 tons, it measured 32.4m in length with a beam of 5.1m. Its main drawback lay in the three lightweight MAN L7 two-stroke diesels that powered it. In terms of reliability and performance, the engines were a total disaster, giving a whole catalogue of problems. The boat was basically a liability and of no real use to the navy. It was sold to Spain along with its five predecessors.

S-7 to S-13 were new designs. The possibility of a future war with France saw the navy requiring a boat with the specifications that would allow it to operate against French ports, thus requiring greater range than the existing models. The existing designs were not capable of upgrading to an additional fuel capacity without adversely affecting their power/weight statistics. The resultant new design was the 86-ton S-7 class, with a length of 32.4m and a beam of 5.1m. Three of these boats (S-7 to S-9) were fitted out with MAN diesels and others (S-10 to S-13) with the more reliable Daimler Benz type.

S-14 to S-17 boats were even larger. These vessels were 34.6m in length with a beam of 5.3m. S-14 and S-15 displaced 93 tons whilst S-16 and S-17 displaced 100 tons. A crew of 18 was required. These boats were powered by MAN 11-cylinder two-stroke diesels, which once again proved to be far from reliable. So exasperated was the navy with the poor reliability of the MAN engines that it decided that in future this

Mid-war high forecastle E-boats

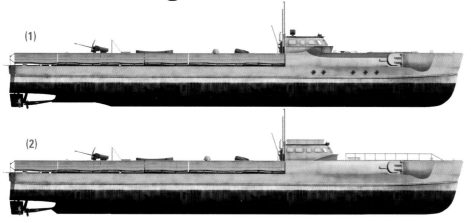

(1) An S-30-type boat in 1942. Note the higher relatively uncluttered foredeck. A base for the machine gun pedestal mount was provided, but this weapon seems rarely to have been fitted. Note how the rear portion of the foredeck curves upwards to the side of the bridge/wheelhouse. In place of the 2cm gun on the afterdeck of earlier types, this boat now carries a 3.7cm gun. **(2)** An S-26 type, with open bridge. Once again, this type rarely seems to have a machine gun fitted, though fittings were provided on the foredeck to allow one to be used.
(Ian Palmer ©
Osprey Publishing)

firm's engines would not be considered for use in E-boats. It is interesting that the MAN diesels proved so unsatisfactory having given such great service in the U-Bootwaffe, whilst, conversely, high performance E-boat engines installed in U-boats (U-180 for example) proved equally unsatisfactory.

S-18 to S-25 comprised a group that was of very similar specification and identical size to the S-14 class but was powered by Daimler Benz MB501 four-stroke diesels, a far more reliable unit.

Mid-War High Forecastle Types

S-26 to 29, 38 to 53, 62 to 133, 159 to 166. The first of the S-26 models were built by Lürssen. Displacing 112 tons, they were 34.9m in length with a beam of 5.3m.
S-30 to 37, 54 to 61. Also built by Lürssen, the S-30 class was marginally smaller than the S-26, displacing 100 tons and having a length of 32.8m and beam of 5.1m. The slightly smaller size was due to the fitting of the 16-cylinder Daimler Benz MB502 engines.

Early high forecastle E-boats of the S-30 class, built by Lürssen. Note the distinctive upsweep to the rear of the torpedo tube casing which identifies this model. Only 16 of the S-30 type were built. E-boats were generally painted a very pale grey known as *Schnellbootweiss*. (ullstein bild via Getty Images)

This E-boat has the high forecastle, the forward part of the torpedo tubes being completely enclosed. Note that canvas dodgers have been fitted over the railings at the side of the vessel to provide some degree of protection from the spray thrown up when the boat is moving at speed. (Author's collection)

Late-War Armoured Bridge Types

S-139 to 150, 167 to 169, 171 to 227, 229 to 260. This class was visually quite similar to the S-26 type, but was 1m longer and was powered by the supercharged Daimler Benz MB511 engine. All had a much lower profile due to the new bridge design. The armoured bridges had in fact begun to be fitted from S-67 onwards in the S-26 series, but were common to all the S-139 and S-170 classes.

S-170 to 228, 301 to 425, 701 to 825. The S-170 class was to be the largest of the E-boats. Displacing 121 tons, they were 35m in length and had a beam of 5.3m. The last batch to be constructed, S-701 to S-825, were also powered by the supercharged MB511 engine.

It is interesting to note that the E-boat War Badge, awarded to E-boat crews after their third combat sortie, was unique amongst such badges in that it was specifically redesigned to reflect new developments in E-boat construction. The first badge, instituted in May 1941, depicted one of the early high forecastle types, but still with the relatively high cabin type of bridge. In 1943, a second type was introduced. The commander of 2.Schnellbootflottille, Kapitän zur See Rudolf Petersen, was involved in producing the design for this second version, which shows the later, sleeker type with the armoured bridge in a form that also imparts a greater impression of the speed of the boat.

Smaller Boats

As well as the larger, powerful S-boat classes, a number of smaller craft were also produced.

LS-boats were intended to be carried on and launched from larger craft (the proposed, though ultimately rejected, Type III U-boat was to carry two such small motor torpedo boats of the LS type). A small number were also allocated to some of the auxiliary cruisers. In the event, from a total of 34 proposed craft, only 15 were actually built. Most ended up being assigned to 21.Schnellbootflottille based in the Aegean. These boats displaced just 13 tons and were only 12.5m in length with a beam of 3.5m. They were powered by two Daimler Benz MB507 diesel engines and required a crew of seven. Armament consisted of two torpedo tubes and one 2cm gun. Not all were actually completed as torpedo boats, some being used as minelayers.

Early-war low forecastle E-boats

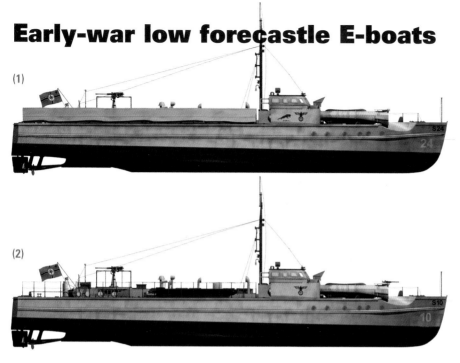

(1)

(2)

At top (1) is S-10, from the group S-7 to S-13 built by Lürssen at Vegesack, and commissioned in March 1935. The low forecastle caused these boats to take on considerable quantities of water when moving at speed. Note the large spray deflectors just ahead of the bridge. (2) shows S-24, also a Lürssen-built boat, commissioned in September 1939, and one of the group S-18 to S-25. Outwardly similar to the previous model, it was around 2m longer, and powered by 20-cylinder Daimler Benz MB501 diesel engines as opposed to the 16-cylinder MB502 engines in the S-10 type.
(Ian Palmer © Osprey Publishing)

KM-boats had a length of 15.6m, a beam of 3.5m and displaced 18 tons. Powered by two BMW petrol engines, they could achieve a top speed of around 30 knots. Two configurations were produced: a minelayer capable of carrying four mines, and a torpedo boat with two stern-mounted torpedo tubes. In both cases, a 7.92mm machine gun was provided as supplementary armament. A total of 36 boats of this type were produced.

Configuration
Hull
Though many of the E-boats differed in external detail as the series was developed, the general structure of the boats was broadly similar.

The E-boats' hulls were of mixed wooden/metal construction, with the keel, longitudinals and deck beams in wood and the frames and diagonal stringers in light metal alloy. The deck superstructures were also made of light metal alloys. The bulkheads were in 4mm- thick steel below the waterline and of slightly thinner light metal alloy above.

Low Forecastle Boats
This type was identified by its low forecastle and exposed torpedo tubes. The tubes passed through a steel bulkhead, forward of which, between the tubes, was positioned a pedestal-mounted machine gun, just ahead of a small breakwater. The boat's inflatable dinghies were usually stored here, being screened to some degree from enemy fire by the torpedo tubes.

S-100 type E-boat

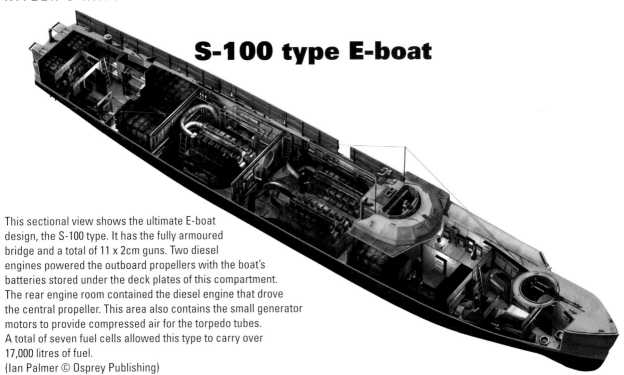

This sectional view shows the ultimate E-boat design, the S-100 type. It has the fully armoured bridge and a total of 11 x 2cm guns. Two diesel engines powered the outboard propellers with the boat's batteries stored under the deck plates of this compartment. The rear engine room contained the diesel engine that drove the central propeller. This area also contains the small generator motors to provide compressed air for the torpedo tubes. A total of seven fuel cells allowed this type to carry over 17,000 litres of fuel.
(Ian Palmer © Osprey Publishing)

RIGHT A late E-boat of the type with an armoured bridge as fitted on the S-38 and S-100 class boats. These were some of the biggest, fastest and most powerfully armed E-boats. Interestingly one such boat, S-130, still survives and is currently undergoing full restoration at the Wheatcroft Collection in the UK. (Author's collection)

To the rear of the bulkhead was the cabin-like bridge/wheelhouse with a mast mounted to its rear. Just abaft the rear of the torpedo tubes the two spare torpedoes were stored on deck, on special cradles. The deck superstructure amidship was over the engine compartment, and was liberally covered with ventilators and skylights.

To the rear of this midship superstructure, the forward end of the aft superstructure had mounted upon it a circular platform with a surrounding guardrail, on which the 2cm Flak C/30 or C/38 was mounted on a pedestal. At the aftermost point on the upper deck could be fitted two depth charge racks, though these were by no means universally used.

High Forecastle Boats

In an attempt to improve the handling characteristics of the E-boats in heavy seas, the forecastles were raised, this having the effect of enclosing the torpedo tubes. The earlier boats fitted with a high forecastle generally had a clear foredeck, though a base for a pedestal mount for a machine gun was provided as per the early models. This weapon, however, rarely seems to have been fitted. The inflatable dinghy was moved back towards the midship area, leaving the rest of the foredeck uncluttered. This early high forecastle design has an instantly recognisable curve to the line of the foredeck just forward of the bridge.

These boats still had a relatively prominent and unprotected bridge/wheelhouse area, to the rear of which was the long midship superstructure on the forward end of whose roof was mounted an inflatable escape raft. On the roof of the superstructure were positioned several ammunition lockers. Just abaft the superstructure was the heavy flak mount comprising a 40mm Bofors, 3.7cm flak gun or quadruple 2cm *Flakvierling*. To the rear of the flak mount was the small after superstructure, the roof of which contained ammunition lockers and smoke generators as well as an entry hatch to the crew accommodation. On the aftermost part of the deck were often located twin depth charge racks, each of which would hold three charges.

Generally, apart from the raised forecastle, the appearance of this type was little changed from the earlier low forecastle models.

Later High Forecastle Boats

Later high forecastle models had significant changes in appearance. The forward gun position, instead of being fully exposed, now became a sunken 'tub', thus providing more cover for the gun crew. The weapon generally mounted here, instead of the machine gun of the earlier models, was a 2cm cannon. On the aft end of the forward superstructure (over the boat's engine room) a twin 2cm flak gun was generally fitted, and the usual heavy flak gun was mounted at the forward end of the aft superstructure. The most obvious change on this type was the bridge.

Whereas early models had an enclosed bridge/wheelhouse, these later models had an open bridge above the wheelhouse, giving this area a somewhat higher profile.

High Forecastle Armoured Bridge Boats

In an attempt to provide more protection for the commander and crew in the wheelhouse, most later boats had a so-called 'Skullcap' armoured bridge fitted (these were also retrofitted to some earlier boats). This had a very low silhouette with chamfered edges and armoured flaps, which could be closed over the vision ports. The foredeck was flat and lacked the upswept curvature of the earlier type just forward of the bridge. A 2cm flak gun (sometimes fitted with an armoured shield) was positioned in a gun tub on the forecastle, level with the torpedo tube doors.

To the rear of the bridge was the midship superstructure on the forward part of which was mounted the boat's binnacle and an inflatable life raft. In the centre of this

Late-war high forecastle E-boats

(1) One of the boats fitted with the excellent quadruple *Flakvierling* 2cm anti-aircraft gun. Although this could throw up a considerable volume of fire, the 2cm shell itself was not particularly powerful and was contemptuously know by the Germans as the 'doorknocker', so poor was its penetrating power. This design, before the advent of the armoured bridge, had an open bridge compartment above the wheelhouse.
(2) A similar boat, but with its canvas dodgers fitted, and with the more powerful 3.7cm flak gun. This gun was far more effective in its penetrating power.
(Ian Palmer © Osprey Publishing)

(1)

(2)

superstructure was a circular platform bearing a twin 2cm gun with armoured shield and, to the rear, a large rubber dinghy and numerous ammunition lockers.

In the space between the midship and rear superstructures was positioned a four-barrelled 2cm *Flakvierling* (alternatively a 3.7cm flak gun or 4cm Bofors). The roof of the rear superstructure contained a hatchway into the interior, ammunition lockers and smoke discharger pots. As with other variants, depth charge racks with the capacity of three charges for each could be mounted.

Armament

The basic forward armament of the E-boat consisted of a forecastle-mounted 7.92mm machine gun, and two bow torpedo tubes (with two spare torpedoes carried). On the afterdeck was mounted a flak gun, originally 2cm but eventually upgraded, and on some boats a complement of depth charges.

Machine Guns

The basic machine-gun armament was the 7.92mm MG38 which had the facility to be belt or magazine fed. Earlier MG08 and MG151 types were also widely used. Both were excellent weapons heavily used by the German Army. The MG38 was effective up to 2,000m and had a cyclic rate of 900 rounds per minute for the MG38 and 1,550 rounds per minute for the MG42. This made these weapons quite devastating. The downside, however, as already found by the army, was that such a high rate of fire required substantial supplies of ammunition to keep the weapon fed. This could be problematic for infantry or other troops in having to carry heavy ammunition containers, but onboard ship this was less of a problem.

On the early, low forecastle boats, the machine gun was fitted to a simple pedestal mount on the deck between the two bow torpedo tubes. The torpedo tube structures gave the machine gunner some degree of protection from enemy fire from the flanks, but the position was totally exposed from the bow. On later boats with the raised forecastle, the

Late-war E-boats with armoured bridges

(1)

(2)

(3)

(1) An S-38 type Lürssen boat from the batch S-38 to S-53, after upgrading and fitting with the armoured bridge. It carries a 2cm bow gun, a twin 2cm gun amidship and a 3.7cm flak gun on the afterdeck. In the centre (2) is shown S-100, sporting the new low-profile armoured bridge, and the typical lack of portholes on late-war boats. At bottom (3) is *S-223* from the largest E-boat class to be built. Measuring 36m, the additional length more easily accommodated the Daimler Benz MB511 supercharged diesel engines, which gave this craft a top speed of 43.5 knots.
(Ian Palmer © Osprey Publishing)

forward gunner's position consisted of a tub sunken into the foredeck, giving a measure of all round cover.

On many of the later boats, the forward machine gun was replaced by a heavier 2cm MG C/38 cannon giving the boat considerably more 'punch' when firing forward. In many cases, however, the option to fire forward would be limited as, when travelling at speed, the bow rose in the water quite significantly, obscuring the gunner's view of the sea in front of him.

A number of dismounted machine guns were also carried and could be fitted to various mounts when necessary.

Flak Guns

Early boats carried a 2cm MG C/30 flak gun on a pedestal mount sited on a circular platform amidship over the engine room. This was the same weapon provided for flak defence on most U-boats in the early part of the war. Its rate of fire was disappointingly low and, as with the U-boats, it was soon replaced by the improved MG C/38. It was magazine fed with a cyclic rate of fire of around 240 rounds per minute and a range of over 12,000m.

Initially, as mentioned above, the bow machine gun was also replaced by a 2cm MG C/38, and this was followed by the fitting of a twin 2cm mount on the aft flak platform. Even this improvement, however, was considered inadequate by most boat commanders. As a result, a small number of selected boats in 2., 4., 5. and 6. Schnellbootsflottillen were armed with captured 4cm Bofors guns in addition to the 2cm flak armament.

The second-type E-boat War Badge, introduced in January 1943 with a more dynamic looking boat. The redesign is said to have been at the request of E-boat personnel supported by the Knight's Cross winner Korvettenkapitän Rudolf Petersen. The design was reworked by the original artist Wilhelm Ernst Peekhaus. (Author's collection)

By late 1944, the gun armament was standardized at one 2cm MG C/38 forward, two twin 2cm flak guns amidship and a 4cm or 3.7cm flak gun astern. In a few cases, quadruple 2cm *Flakvierling* mounts were fitted astern, giving some boats a fairly hefty armament of ten 2cm cannon. Though impressive on paper, the penetrating power of the 2cm weapon was poor, leading to them being contemptuously referred to as 'doorknockers' by the Germans.

No matter what the armament fitted to E-boats, they would rarely come out best in a contest with enemy aircraft. The E-boat itself, though light and fast, could hardly be considered a stable gun platform. Many wartime close-up photos of E-boats show the hulls covered with small patches where the structure had been peppered with small-arms fire or shrapnel.

Torpedoes

The main armament of the E-boat was the torpedo. All E-boats carried two bow tubes, with two spare torpedoes carried in racks on deck just behind the tubes from where they could be quickly loaded. The standard torpedo carried was the 53.3cm G7a. Some 7.2m in length and weighing 1,530kg, this weapon was steam driven. Its single propeller drove it along at a maximum speed of 44 knots, giving it a range of 6,000m. At its optimum lower speed of 30 knots, its range extended to 14,400m. In the nose of the torpedo was the warhead, typically with 280kg of mixed explosive (trinitrotoluene, hexanitrophenylamine and powdered aluminium). Into this was set a detonator with a small propeller. This propeller was in effect a timing mechanism, which charged the detonator whilst spinning, as the torpedo sped through the water. The detonator would not fully charge until it had covered about 30m, ensuring against premature detonation damaging the boat that had launched it. The detonator on the G7a was a contact type, activated by physical contact with the target.

Around half the length of the torpedo was taken up by a compressed-air cylinder. This was followed by a fuel tank and a combustion chamber in which the air and fuel mix was ignited, driving a small four-cylinder engine that in turn powered the torpedo's propeller. Exhaust gases were vented through the hollow bore of the prop shaft. The torpedo was fitted with a gyroscope controlling its rudders to ensure it kept on course, and a depth gauge that controlled its dive planes. The torpedo was extremely expensive, costing well over 20,000 Reichsmarks each, and was a highly sensitive piece of equipment. Fortunately for the E-boats, its use on a surface ship was not beset by quite the same level of technical problems as was suffered by U-boats when launching the torpedo from a submarine.

The visible stream of bubbles caused by the vented exhaust gases could be problematic in the use of the G7a by U-boats, giving a sharp-sighted lookout an approximate bearing on the submarine which launched it, but such considerations were of little significance for their use by surface ships.

The more advanced, electrically driven G7e, widely used on U-boats, was not carried by E-boats. However, the advanced, long-range torpedo (the T3d) with a range of up to 57,000m, but a slow speed of just 9 knots and carrying a 281kg warhead, was used in limited numbers by E-boats attacking the Allied beachhead in Normandy. This allowed the E-boats to fire their torpedoes from a safe distance. The torpedoes would run true until reaching the target area, after which they would circle until hitting a target. The T5 homing torpedo was also used by E-boats in the latter part of the war, but without significant results.

Mines

Mines were another very important addition to the armoury of the E-boats. Those predominantly used were the RMA and RMB types, though captured Russian-made MO8 mines were also used. The torpedo-tube-launched TMB as used in the U-boat arm was also used to good effect by the E-boats, as were LMB and LMF types (acoustic/magnetic). A good number of the sinkings achieved by the E-boats were by the use of mines.

Schnellbootwaffe Organization

The E-boats had originally fallen under the command of FdT (*Führer der Torpedoboote* or Flag Officer Torpedo Boats) though it should be pointed out that the term torpedo boats used here related to the larger vessels that resembled a small destroyer. In 1942, the torpedo boats passed into the command of the FdZ (*Führer der Zerstörer* or Flag Officer Destroyers) and the navy's E-boat forces came under the control of the newly appointed Flag Officer E-boats, known as the *Führer der Schnellboote,* or FdS.

E-boats were organized into flotillas, of which there were eventually a total of 14, and which ultimately operated in four main theatres: the English Channel/North Sea, the Baltic/Far North, the Black Sea, and the Mediterranean/Aegean. Some E-boats were committed for use in the Baltic during the invasion of Poland, but so quickly was the Polish Navy subdued that they saw little or no action.

A specific training flotilla for E-boat crews was formed in July 1942, as the Schnellbootsschuleflottille at Swinemünde. This training establishment was divided into two sections: 1.Abteilung at Swinemünde-Eichstaden, and 2.Abteilung at Kaseburg. It was enlarged into the Schnellbootslehrdivision, itself comprised of three

Sanitätsmaat (Petty Officer) Rolf Kölbel served on U-129 as well as on E-boats. He wears the second type E-boat War Badge immediately under his U-boat Badge. The wearing of more than one war badge was not unusual as sailors often moved between branches and earned new awards. (DUBM)

Service Theatres of the E-boat Flotillas	
English Channel/North Sea	1., 2., 3., 4., 5., 6., 7., 8., 9., 10., 11.
Baltic/Far North	1., 2., 3., 5., 6., 7., 11., 21., 22.
Black Sea	1.
Mediterranean/Aegean	3., 7., 21., 24.

Most of these E-boat flotillas operated as autonomous units with the exception of those operating in the Mediterranean, which were formed into 1.Schnellbootsdivision.

The *Kriegsabzeichen für Minensuch-, U-Bootsjagd- und Sicherungsverbände* (War Badge for Minesweeper, Sub-Chaser and Security Units). It was unusual amongst naval war badges in that it did not show a type of vessel or weapon, but rather an action – that of an underwater mine exploding. Introduced on 31 August 1940, it was designed by artist Otto Placzek of Berlin. (Author's collection)

training flotillas in November 1943. 1.Schnellbootsschuleflottille was formed in November 1943 and based in the Baltic with the escort ship *Adolf Lüderitz*, 2.Schnellbootsschulefottille was formed in April 1944 and served in both Norwegian and Baltic waters with the escort ship *Tsingtau* and 3.Schnellbootsschuleflottille was formed in June 1944 and based in Kurland with the escort ship *Carl Peters*. Initially, each E-boat flotilla had its own tender/escort ship.

The Security Branch (*Sicherungsverbände*)

In the simplest terms, the navy under the *Oberkommando der Kriegsmarine* (Naval High Command) was split into three main operational commands: the *Flottenchef*, covering the major combat units of the Fleet, and the *Kommandierender Admiral der Marinestationen der Nordsee* and *Kommandierender Admiral der Marinestationen der Ostsee* (the Commanding Admirals of the North Sea and Baltic Naval Stations). Under these latter two senior commands came the *Befehlshaber der Sicherung der Nordsee* and *der Ostsee*, Commanders of Security in the North Sea and Baltic.

On the outbreak of war in September 1939, the position of Befehlshaber der Sicherung was held by a flag officer with the rank of Konteradmiral. As more and more territory, and thus coastal waters, fell under German control, so new senior naval commands were established (e.g. in Paris, Oslo, Sofia, and so on), and each had a number of units of the Sicherungsverbände under its control. In November 1944, as German-controlled waters rapidly shrank, Sicherungsverbände units were grouped under the command of the *Befehlshaber der Sicherungstreitkräfte* or Commander of Security Forces. Below these senior levels in the chain of command came the positions of *Führer der Minensuchboote* and *Führer der Vorpostenboote*, Commanders of Minesweepers and of Patrol Boats.

For the greater part of the war those naval units (usually of flotilla size) responsible for minesweeping, minelaying, patrol and escort work were grouped into Security Divisions or *Sicherungsdivisionen* – of which 11 were ultimately created, plus one training unit, the *Sicherungslehrdivision*. For example, in 1941, 1.Sicherungsdivision comprised the following units:

- 15.Minensuchflottille (Minesweeper Flotilla)
- 22.Minensuchflottille
- 32.Minensuchflottille
- 34.Minensuchflottille
- 13.Vorpostenflottille
- 20.Vorpostenflottille
- Minenräumschiff 12
- Sperrbrecher 145, 147, 148 and 149

As early as 1940, a special badge was introduced to recognize the service of personnel involved in such essential duties. Designed by the respected Berlin graphic artist Otto Placzek, it was authorized on 31 August 1940 by Grossadmiral Raeder, and entitled the *Kriegsabzeichen für Minensuch-, U-Bootsjagd- und Sicherungsverbände* (War Badge for Minesweeper, Sub-Chaser and Security Units). Awards began on 11 September of that year, the badge being available to those who had completed a minimum of three combat missions. Like the other war badges of the armed services, this was issued together with an award document; it was recorded in the individual's pay book and service records, and was worn on the left breast of uniforms.

The metal badge consisted of a vertical oval wreath of Oak Leaves topped by the eagle with a tiny swastika in its talons. In the centre of the wreath was a waterspout rising from the sea, which could indicate either a detonating mine in the mine-clearing role, or a detonating depth charge in the sub-chaser role. The wreath and eagle were gilded, surrounding a silvered waterspout on a toned silver sea. The reverse featured either a vertical or horizontal hinged pin fitting.

M-19, an M35-type minesweeper serving with 3.Minensuchflottille. This type, the first of the modern minesweeper types, formed the vast bulk of the Kriegsmarine's minesweeper force along with the M40. Almost half of those built were lost in action. Some of those that survived went on to serve in the post-war Bundesmarine. (Author's collection)

Minesweepers (*Minensuchboote*)

At the time the Kriegsmarine was formed in 1935 many of its existing minesweepers were rather elderly veterans of World War I. The first modern class to be introduced was the Minensuchboot M35. This proved to be a successful and highly seaworthy vessel with a relatively powerful armament for vessels of this category. It was, however, of fairly complex construction and expensive to produce. The powerplant required extensive and careful maintenance by skilled technicians, a situation that may have been acceptable in peacetime but was less so after wartime manpower demands put great pressure on the numbers of such skilled personnel available. During the latter part of the war the fact that these vessels had oil-fired boilers also restricted their use due to fuel shortages.

Minesweepers were not named, but were given a pennant number prefixed with the letter 'M'.

Minensuchboot M35
The M35 was constructed by a number of different shipyards, and a total of 68 were built. Of this number just over 30 were lost in action during the war. Those that survived were distributed post-war amongst the Allies, with 17 given to the US Navy, 13 to the Soviets and five to the Royal Navy. The US Navy returned five of its M35s to the new German Bundesmarine in the mid 1950s.

M35 Production		
Stülken, Hamburg	M1–3, 10, 13–16, 25–28	Total: 12
Oderwerke, Stettin	M4–6, 11, 17–19, 29–32, 151–156	Total: 17
Flenderwerke, Lübeck	M7–9, 12, 20–24	Total: 9
Lübecker Maschinenbaugesellschaft, Lübeck	M33–34, 81–85	Total: 7
Schichau, Elbing	M35–36	Total: 2
Atlas Werke, Bremen	M37–39	Total: 3
Rickmerswerft, Wesermünde	M101–104	Total: 4
Lindenau, Memel	M131–132	Total: 2
AG Neptun, Rostock	M201–206	Total: 6
Deutsche Werft, Hamburg	M251–256	Total: 6
		Total built: 68

M35 Specifications			
Length	68m	Powerplant	2 x Lentz 3,200hp expansion engines
Beam	8.7m	Top speed	18 knots
Displacement	870 tons	Endurance	5,000 nautical miles
Armament	• 2 x 10.5cm gun • 1 x 3.7cm flak • 2 x 2cm flak • 4 x depth charge launchers up to 30 mines	Complement	107

Minensuchboot M35

Sectional view of an M35 minesweeper. (1) Visible towards the aft end of the deck are a number of mines on their wheeled trolleys. (2) Main armament consisted of a single turret mounted 10.5cm gun forward and aft. (3) The 3m rangefinder which controlled the main armament is mounted on the bridge. (4) Slung from 'goalpost' davits on the starboard side just aft of the funnel is a large motor pinnace, and a small jollyboat is carried on the port side. (Ian Palmer © Osprey Publishing)

Better armed than many enemy types, the German minesweeper was capable of more than just laying or clearing mines. Victory markings on the bridge of this minesweeper show it has shot down or damaged nine enemy aircraft and one gunboat. (Author's collection)

Minensuchboot M40

This type was of similar specification to the M35 but utilized a simpler method of construction, and featured coal-fired rather than oil-fired boilers, making them less dependent on Germany's dwindling oil reserves in the second half of the war. A total of 131 of the class were built, predominantly in shipyards in occupied Holland. These boats did not replace the M35 class, production of which continued.

As with the M35 type, these boats were eventually up-gunned, the ultimate version carrying one 10.5cm gun, two twin and one single 3.7cm flak, one 2cm *Flakvierling*, two twin 2cm flak and two machine guns.

Around half of the M40 boats built were lost in action during the war; of those that survived 25 went to the US Navy, 30 to the Soviets and 13 to the Royal Navy. As with the M35s, five of the boats that had served in the US Navy were returned to the new *Bundesmarine* in the 1950s. Interestingly, a handful of this highly successful type were still serving in the Romanian Navy in the mid 1990s.

M40 Specifications			
Length	62.3m	**Powerplant**	2 x 2,400hp expansion engines
Beam	8.9m	**Top speed**	17 knots
Displacement	775 tons	**Endurance**	4,000 nautical miles
Armament	1 x 10.5cm gun 1 x 3.7cm flak 2 x 2cm flak 4 x depth charge launchers up to 30 mines	**Complement**	74

M40 Production		
Atlas Werke, Bremen	M261–267	Total: 7
Rickmerswerft, Wesermünde	M271–279	Total: 9
Lindenau, Memel	M291–294	Total: 4
Unterweser Schiffsbaugesellschaft, Lehe	*M301–307*	Total: 7
Oderwerke, Stettin	–	Total: 8
Lübecker Maschinenbaugesellschaft, Lübeck	M329–330	Total: 2
AG Neptun, Rostock	M341–348	Total: 8
Schichau, Elbing	M361–377	Total: 17
Elsflether Werft, Elsflether	M381–389	Total: 9
Rotterdamsche Droogdok, Rotterdam	M401–408	Total: 8
Königliche Mij, De Schelde, Vlissingen	M411–416	Total: 6
Wilton Fijenoord, Schiedam	M421–428	Total: 8
Nederlandsche Scheepsbouw, Amsterdam	M431–438	Total: 8
Naamlooze Vennootschap Maschinefabriken & Scheepwerft	M441–446	Total: 6
NV Werft Gusto, Schiedam	M451–456	Total: 6
Nederlandsche Dok, Amsterdam	M459–463	Total: 5
Vd Giessen & Zones Scheepwerven, Krimpen	M467–471	Total: 5
J. & K. Smidt, Kinderdijk	M475–476	Total: 2
Boele's Scheepswerven & Maschinefabrik, Bolnes	M483–484	Total: 2
Verschure & Co Scheepswerven, Amsterdam	M486	Total: 1
NVL Smit & Zoon, Kinderdijk	M489	Total: 1
Scheepsbouwerft Gebr, Bolnes	M495–496	Total: 2
		Total built: 131

Minensuchboot M43

This final minesweeper type to be built for the Kriegsmarine made use of prefabricated sections, so construction could be dispersed and only final assembly required shipyard facilities. Although more than 160 were ordered only 17 were ultimately built, though a number of others were in various stages of completion when the war ended. Far more powerfully armed and, like the M40s, equipped with coal-fired boilers, examples of these vessels served on into the 1960s.

M43 Specifications			
Length	67.8m	Powerplant	2 x 2,400hp expansion engines
Beam	9m	Top speed	17 knots
Displacement	821 tons	Endurance	3,600 nautical miles
Armament	• 2 x 10.5cm guns • 2 x 3.7cm flak • 1 x 2cm *Flakvierling* • 4 x depth charge launchers up to 24 mines	Complement	90

M43 Production	
AG Neptun, Rostock	M601–612 Total: 12
Schichau, Königsberg	M801–805 Total: 5
	Total built: 17

Operational deployment of minesweepers

Minesweepers served on every front on which the Kriegsmarine was involved, from the Arctic to the Mediterranean. In the list that follows, 'Channel' refers to the English Channel, and active dates which conclude after 1945 refer to units that were maintained post-war for mine-clearing under Allied control.

Minesweeper Flotillas

Flotilla	Location	Active	Flotilla	Location	Active
1.Minensuch-Flottille	Baltic/North Sea	1924–45	22.Minensuch-Flottille	North Sea/Norway/Baltic	1942–45
2.Minensuch-Flottille	Baltic/North Sea	1936–44	23.Minensuch-Flottille	Norway/Baltic	1942–47
3.Minensuch-Flottille	Norway/Baltic	1940–45	24.Minensuch-Flottille	Channel Islands	1942–45
4.Minensuch-Flottille	North Sea/Atlantic coast	1939–45	25.Minensuch-Flottille	North Sea/Norway/Baltic	1942–45
5.Minensuch-Flottille	Norway/North Sea/Baltic	1940–47	26.Minensuch-Flottille	French coast	1943–44
6.Minensuch-Flottille	North Sea/Atlantic coast	1939–44	27.Minensuch-Flottille	North Sea/Holland	1943–45
7.Minensuch-Flottille	Baltic/North Sea	1939–45	28.Minensuch-Flottille	Atlantic coast/Channel	1943–44
8.Minensuch-Flottille	Atlantic coast	1941–45	29.Minensuch-Flottille	Kattegatt/Skagerak	1943–45
9.Minensuch-Flottille	Norway	1943–47	30.Minensuch-Flottille	Norway	1943–45
10.Minensuch-Flottille	Atlantic coast	1943–44	31.Minensuch-Flottille	Holland/Baltic	1940–45
11.Minensuch-Flottille	North Sea/Baltic/Norway	1939–45	32.Minensuch-Flottille	Holland	1940–44
12.Minensuch-Flottille	Baltic/North Sea	1939–47	34.Minensuch-Flottille	Holland	1940–45
13.Minensuch-Flottille	Baltic/North Sea	1939–42	36.Minensuch-Flottille	Holland/Baltic	1940–45
14.Minensuch-Flottille	North Sea	1939–41	38.Minensuch-Flottille	Channel/Holland/Kattegat	1940–45
15.Minensuch-Flottille	Baltic/Norway	1939–43	40.Minensuch-Flottille	French coast	1940–44
16.Minensuch-Flottille	North Sea/Channel	1939–43	42.Minensuch-Flottille	French coast	1940–44
17.Minensuch-Flottille	Baltic/North Sea/Norway	1939–42	44.Minensuch-Flottille	French coast	1940–44
18.Minensuch-Flottille	North Sea/Channel /Norway	1939–42	46.Minensuch-Flottille	French coast	1942–45
			52.Minensuch-Flottille	Norway	1941–45
19.Minensuch-Flottille	Baltic/Norway	1939–43	54.Minensuch-Flottille	Norway	1940–44
21.Minensuch-Flottille	North Sea/Norway/Baltic	1942–45	56.Minensuch-Flottille	Norway	1940–45
			70.Minensuch-Flottille	Mediterranean	1943–44

Motor Minesweepers (*Räumboote*)

The *Räumboote* (R-boats) were basically small motor minesweepers for inshore work, often doubling as patrol boats or escorts. The first was ordered in 1930 from the firm of Lürssen, the principal manufacturer of S-boats, and indeed there was a resemblance in appearance between R-boats and S-boats, the principal difference being that the former did not carry torpedoes. The first batch consisted of 16 boats, with R1–R8 displacing 43 tons and R9–R16 increased to 52 tons. Armament consisted of only a single heavy machine gun and up to six mines. These earlier boats can be easily

RIGHT A typical *Räumboot* – a multi-purpose vessel used as a patrol boat, sub-chaser or minesweeper. Manufactured by the same firms which made the E-boats, these excellent little vessels gave sterling service throughout the war. A large number were produced and many survived to serve after the war. (Author's collection)

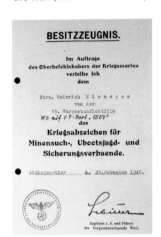

ABOVE An award document for the Minesweeper Badge to Steuermann Heinrich Niemeyer, an NCO on a Vorpostenboot VP-1507 and who progressed to become an officer and commander of first U-547, then U-1233. Sinking two merchants and a warship, he earned the German Cross in Gold. (Author's collection)

identified in photographs by the raised forecastle in contrast to the flush-decked appearance of later boats.

A larger version was introduced in 1934; R17–R24 displaced 120 tons and carried two 2cm guns and up to eight mines. In 1936 a similar, slightly smaller variant but with greater draft appeared, numbered R21 to R40. Both 1934 and 1936 types remained in production during the war. An even larger version, displacing 165 tons, was brought into service in 1942; more than 200 were ordered but only around 75 completed. This type had a heavier armament of one 3.7cm and two 2cm guns.

One interesting development of the R-boat arose from the need for small, shallow-draft vessels for use in the narrow fjords of occupied Norway. In October 1940 the officer commanding one unit, Kapitänleutnant Hans Bartels, commissioned the construction of his own highly successful small vessels based on Norwegian fishing-boat designs. These 12 boats were called *Zwerge* ('dwarves') and were to become known as the *Tigerverband*, all vessels flying a pennant bearing a snarling tiger's head over crossed swords. To foster unit morale Bartels even had a small commemorative pin made with this emblem, which was awarded with a special certificate to members of the unit.

Despite his success, higher command did not appreciate junior officers acting on their own initiative in this way, and Bartels found himself posted as first officer to the destroyer Z-34.

Outpost or Patrol Boats (*Vorpostenboote*)

Vorpostenboote, literally 'outpost boats', was an all-encompassing term used for a wide variety of vessels used for patrol work, forming outer protective screens for convoys and guarding numerous smaller ports. These were primarily former whaling and fishing vessels, and included large numbers of so-called 'booty ships' confiscated or captured from defeated nations. So great was the number and variety of vessels used in these roles that when studying photographs of VP-boats it is difficult to find two that are identical. These boats were organized in 33 *Vorpostenbootflottillen*, operating in the following areas:

Räumboote Flotillas

Flotilla	Location	Active
1.Räumbootsflottille	Baltic/North Sea/Channel	1939–47
2.Räumbootsflottille	North Sea/Channel	1939–44
3.Räumbootsflottille	Baltic/North Sea/Channel/Black Sea	1939–44
4.Räumbootsflottille	North Sea	1940–45
5.Räumbootsflottille	Baltic/North Sea	1939–45
6.Räumbootsflottille	Channel/Mediterranean/Adriatic	1941–45
7.Räumbootsflottille	Channel/North Sea	1940–46
8.Räumbootsflottille	North Sea/Channel	1942–46
9.Räumbootsflottille	Channel	1942–47
10.Räumbootsflottille	Channel	1942–44
11.Räumbootsflottille	Channel	1939–40, 1942–44
12.Räumbootsflottille	Channel/Adriatic/Aegean	1942–45
13.Räumbootsflottille	North Sea	1942–57
14.Räumbootsflottille	Channel/Baltic/North Sea	1943–46
15.Räumbootsflottille	Baltic/North Sea	1944–45
16.Räumbootsflottille	Norway	1944–47
17.Räumbootsflottille	Baltic/Channel	1944–47
21.Räumbootsflottille	Norway	1943–46
25.Räumbootsflottille	North Sea	1943–46
30.Räumbootsflottille	Black Sea	1943–44

Vorpostenboot Flotillas

Area	Flotillas
Baltic	1, 3, 5, 7, 9, 11, 13, 15, 17, 19
North Sea	2, 4, 6, 8, 10, 12, 14, 16, 18, 20
France	2, 4, 6, 7, 15, 18
Holland	8, 11, 13, 14, 20
Denmark	9, 10, 16, 18, 19
Norway	63, 64, 65, 66, 67, 68
Mediterranean	70

ABOVE A *Zimmermannsmaat* (Carpenter) wearing the Minesweeper Badge. The anchors on his collar tabs indicate he is serving as a war correspondent. Many sailors 'cut their teeth' serving on minesweepers before going on to other branches. This badge was often seen worn in conjunction with other war badges earned on different types of vessel. (DUBM)

LEFT The Vorpostenboote, were small patrol boats very often converted from civilian trawlers. Although some were purpose built, the majority were of non-military origin pressed into service as well as foreign vessels which had been captured. Surviving examples of these robust little vessels were also used in post-war mine clearing. (DUBM)

As well as captured and requisitioned former civil vessels, a number of purpose-built types were constructed, based on civilian fishing boat designs, these being known for being extremely sturdy and seaworthy. Such vessels were designated as *Kriegsfischcutter,* and as well as patrol work they might be used for minesweeping and anti-submarine duties.

Sub-Chasers (*U-Jagd boote*)

Although a small number of dedicated sub-chaser units (*Unterseebootsjagdflottillen*) were formed, the bulk of anti-submarine operations were carried out by a mixture of minesweepers and VP-boats rather than by vessels specifically designed as anti-submarine warships. It had originally been intended that a range of such purpose-built ships would be constructed, and specifications were drawn up. It was eventually decided, however, that given the size and specification of the proposed vessels, and the issues of shipyard availability and the need not to waste time and resources on unnecessary diversification, that the task of anti-submarine work could be undertaken by existing vessels, particularly the M35 minesweeper. With no specific type of purpose-built sub-chaser vessel, the term was used to describe any boat allocated to such duties.

Unterseebootsjagd Flottillen		
Flotilla	**Location**	**Active**
1.U-Bootsjagd-Flottille	Black Sea/Baltic	1943–44
2.U-Bootsjagd-Flottille	Adriatic	1944
3.U-Bootsjagd-Flottille	Black Sea/Baltic	1944
11.U-Bootsjagd-Flottille	Baltic/Norway	1939–45
12.U-Bootsjagd-Flottille	North Sea	1939–45
14.U-Bootsjagd-Flottille	Norway/France	1940–45
17.U-Bootsjagd-Flottille	Norway	1939–45
21.U-Bootsjagd-Flottille	Aegean	1941–44
22.U-Bootsjagd-Flottille	Western Mediterranean	1942–45
23.U-Bootsjagd-Flottille	Black Sea	1944

General-Purpose Boats (*Mehrzweckboote*)

Orders for the production of a new class of escort boat were given in March 1943. The new vessel was effectively to be a more powerful version of the R-boat with heavier armament including, significantly, torpedoes. The new vessel was intended to replace a number of other types such as R-boats and VP-boats. The result was a stylish, 290-ton boat, 52m long and with a 7.2m beam. A single 6-cylinder diesel engine would give it a speed of just 14 knots, sufficient for its role of escorting slower vessels.

Armament consisted of two 8.8cm, one 3.7cm and eight 2cm flak guns. Two torpedo tubes were fitted, emerging from the hull near the bow in a somewhat similar manner to those on S-boats.

It was originally intended that 12 boats would be built by the Stülcken yard in Hamburg, but in the event only one was ever completed, MZ1. This boat was built in a conventional manner, but it was intended that future boats would be assembled from prefabricated sections. MZ1 was launched on 16 April 1944 and was well received. Had Germany's military and industrial situation not been so bad by this date it is likely that significant numbers of this new type would have been constructed, but all that existed by the end of the war was MZ1 and the keels of three more partially constructed boats. Records of MZ1's use and eventual fate are virtually non-existent. It is believed that it was captured by British forces when Eckernförde fell, but there seems to be no record of what befell it.

Barrier-Breakers (*Sperrbrecher*)

The purpose of the *Sperrbrecher,* rather than to clear minefields, was to escort ships into and out of German-held ports along cleared paths through defensive minefield barriers, and to detonate any mines that might have been laid by the enemy in these clear paths.

Most Sperrbrecher began their lives as merchant vessels, and were crewed by merchant seamen with a small cadre of naval personnel. These were termed 'Special Purpose Merchant Ships' (*Handelsdampfer zb V*). Others were crewed entirely by naval personnel. Both German-built and captured foreign vessels were pressed into service as *Sperrbrecher*. It was typical for a Sperrbrecher to have its hold filled with buoyant material to help keep it afloat should it run into a mine, and for the bows to be significantly strengthened. Nevertheless, the detonation of a powerful mine could easily break the back of a ship, so service on this type of vessel must have required strong nerves on the part of its crew. Photos of Sperrbrecher will often show a metal beam set just forward of the bow, intended to detonate any mine before it touched the hull itself.

The Sperrbrecher or barrier-breaker. These ships sailed as 'pathfinders' clearing a way through minefields so that warships could pass in safety. With reinforced hulls, magnetic mine clearing equipment and with their hulls filled with bouyant material they would in many cases absorb damage that would sink other ships. (Author's collection)

191

Armament on each Sperrbrecher varied; as they were never expected to engage enemy surface ships it tended to consist primarily of anti-aircraft guns, but these might be numerous. Typical armament in the second half of the war might comprise two 10.5cm, six 3.7cm and 14 x 2cm guns. In addition, many Sperrbrecher were equipped with barrage balloons.

Barrier-breakers were organized into a total of seven *Sperrbrecher-Flottillen*. Like the minesweepers, more than one unit remained in service after the war, making safe the waters around Europe's coasts.

Escort Boats (*Geleitboote*)

A distinction must be drawn between improvised and purpose-built escorts. A class of fleet escorts (*Flottenbegleiter*) were planned and built, their pennant numbers being prefixed with 'F'. However, only ten were ever constructed.

Sperrbrecher-Flottillen		
Flotilla	**Location**	**Active**
1.Sperrbrecher-Flottille	Baltic/German Bight	1940–46
2.Sperrbrecher-Flottille	Channel/Bay of Biscay	1939–44
3.Sperrbrecher-Flottille	Baltic	1940–46
4.Sperrbrecher-Flottille	Channel	1941–43
5.Sperrbrecher-Flottille	–	never operational; existed only 1 month
6.Sperrbrecher-Flottille	Bay of Biscay	1941–44
8.Sperrbrecher-Flottille	North Sea/Channel	1941–45

Sperrbrecher in Kiel harbour, 1941. These were usually re-purposed merchant ships and often carried extensive camouflage schemes. They also carried significant defensive armament. These ships suffered heavy losses during the war with around 50 per cent losses, though several survived to service as merchant ships once again. (Sobotta/ullstein bild via Getty Images)

Flottenbegleiter Construction

Germaniawerft, Kiel	F1 to F6	Total: 6
Blohm & Voss, Hamburg	F7 to F8	Total: 2
Kriegsmarinewerft, Wilhelmshaven	F9 to F10	Total: 2
	Total built: 10	

Flottenbegleiter Specifications

Length	68m	**Powerplant**	2 x 14,000hp turbines
Beam	8.7m	**Top speed**	18 knots
Displacement	870 tons	**Endurance**	5,000 nautical miles
Armament	• 1 x 10.5cm gun • 1 x 3.7cm flak • 4 x 2cm flak • 4 x depth charge launchers up to 30 mines	**Complement**	24

The first was launched in December 1935 and the last by March 1938. The principal purpose for which they were designed was to act as an inner escort screen for the 'pocket battleships' *Deutschland*, *Admiral Graf Spee* and *Admiral Scheer*. Due to technical problems with the type of high-pressure boilers installed in these vessels, they were not considered successful and no more were ordered. They were organized into two flotillas.

Due to their limitations, it was decided that these vessels could best be employed as minesweepers; but problems during exercises raised questions over their speed, manoeuvrability and endurance as well as the reliability of their engines, and led to the

Geleitflottille

1.Geleitflottille	F1, F2, F5, F6, F9, F10
2.Geleitflottille	F3, F4, F7, F8

This shot shows a fleet escort, or Flottenbegleiter, a type of which only ten were commissioned. These were purpose-built escort vessels rather than other types pressed into the role. They were an unsuccessful type, suffering from poor stability and sea-keeping as well as frequent power plant breakdowns. Half survived the war but were soon scrapped. (Author's collection)

disbandment of 2.Geleitflottille. The Geleitboote were finally judged to be of so little effective value that even before the outbreak of war it was decided to delegate them to various non-combat duties.

However, the outbreak of war in September 1939 put paid to these plans. Under wartime conditions the navy had to make the best it could of these boats; but by December, F9 had been lost when torpedoed by a British submarine, and the others

Geleitboote Flotilla Intended Duties, 1939	
F1	Allocated as a command ship to Führer der Minensuchboote Ost
F2, F4, F7	Converted into torpedo-recovery vessels
F3, F6	Converted into tenders, with most armament removed and extra accommodation added
F5, F8, F9, F10	Allocated to the Anti-Submarine Warfare School as training vessels

had performed so badly that the plan to remove them from operational service was revived. Any thoughts of trying to refit and improve these boats was quickly discarded as a waste of dockyard time and resources.

Accordingly, F2, F5, F7, F8 and F10 were simply handed over to the U-boat arm for use as torpedo recovery vessels and submarine escorts. F1 was allocated to the *Führer der Zerstörer* (Head of Destroyers) as a tender/command vessel; F3, allocated to the *Führer der Minensuchboote* (Head of Minesweepers) in the same role, was sunk by rocket-firing aircraft in May 1945. F4 served as a trials vessel with *Sperrversuchskommando* (Experimental Mine Command) and *Torpedoversuchsanhalt* (Experimental Torpedo Command), but returned to minelaying in 1944. F6 took part in the attack on Norway, allocated to the Führer der Minensuchboote (West); it saw service in minelaying and escort duties throughout the war, eventually being sunk by Allied aircraft during an attack on Wilhelmshaven in April 1945.

Despite their serious limitations these ships were relatively fortunate in that six of the ten survived the war, and a number served on under the less demanding needs of peacetime; indeed, F7 served in the Soviet Navy until at least 1956.

Although these purpose-built Flottenbegleiter were a complete failure, the concept of allocating vessels into units specifically tasked with escort work survived them. In all seven flotillas were created and deployed operationally.

There were several additional small units under the control of the Sicherungsverbände. *Netzsperrverband* units maintained the boom defence nets around German ports and naval bases. The vessels were classed as *Netzleger* (netlayers) and *Netztender*. The flotillas into which these units were formed were designated by area rather than number, i.e. *Netzsperrflottille Nord*.

Hafenschutzflottillen (harbour-protection flotillas) were generally formed of small craft such as armed trawlers and armed tugboats and, as the name suggests, were permanently based in ports to protect the installations. There were three such flotillas

Geleitflottille Deployment			
1.Geleitflottille (reformed)	Adriatic	1944–45	
2.Geleitflottille (reformed)	Adriatic	1944–45	
3.Geleitflottille	Mediterranean	1943–44	
4.Geleitflottille	Mediterranean	1943–44	
5.Geleitflottille	Baltic	1945	
30.Geleitflottille	Black Sea	1943–44	
31.Geleitflottille	Black Sea	1942–44	

based in major German naval bases: Hafenschutzflottille Cuxhaven, Hafenschutzflottille Wilhelmshaven and Hafenschutzflottille Borkum.

Torpedo Boats

To British and American ears the term torpedo boat conjures up images of the MTB (Motor Torpedo Boat) or PT-boat (Patrol Torpedo Boat) – a small, fast, motor-launch type of vessel relying on its high speed to survive attacks on enemy shipping. Nothing could be further removed from the reality of a German *Torpedoboote*, which in fact was a small destroyer akin to the US destroyer escort.

M23 and M24 Boats

On the outbreak of war the bulk of the Kriegsmarine's torpedo boat fleet was made up of vessels that had been built in the second half of the 1920s and were already somewhat dated. All were built at the Marinewerft in Wilhelmshaven; the first batch of six were designated as the Raubvogel (Wild Bird) class, and named accordingly as follows: *Möwe* (Seagull), *Seeadler* (Sea Eagle), *Greif* (Griffon Vulture), *Albatros*, *Kondor* and *Falke* (Falcon). A second batch of six, the Raubtier (Wild Animal) class, consisted of the following: *Wolf*, *Iltis* (Polecat), *Luchs* (Lynx), *Tiger*, *Jaguar* and *Leopard*.

M23 (Raubvogel class) Specifications			
Length	87m	**Powerplant**	2 x Schichau 23,000hp turbines
Beam	8.3m	**Top speed**	33 knots
Displacement	898 tons	**Endurance**	1,800 nautical miles
Armament	• 3 x 10.5cm guns • 4 x 3.7cm flak • 4 x 2cm flak • 6 x torpedo tubes • 4 x depth charge launchers • up to 30 mines	**Complement**	120–130

M24 (Raubvogel class) Specifications			
Length	92.6m	Powerplant	2 x Schichau 23,000hp turbines
Beam	8.6m	Top speed	34 knots
Displacement	933 tons	Endurance	2,000 nautical miles
Armament	• 3 x 10.5cm guns • 4 x 3.7cm flak • 4 x 2cm flak • 6 x torpedo tubes • 4 x depth charge launchers • up to 30 mines	Complement	120–130

M35 Boats

Despite various improvements and refits it was clear that a more modern type would be required, and in 1935 a new design was approved for construction. Between 1936 and 1942 a total of 21 of these M35 types (including an improved but basically similar variant introduced in 1937) were built. This class were not named but identified by a pennant number prefixed with 'T' for 'Torpedoboot':

M35 Class Specifications			
Length	84m	Powerplant	2 x Wagner 31,000hp turbines
Beam	8.6m	Top speed	34.5 knots
Displacement	859 tons	Endurance	1,070 nautical miles
Armament	1 x 10.5cm gun 1 x 3.7cm flak 2 x 2cm flak 6 x torpedo tubes 4 x depth charge launchers up to 30 mines	Complement	117

M35 Construction		
Schichau, Elbing	T1–4, T9–10, T13–21	Total: 15
Deschimag, Bremen	T5–6, T11–12	Total: 6
	Total built: 21	

There were nine torpedo boat flotillas numbered sequentially 1–7 and 9–10, the 8th Flotilla never becoming operational.

M23/M24 and M35 Deployments

The M23 and M24 torpedo boats were active during the Spanish Civil War as part of Germany's 'non-intervention' patrols. All vessels of both classes were also involved in escort work for the invasion fleet during the attack on Norway in April 1940. By the

COASTAL AND OTHER VESSELS

Torpedobootsflottille Deployment

1.Torpedobootsflottille (formed pre-war)

1939–April 1941	North Sea and English Channel
April–August 1941	Baltic
August 1941	Stood down

2.Torpedobootsflottille (formed pre-war)

1940–41	Operational in Channel
1941	Operational in Baltic
1942–43	Defensive minelaying in Western waters
1943–44	Training flotilla
1944–45	Escort service in Baltic

3.Torpedobootsflottille (formed April 1941)

1941–42	Working-up and training exercises
1942	Minelaying in Western waters
1943–44	Training duties with Torpedo School, and combined operations with U-boats in Baltic
1944–45	Patrol and security duties in eastern Baltic and Skagerak

4.Torpedobootsflottille (formed February 1943)

1943–44	Minelaying and escort duties in Western waters
April 1944	Stood down

5.Torpedobootsflottille (formed pre-war)

1939–40	Defensive minelaying, escort duties and anti-shipping operations in Western waters
1940	Invasion of Norway; escort and security duties in Skagerak
1941–44	Escort duties; offensive and defensive minelaying in Western waters
1944	Based on French Channel coast; all ships destroyed during Normandy invasion campaign
1944–45	Re-formed; served in Finnish waters and eastern Baltic escorting evacuation operations

6.Torpedobootsflottille (formed pre-war)

1939–40	Minelaying, escort and anti-shipping operations in Western waters
1940–41	Security and escort duties during invasion of Norway; minelaying and escort duty
February 1941	Stood down

7.Torpedobootsflottille (formed November 1943)

1943–44	Operational in Finnish waters, and defensive minelaying in Baltic
August 1944	Stood down

9.Torpedobootsflottllle (formed late summer 1943)

1943–44	Operational in Aegean
October 1944	Stood down

10.Torpedobootsflottille (formed January 1944)

1944–45	Operational in Mediterranean

end of that campaign four of the 12 vessels had been lost, and the remaining eight were thereafter grouped together in 5.Torpedobootsflottille. During the second half of 1940 the flotilla was heavily involved in minelaying operations in the English Channel, and also in 'hit and run' attacks on British merchant shipping.

Five of these warships – *Seeadler, Kondor, Falke, Iltis* and *Jaguar* – were also involved in Operation *Cerberus* (the 'Channel Dash'), escorting the battleships *Scharnhorst* and *Gneisenau*, and the heavy cruiser *Prinz Eugen*, during their run eastwards through the English Channel in February 1942; *Jaguar* was severely damaged by British aircraft during this operation. On 14/15 May 1942, *Seeadler, Iltis, Kondor* and *Falke* formed part of the escort screen for the auxiliary cruiser *Stier* as it broke out into the Atlantic through the Channel. The German ships came under fire from both longrange coastal artillery at Dover and from British MTBs, and both *Iltis* and *Seeadler* were sunk.

The remainder of these elderly boats continued to give good service until the summer of 1944, when they were all destroyed in Allied bombing raids connected with the Normandy invasion. The individual fates of the M23 and M24 class are given below.

The more modern M35 torpedo boat design was certainly more stylish in appearance than that of their elderly forerunners, but the use of high-pressure turbines as fitted in the larger German destroyers resulted in their suffering similar technical problems. They were also poor seagoing vessels, and could not be used for minelaying except in calm weather; one of their perceived positive points had been their anticipated ability to carry out high-speed, short-range minelaying sorties. In addition to their other shortcomings, they also had relatively light armament. Most of them were relegated to non-combat duties, assigned to U-boat training flotillas in the Baltic.

The M35 torpedo boats first became operational in late 1940 with 1.Torpedobootsflottille, which had been created a year earlier; it had taken this length of time to deliver the boats allocated to the flotilla in serviceable condition following numerous powerplant failures.

This flotilla was disbanded in August 1941. During its short life T1 was severely damaged after running aground; T2 had to spend several months in dock for repairs when it was damaged by a bomb dropped by a British aircraft while escorting a

M23 and M24 Boats Operational History			
Vessel	Launched	Commissioned	Fate
Möwe	March 1926	October 1926	Sunk at moorings in Le Havre during air raid, 15 June 1944
Seeadler	July 1926	May 1927	Sunk in action with British MTBs in the Channel, 13 May 1942
Albatros	July 1926	May 1927	Beached May 1940 after running on to a reef
Greif	July 1926	March 1927	Sunk in Seine estuary during air raid, 23 May 1944
Kondor	September 1926	July 1927	Sunk at moorings in Le Havre during air raid, 31 July 1944
Falke	September 1926	August 1927	Sunk at moorings in Le Havre during air raid, 15 June 1944
Wolf	October 1927	November 1928	Sunk by British mine off Dunkirk, 8 January 1941
Iltis	October 1927	October 1928	Sunk in action with British MTBs in the Channel, 13 May 1942
Luchs	March 1928	April 1929	Sunk in North Sea by British submarine HMS *Swordfish*, 26 July 1940
Tiger	March 1928	January 1929	Sunk in collision with German destroyer *Max Schulz*, 25 August 1939
Jaguar	March 1928	June 1929	Sunk at moorings in Le Havre during air raid, 15 June 1944
Leopard	March 1928	June 1929	Sunk in collision with German minelayer Preussen, 1 April 1940

minelaying mission; T3 was sunk during a bombing raid on Le Havre (though it was later raised); and T6 was lost when it ran onto a mine.

The 2.Torpedobootsflottille began operations in the summer of 1940. Shortly after the flotilla moved to France, T11 was severely damaged in a bombing attack and subsequently spent several months in repair dock. Availability of operational boats was a constant problem, since regular visits to the dockyard for repairs were required. The flotilla did perform some useful tasks, particularly in the escort role, and was involved in the successful 'Channel Dash'; but from mid 1943 to mid 1944 no operational sorties were undertaken. T2 and T4 were sunk during a bombing raid on Bremen, and although refloated they never returned to service. Although T3 did succeed in sinking a Soviet submarine in January 1945, the late stages of the war were spent on escorting convoys in the Baltic; during one such mission both T3 and T5 were sunk by mines laid by a Soviet submarine.

M39 Boats

The largely unsuccessful M35 class would be followed by an even larger type known as the M39 or Fleet Torpedo Boats (*Flotten-Torpedoboote*). Construction was again shared between Schichau and Deschimag, but in the event only the batch of 16 awarded to the Schichau yard at Elbing were completed, and numbered T22 to T36.

T35, an M39 'Elbing'-class Torpedoboot, at speed, shown here after its surrender when it was taken to the USA for trials. A huge improvement on the M23, larger and with more powerful armament, the M39 class were excellent warships. Unfortunately for the Kriegsmarine only 16 were built. (NHHC)

M39 Flotten-Torpedoboote Specifications			
Length	102.5m	Top speed	30 knots
Beam	10m	Endurance	2,400 nautical miles
Displacement	294 tons		
Armament	• 4 x 10.5cm guns • 4 x 3.7cm flak • 2 x 2cm flak • 6 x torpedo tubes • 4 x depth charge launchers • up to 50 mines	Complement	198

After the problems suffered by the M35 type the M39 'Elbing'-class boats were a massive improvement, and true multi-role warships rather than simply torpedo boats. Bigger and heavier than their predecessors, this class was almost a hybrid between the smaller torpedo boats and the larger destroyers; they were seaworthy, fast and highly manoeuvrable. Much of the work performed by this class was on escort duties and they were certainly capable of giving a good account of themselves. Since most of the ports in the West had been lost by the time the last five were commissioned, those spent their active careers in the Baltic.

M39 Boats Operational History		
Vessel	Commissioned	Fate
T22	February 1942	Sunk with loss of 143 crew when it ran onto one of its own mines, 18 August 1944
T23	June 1942	Survived the war; taken into service by the British in 1946
T24	October 1942	Sunk with loss of 18 crew by British air attack, 24 August 1944
T25	December 1942	Sunk with loss of 85 crew during engagement in Bay of Biscay with British destroyers HMS *Glasgow* and *Enterprise*, 28 December 1943
T26	February 1943	Lost with 90 crew in same engagement as *T25*
T27	April 1943	Ran aground after engagement with Canadian destroyer off Breton coast, later destroyed by Allied aircraft; most of its crew survived
T28	June 1942	Survived the war; taken into service by the British in 1945
T29	August 1943	Sunk with loss of 137 crew by gunfire and torpedoes from British cruiser HMS *Black Prince* and destroyers HMS *Haida, Huron, Ashanti* and *Athebascan*, 26 April 1944
T30	October 1943	Sunk with loss of 114 crew when it ran into German minefield, 18 August 1944
T31	February 1944	Sunk with loss of 82 crew by torpedo from Soviet MTB, 20 June 1944
T32	May 1944	Sunk with loss of 137 crew when it ran into German minefield, 18 August 1944 (see *T30*)
T33	June 1944	Survived the war; taken into service by the Soviet Navy
T34	August 1944	Sunk with loss of 62 crew off Cap Arcona by torpedo from Soviet submarine *L3*, 20 November 1944
T35	October 1944	Survived the war; taken into service by US Navy
T36	December 1944	Sunk with loss of 63 crew by mine and Soviet aircraft off Usedom, 4 May 1945

Probably the best known of the German supply ships was the *Altmark*. With 300 British prisoners on board, being those taken from ships sunk by the raider *Graf Spee*, it was cornered in a Norwegian fjord by the destroyer HMS *Cossak* on 16 February 1940 and the prisoners rescued. (Keystone/Getty Images)

Fleet Auxiliary Supply Ships (*Tross-Schiffe*)

In common with other nations, the German Navy commandeered many merchant vessels for military use. These were classified into a whole range of supply ship classes, many of which retained their original merchant navy crews on temporary secondment to the Kriegsmarine for the duration of hostilities. A typical example was the *Jan Wellem*, the mothership of the German whaling fleet, which served with its original merchant navy crew in the invasion of Norway and was severely damaged at Narvik.

However, there were also a small number of purpose-built fleet auxiliaries of the Dithmarschen class, produced in 1936 and 1937. It had originally been intended that these ships could double as auxiliary cruisers; it was later decided that their role as supply ships was too valuable to divert them onto combat duties as auxiliary warships, but their original intended role was reflected in the manner in which their main

As well as the navy's own ships, merchant vessels were used by the Kriegsmarine to bring supplies through the Allied blockade. One successful blockade runner shown here was the *Anneliese Essberger*. After reaching Germany, many of their crews were drafted into the Kriegsmarine. This ship was intercepted during its second blockade-breaking attempt and scuttled by its crew on 21 November 1942. (W. E. Frost via Vancouver City Archives)

ABOVE Crews of ships which successfully ran the Allied blockade and brought much-needed supplies back to Germany were awarded the *Abzeichen für Blockadebrecher* (Blockade Runners Badge). This badge was awarded to both merchant navy and Kriegsmarine personnel. It was designed by Otto Placzek of Berlin. (Author's collection)

ABOVE RIGHT The supply ship *Dithmarschen*, one of only five of its class built, survived the war and was handed over to the USA where it served as the USS *Conecuh*. This image shows it with a bow gun platform added by the US Navy. It is testament to the quality of this class of vessel that it remained in service until 1960. (NHHC)

RIGHT Award Document for the Blockade Breaker Badge awarded to a merchant navy officer, the First Engineer on the tanker *Jan Wellem*, supporting the invasion of Norway recognizing the subsequent safe return to Germany through the Allied blockade. This officer was also one of a small number of merchant navy personnel awarded the Narvik Shield.

armament was concealed behind collapsible panels. As indicated by their official designation as *Flottentross-schiffe*, these vessels came under the control of Fleet command via the *Chef des Tross-schiffverbandes* headquartered in Wilhelmshaven, and not the *Sicherungsverbände*. These ships would typically carry fuel, ammunition, food, machine parts and even mail from home. The crews were Kriegsmarine personnel, but were recruited for the navy from experienced merchant seamen who, already possessing all the seamanship skills required, simply needed to be put through an abbreviated military training programme.

A total of five new supply ships were built: *Dithmarschen*, *Uckermark* (originally *Altmark*), *Nordmark* (originally *Westerwald*), *Ermland* and *Franken*. Only *Dithmarschen* and *Nordmark* survived the war, the former serving with the US Navy until scrapped in 1960, and the latter with the Royal Navy until 1955.

Dithmarschen Class Specifications				
Length	178m	**Powerplant**	2 x Wagner turbines	
Beam	22m	**Top speed**	21 knots	
Displacement	20,860 tons	**Endurance**	12,500 nautical miles	
Armament	• 3 x 15cm guns • 2 x 3.7cm flak • 4 x 2cm flak	**Complement**	100–200	

Tenders/Escorts

Flotillas of smaller vessels such as S-boats and U-boats, which often moved location through various ports in Germany and, during wartime, through occupied Europe, needed a larger support vessel providing feeding, medical treatment, supplies and accommodation facilities. This requirement led to the construction of a number of purpose-built tenders; the exact nomenclature used often changed, though the basic purpose remained. The designation as a tender or escort related to the type of duties performed rather than the type of ship. Tenders were classed as either simply 'Tender', or *Flottentender, Stationstender, Unterseebootstender*, and so forth. As an example of how designations might change for the same ship, the *Saar* will be found referred to as both a Fleet Tender (Flottentender *Saar*) and as a Submarine Escort Ship (U-Bootsbegleitschiff *Saar*). Examples of some of the more important vessels of this type are provided below.

Wilhelm Bauer

Built by Howaldtswerke in Kiel, *Wilhelm Bauer* was the first ship of its class to be completed; it was launched in December 1938 and commissioned in April 1940. In July it became the depot ship for 27.Unterseebootsflottille, and in March 1945 for 25.Unterseebootsflottille. It was bombed and sunk on 8 April 1945, and raised and scrapped in 1950.

The U-boat tender *Waldemar Kophamel*, with two Type VII boats moored alongside. It served as depot ship for both 27. and 24. Unterseebootsflottille. Bombed and sunk in shallow water in December 1944 it was later raised by the Soviets and served as the *Kuban* until 1978. (Author's collection)

Miscellaneous Vessels

(1) Schnellbootsbegleitschiff *Carl Peters*. In keeping with its largely static role its armament consists of anti-aircraft guns.
(2) *Sperrbrecher*. A large number of different types were used in the role of 'barrier-breaker', leading warships in and out of port through minefield lanes.
(3) *Tross-schiff* (Dithmarschen class). This is a typical example of the Dithmarschen-class naval supply ship; all vessels within the class were built to near-identical specifications.
(4) *Lazarettschiff* (hospital ship) *Robert Ley*. Built as a cruise liner for the *Kraft durch Freude* ('Strength through Joy') movement. It is shown here in its guise as a hospital ship in late 1939.
(Ian Palmer ©
Osprey Publishing)

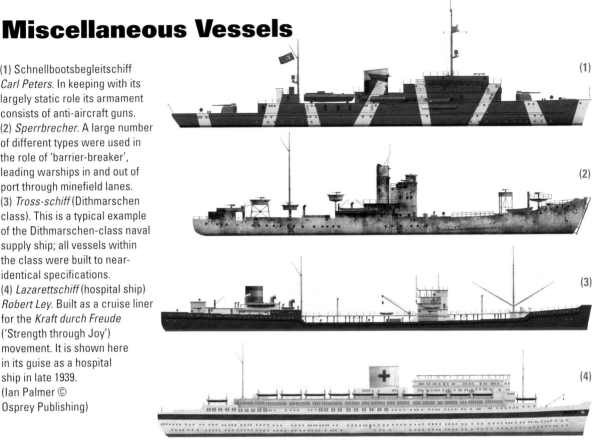

(1)
(2)
(3)
(4)

Wilhelm Bauer Specifications			
Length	132.7m	Powerplant	4 x MAN diesels
Beam	16m	Top speed	20 knots
Displacement	5,600 tons	Endurance	9,000 nautical miles
Armament	• 2 x twin 10.5cm guns • 1 x 4cm flak • 2 x 3.7cm flak • 4 x 2cm flak	Complement	289

Waldemar Kophamel

Launched in May 1939 and commissioned in October 1940, its first allotted task was as depot ship for 27.Unterseebootsflottille. In February 1941 it took over responsibility for 24.Unterseebootsflottille, before returning to its original charges in February 1942. Bombed and sunk by Allied aircraft in December 1944, it was raised by the Soviets in 1950 and taken on strength by the Soviet Navy, serving as the Kuban; it was eventually scrapped in 1978.

Waldemar Kophamel Specifications			
Length	132.7m	**Powerplant**	4 x MAN diesels
Beam	16m	**Top speed**	20 knots
Displacement	5,600 tons	**Endurance**	9,000 nautical miles
Armament	• 2 x twin 10.5cm guns • 1 x 4cm flak • 2 x 3.7cm flak • 4 x 2cm flak	**Complement**	289

Otto Wünsche

Launched in May 1940 but not commissioned until November 1943, _Otto Wünsche_ was the last of the Howaldtswerke-built Willhelm Bauer class. Its assignment until just before the end of the war was as depot ship with 27.Unterseebootsflottille, joining 26.Unterseebootsflottille thereafter. It survived the war, being taken into service by the Soviet Navy as the _Pechora_; it ended its life as an accommodation ship, but was not finally scrapped until 1977.

Otto Wünsche Specifications			
Length	139m	**Powerplant**	4 x MAN diesels
Beam	16m	**Top speed**	21 knots
Displacement	5,900 tons	**Endurance**	9,000 nautical miles
Armament	• 2 x twin 10.5cm guns • 1 x 4cm flak • 2 x 3.7cm flak • 4 x 2cm flak	**Complement**	289

Carl Peters

Built by the Neptun yard in Rostock, _Carl Peters_ was commissioned in January 1940 and became the depot ship for 1.Schnellbootflottille. Its home base was in Kiel but operational deployment of its designated flotilla saw it based variously at Rotterdam and IJmuiden in Holland, and at Abo in Finland. In April 1942 it took over 5.Schnellbootflottille and served with them in Norwegian waters, based first at Trondheim and then at Bodø. Remaining in Norway until December 1943, it returned to German waters to assist in the working-up of 21.Schnellbootflottille.

After a brief period of operational duty in early 1944 it returned to the training role, in which it remained until the end of the war. _Carl Peters_ was sunk just a few days after the war when it ran onto uncleared mines.

Carl Peters Specifications			
Length	114m	**Powerplant**	4 x MAN diesels
Beam	14.5m	**Top speed**	23 knots
Displacement	3,600 tons	**Endurance**	12,000 nautical miles
Armament	• 2 x twin 10.5cm guns • 2 x 8.8cm flak • 1 x 4cm flak • 6 x 3.7cm flak • 8 x 2cm flak	**Complement**	225

Adolf Lüderitz

Sister ship to *Carl Peters*, the *Adolf Lüderitz* was commissioned in June 1940 and became the depot ship for 3.Schnellbootflottille. It was based in Rotterdam until the opening of Operation *Barbarossa* in mid 1941, when 3.Schnellbootflottille moved to the Baltic. In late 1941 it sailed for Norway to become depot ship for 8.Schnellbootflottille at Semskefjord and Kirkenes, and later for 6.Schnellbootflottille at Tromsø. Latterly, *Adolf Lüderitz* served as a wireless communications ship for U-boats operating out of Norway, before returning to Germany for a refit in February 1943. On completion of the refit it joined the S-Boot training flotilla and subsequently the S-Bootelehrdivision, where it remained until the end of the war. *Adolf Lüderitz* was allocated to the Soviet Union, and served as the *Paysherd*.

Adolf Lüderitz Specifications			
Length	114m	**Powerplant**	4 x MAN diesels
Beam	14.5m	**Top speed**	23 knots
Displacement	3,600 tons	**Endurance**	12,000 nautical miles
Armament	• 2 x 10.5cm guns • 1 x 4cm flak • 6 x 3.7cm flak • 8 x 2cm flak	**Complement**	225

Tsingtau

Built by Blohm & Voss in Hamburg, *Tsingtau* was launched in June 1934 and commissioned in September of that year. It was the first tender to be purpose-built as a support ship for the *Schnellboote*, but on the outbreak of war it actually served as a training ship for anti-aircraft crews. It eventually reverted to its intended role, and survived the war unscathed, going on to serve post-war with the German Mine Sweeping Administration (GMSA) under British control. It was eventually broken up in Great Britain in 1950.

The E-boat tender *Tsingtau*. One of the smaller tenders, *Tsingtau* also acted as a flak gunnery training ship. It survived the war and was used under British control for mine clearing operations in the North Sea as part of 4th Minehunting Division. It was eventually scrapped in 1950. (Author's collection)

Tsingtau Specifications

Length	87.5m	**Powerplant**	4 x MAN diesels
Beam	13.5m	**Top speed**	17.5 knots
Displacement	2,400 tons	**Endurance**	8,500 nautical miles
Armament	• 2 x 8.8cm guns • 8 x 2cm flak	**Complement**	149

Tanga

Another product of the Neptun yard, this ship was built for export to China, but the Japanese invasion of that country prevented delivery. The vessel was taken over by the German Navy and commissioned as the *Tanga* in January 1939. It took over the 2.Schnellbootflottille, operating in the Baltic until the beginning of 1940 and thereafter moving to Wilhelmshaven. Moving to the 6.Schnellbootflottille in March 1941, it remained with this training unit until moved to Norway in October 1941. It remained there for a year serving as a radio communications vessel for Kriegsmarine cruisers operating from Norway, returning to Germany in October 1942 for a refit. After its completion it joined the S-Bootlehrdivision, remaining as a depot ship for training units until January 1945; it then took over 11.Schnellbootflottille until the end of the war.

Thereafter, the *Tanga* operated with the GMSA for two years, before being passed to the US Navy. It remained in American hands for a little over a year before transferring to the Danish Navy, with which it had a long and successful career until finally broken up in 1967.

Tanga Specifications

Length	87.5m	**Powerplant**	4 x MAN diesels
Beam	13.5m	**Top speed**	17 knots
Displacement	2,490 tons	**Endurance**	8,500 nautical miles
Armament	• 2 x 8.8cm guns • 8 x 2cm flak	**Complement**	149

Hela

Built by Stückelenwerft in Hamburg, *Hela* was launched in December 1938 and commissioned in October 1940. Designated as a fleet tender (*Flottentender*), it served throughout the war as a fleet command ship. Apart from minor damage suffered during an air raid in April 1945 it survived unscathed, and was taken over by the Soviets, serving as the *Angara*. Damage sustained during a fire in 1995 led to its being deactivated and serving as an accommodation ship. It appears that it has been refitted in more recent times– the sole remaining Kriegsmarine depot ship from World War II.

Hela Specifications			
Length	100m	**Powerplant**	4 x MAN diesels
Beam	12m	**Top speed**	21 knots
Displacement	2,520 tons	**Endurance**	2,000 nautical miles
Armament	• 2 x 10.5cm guns • 2 x 3.7cm flak • 2 x 2cm flak	**Complement**	224

Saar

Built by Germaniawerft in Kiel and commissioned in October 1934, the *Saar* was the first purpose-built tender/support ship, and on being accepted into the navy took up its post as depot ship for 2.Unterseebootsflottille 'Saltzwedel'. During 1935 it served briefly as command ship for the U-boat training programme, before returning to its original role, at first with 1.Unterseebootsflottille 'Weddigen' before returning in 1937 to 2.Unterseebootsflottille.

Following the outbreak of war the *Saar* took part in the invasion of Norway, serving as support ship to all of the U-boat units involved. By the end of the war it was serving as command ship for the *Führer der Unterseeboote Ost*, and after the end of hostilities was handed over to the USA. In 1947 it passed to the French Navy, where it served as a workshop ship under the name *Gustave Zede*.

Saar Specifications			
Length	100.5m	**Powerplant**	2 x 4,800hp diesels
Beam	13.5m	**Top speed**	18.3 knots
Displacement	3,250 tons	**Endurance**	7,265 nautical miles
Armament	• 3 x 10.5cm flak • 8 x 2cm flak	**Complement**	228

Accommodation Ships (*Wohnschiffe*)

The coming of war naturally freed up many German ships that had previously been used for leisure cruises, while the navy found itself in need of accommodation for its sailors as the service expanded. The passenger ships had their bright civilian livery painted over with drab camouflage colours and were given a new career as accommodation ships, often for the crews of U-boat flotillas. Others were used as hospital ships.

The two most important ships in this category were undoubtedly the ocean liners *Wilhelm Gustloff* and *Robert Ley*, which are often referred to as the world's first purpose-built cruise liners. Built for the *Kraft durch Freude* ('Strength through Joy') movement run by the Nazi DAF (German Labour Front – the Party organization that replaced free trade unions), these ships carried the movement's members on holiday cruises until 1939, when Germany's military needs saw both ships pressed into service with the Kriegsmarine.

Wilhelm Gustloff/Robert Ley Specifications			
Length	208.5m	**Powerplant**	6 x 6-cylinder MAN diesels
Beam	23.6m	**Top speed**	15.5 knots
Displacement	25,484 tons	**Endurance**	12,000 nautical miles
Armament	• 3 x 10.5cm flak • 8 x 2cm flak	**Powerplant**	6 x 6-cylinder MAN diesels

Wilhelm Gustloff

Built by Blohm & Voss in Hamburg, and launched in May 1927, the *Wilhelm Gustloff* first served in a military role at the end of May 1939 when it transported members of the Condor Legion, who had been serving in the Spanish Civil War, from Vigo back to Hamburg. On the outbreak of war it was for some time pressed into service as a hospital ship. Latterly, the *Gustloff* was employed as an accommodation ship for men of the 2.Unterseebootslehrdivision in Gotenhafen. As the Red Army approached East Prussia in January 1945, it was decided that it would be one of the vessels used to evacuate a mixture of Kriegsmarine personnel, wounded soldiers and civilian refugees from the Samland peninsula north of Königsberg west down the Baltic to safety at Kiel. Its normal capacity was 1,465 passengers; although exact numbers can never be known, it is thought that when it departed on 30 January 1945 it was crammed with around 10,580, of whom about 8,950 were civilians.

Escorted by the torpedo boat *Möwe*, the *Wilhelm Gustloff* was running with its navigation lights illuminated, trying to avoid a collision with a minesweeper flotilla thought to be operating in the vicinity. Just east of Leba the lights attracted the attention of the Soviet submarine S-13, which fired three torpedoes; all of them hit the

The former cruise liner *Wilhelm Gustloff*. It was taken over by the Kriegsmarine and after some brief service as a hospital ship, became an accommodation ship for U-boat crews. It was sunk by the Soviet submarine S-13 when evacuating refugees from East Prussia, resulting in the greatest maritime loss of life ever. (ullstein bild via Getty Images)

liner, which sank within 45 minutes. The most recent estimates suggest that despite the rescue efforts of naval vessels that rushed to the site, around 9,400 souls were lost in the freezing Baltic waters that night, making the *Gustloff* tragedy the worst single sea disaster in recorded history.

Robert Ley

Launched in March 1938, the *Robert Ley* had a wartime career very similar to that of its sister ship. It was used to bring members of the Condor Legion back to Germany in May 1939, and on the outbreak of hostilities was converted for use as a hospital ship. Subsequently it served as an accommodation ship at Neustadt, with 1.Unterseebootslehrdivision and 21.Unterseebootsflottille. In the closing stages of the war *Robert Ley* was also used for the evacuation of wounded soldiers and civilian refugees from the Baltic coast. It was seriously damaged during a bombing raid while berthed in Hamburg on 9 March 1945. After the war it was taken to Britain and scrapped.

Miscellaneous Vessels

The Kriegsmarine naturally had large numbers of miscellaneous vessels, many of which were built in very small numbers or were even 'one-off' types for special purposes. They included the following.

Aviso Grille (State Yacht)

Built by Blohm & Voss and commissioned in May 1935, *Aviso Grille* was Germany's state yacht. It was used on a number of occasions by Hitler to host visiting foreign dignitaries during naval reviews and other formal occasions, as well as making several goodwill visits to various countries including Great Britain. *Grille* was used as a test-bed for the high-pressure steam turbines being produced for the navy's new destroyers.

The German state yacht *Aviso Grille*. Often referred to as Hitler's Yacht, despite the fact he hated the sea and was rarely to be seen aboard the ship. It served during the war primarily as a minelayer and as a training ship. It survived the war and was eventually scrapped in 1951. (Heinrich Hoffmann/ullstein bild via Getty Images)

On the outbreak of war it reverted to an operational military role, and was used to lay mines off the French coast. It was later transferred to the Baltic, and from its base at Swinemünde it carried out predominantly patrol work. Thereafter it was used for gunnery training duties until the invasion of the Soviet Union in June 1941 when it once again took up minelaying duties, this time in the Baltic, before returning to gunnery training. After a refit in 1942 it sailed for Norwegian waters, where it remained as a base ship for the remainder of the war.

Grille passed into British hands at the end of the war and was subsequently sold off into civilian ownership. It was eventually scrapped in the USA in 1951.

Aviso Grille Specifications			
Length	135m	**Powerplant**	2 x Blohm & Voss steam turbines
Beam	13.5m	**Top speed**	26 knots
Displacement	3,430 tons	**Endurance**	9,500 nautical miles
Armament	• 2 x 10.5cm guns • 2 x 3.7cm flak • 2 x 2cm flak • up to 228 mines	**Complement**	250

Versuchsboote (Test Boats)

Literally 'test boats', these were generally old ships, usually veterans of World War I which were too outdated for operational use and were simply retained as test-beds for new equipment or methods. Some did see occasional active service, however, being used as support vessels during the invasions of Norway and Denmark. A few of the newer boats also saw service throughout the war; for example, Versuchsboot *Pelikan*, a former mine warfare test boat of the *Kaiserliche Marine*, served on convoy escort duties in the Kattegat throughout the war, and was considered worth being taken over by the Americans in 1945.

Some of these vessels, like *Pelikan* and *Claus von Bevern*, had been built as warships; others had civilian origins – like the *Welle*, built as a fishing boat. These boats were simply classed together by purpose rather than by design or type. Thirteen vessels were so designated, as follows: Versuchsboote *Acheron, Arkona, Claus von Bevern, Grille, Hecht, Johann Wittenborg, Nautilus, Otto Braun, Pelikan, Störtebecker, Strahl, Sundewall* and *Welle*.

Schulschiffe (School Ships)

In addition to existing older ships inherited from the Kaiserliche Marine and Reichsmarine, two newly built vessels were designated as school ships – the *Brummer* and *Bremse*.

Brummer was launched in May 1935 at Deschimag in Bremen and commissioned in February 1936. As well as its intended duties in training anti-aircraft crews, it was planned that when necessary it could act as an auxiliary minelayer, and in that capacity could carry up to 450 mines. *Brummer*'s main armament consisted of twin 10.5cm heavy flak mounts of the same type as used on most of Germany's heavy warships. It is interesting to note that it was used as a test-bed for the new high-pressure steam turbines that would be fitted into Germany's destroyer fleet, and that on *Brummer* they were found to work well, in contrast to their highly problematic performance on the destroyers.

Serving initially at the Küstenartillerieschule at Swinemünde, on the outbreak of war *Brummer* transferred to minelaying duties and in April 1940 was allocated to the invasion forces being assembled for the invasion of Norway and Denmark. On 14 April it was hit by torpedoes from the British submarine HMS *Starlet*, and the resultant explosion blew off almost the entire foredeck. Despite several hours of desperate attempts to save it, the *Brummer* rolled over and sank early on 15 April.

Brummer Specifications			
Length	113m	**Powerplant**	2 x 8,000hp high-pressure steam turbines
Beam	13.5m	**Top speed**	23 knots
Displacement	3,010 tons	**Endurance**	2,400 nautical miles
Armament	• 8 x 10.5cm flak • 2 x 8.8cm flak • 8 x 3.7cm flak • 4 x 2cm flak	**Complement**	238 (including trainees)

Considerably smaller than *Brummer*, the *Bremse* was launched in January 1931 at the Kriegsmarine Werft in Wilhelmshaven and commissioned into the navy in July 1932.

Until 1939, *Bremse* served in its intended role as a training ship for naval anti-aircraft crews. On the outbreak of war it was allocated to escort duties for minelaying and troop ships in the Baltic before returning briefly to training duties.

In April 1940, however, like *Brummer*, it was allocated to the invasion forces for Operation *Weserübung*. During the invasion of Norway it suffered three direct hits from heavy shore batteries, but was able to land the troops it was carrying and continue, sinking some minor Norwegian naval vessels before running aground. It was forced into Stavanger for repairs and was out of action for three months before it could return to Germany.

Bremse was operating in the North Sea when, on 30 July 1941, it came under heavy attack by Fairey Albacore torpedo bombers and Fairey Fulmar fighters from the British carrier HMS *Victorious*, but escaped any serious damage. In early September 1941, operating from a base in Norway, *Bremse*, together with an armed trawler and a torpedo boat, was escorting a convoy heading towards the Murmansk front when, on the night of 8 September, the convoy was intercepted by a British naval force consisting of the cruisers HMS *Aurora* and *Nigeria* supported by destroyers. The German warships engaged, but in the nocturnal artillery duel that followed all three of them were sunk; *Bremse* took 160 of its crew down with it. The sacrifice of the three small warships allowed the convoy to escape unscathed.

ABOVE LEFT Built as a civilian freighter, *Mars* was taken over by the Kriegsmarine in 1938 as a training ship for naval anti-aircraft artillery, carrying light and medium anti-aircraft guns. It was based at the coastal artillery school in Swinemünde. While in dock at Stettin it was hit by RAF bombers and burned out. (DUBM)

ABOVE RIGHT A purpose-built gunnery training ship, *Bremse* was also a test-bed for new power plants. In wartime it was allocated to convoy escort duty and was sunk by British cruisers HMS *Nigeria* and HMS *Aurora* whilst escorting German troopships in Norwegian waters in September 1941. (DUBM)

Bremse Specifications			
Length	103.5m	**Powerplant**	2 x 8-cylinder 28,000hp MAN diesels
Beam	9.5m	**Top speed**	29 knots
Displacement	1,870 tons	**Endurance**	8,000 nautical miles
Armament	• 4 x 12.7cm guns • 4 x 3.7cm flak • 8 x 2cm flak	**Complement**	290 (including trainees)

Apart from these two purpose-built Artillerieschulschiffe, the following older vessels were also classed as Schulboote: Artillerieschuleboot *Hay*, Artillerieschulboot *Fuchs*, Artillerieschulboot *Jungmann* and Artillerieschulboot *Delphin*.

There was also a diver training boat, Taucherschulboot *Taucher*, and two designated simply as school boats – Schulboot *Spree* and Schulboot *Freyr*. Schulboot *Spree* was for a time the home of the so-called Unterseebootsabwehrschule which, despite being named as an anti-submarine warfare school, was actually an establishment for secretly training new U-boat crews before Germany began openly rearming. Both *Spree* and *Freyr* were former fishing vessels taken over by the military.

Fischereischutzboote (Fishery Protection Boats)

Three Kriegsmarine vessels were designated for fishery protection duties, these being Fischereischutzboot *Zieten*, and the sister ships Fischereischutzboot *Elbe* and Fischereischutzboot *Weser*. Both *Elbe* and *Weser* were built in 1931 and served in the fishery protection service until 1938, at which point they and *Zieten* were refitted as tenders for R-boats. They saw service in the English Channel, the Baltic and in Norway. After the war they served with the GMSA, operating out of Cuxhaven; *Elbe* was handed over to the USSR in December 1945.

Vermessungsschiffe (Oceanic Research Ships)

Two vessels were designated as oceanic research ships, Vermessungsschiff *Meteor* and Vermessungsschiff *Panther*. Both were veterans of World War I, originally built as gunboats for the Kaiser's navy. The Kriegsmarine made use of such boats before the outbreak of war (the *Meteor* completed research trips to study the Gulf Stream and the waters of the far North Atlantic), but by September 1939 both had been decommissioned. *Meteor* was brought back into service in 1940 and remained in use as a research ship, based first in Denmark and then in Norway; it ended the war back in Germany, where it was handed over to the USSR.

Segelschulschiffe (Sailing Training Ships)

Germany's sail training programme for officers and cadets suffered a tragedy when in 1932 the sailing ship *Niobe* capsized in a storm with considerable loss of life. A programme of construction resulted in the appearance in the late 1930s of three new sister ships of a new class of three-masted barques: the *Albert Leo Schlageter*, the *Horst Wessel* and the *Gorch Fock*. These beautiful ships were to be responsible for training a new generation of naval officer cadets in seamanship over the next few years, carrying out goodwill cruises to a number of foreign ports throughout the world.

After the outbreak of war brought its sail-training voyages to an end, *Albert Leo Schlageter* remained in port where it

Built as a maritime survey ship, *Meteor* had been deactivated in 1939 but was brought back into service in 1940 and was later used as a tender serving in the Baltic. It survived the war and was handed over to the Soviet Union and returned to its intended role as a survey ship, renamed *Ekvator*. (DUBM)

served as an administration ship – in effect, floating offices. However, it was recalled to service in the Baltic in 1944, and in November of that year ran onto a Soviet mine and had to be towed back to port. It was in Flensburg at the end of the war, and was handed over to the US Navy, who retained it for three years before selling it to Brazil. It remained there until 1961, when it was sold on to Portugal, and is still in service to this day as the *Sagres*.

On the outbreak of war, *Horst Wessel*'s training duties were severely curtailed though not completely stopped, and it began a new role as a military transport ship; during operations in the Baltic it was even credited with shooting down three Soviet aircraft. After repairs and refitting in Wilhelmshaven at the end of the war, *Horst Wessel* was handed over to the US Navy, and in 1946 was commissioned into the US Coastguard as the Coastguard Cutter *Eagle*; it is still in service today.

The sail training ship *Horst Wessel*, seen here in 1946 after its capture, but still bearing the huge bronze eagle and swastika figurehead. Taken over by the US Coastguard as a training ship, it remains in service to this day as the USCGC *Eagle*. (NHHC)

On the outbreak of war *Gorch Fock*, like its sister ship *Albert Leo Schlageter*, was used as a floating administrative office, based in Stralsund. It was formally reactivated in April 1944; and in May 1945, as Soviet forces approached, was taken into shallow waters near Rügen and scuttled. However, it was raised by the Soviets and completely repaired and refitted; it served its new masters as the *Tovarisch*, taking part in many international 'Tall Ships' races. On the break-up of the Soviet Union it found itself under Ukrainian ownership. In 1995 it was sold and taken to Great Britain for a complete refit; from there it was sold once again, to German owners, returning to its country of origin and being renamed *Gorch Fock*. It is currently a museum ship. It is interesting to note that Germany commissioned a new *Gorch Fock* in 1958, built to the same plans as the original with only a few modifications to bring it up to modern safety specifications. All of the class carried around 2,000m² of sail as well as the diesel auxiliary engine, and were fitted with a small number of 2cm flak guns for weapons training.

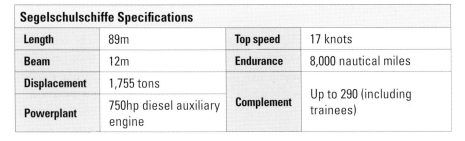

Segelschulschiffe Specifications			
Length	89m	**Top speed**	17 knots
Beam	12m	**Endurance**	8,000 nautical miles
Displacement	1,755 tons	**Complement**	Up to 290 (including trainees)
Powerplant	750hp diesel auxiliary engine		

ABOVE The former Imperial Navy battleship *Hessen*, stripped of all armaments and much of its superstructure in 1935, served in the Kriegsmarine mainly as a radio-controlled target ship. It survived the war and was taken over by the Soviet Union where it continued in the same role, renamed *Tsel*. (NHHC).

BELOW The *Nymphe*, a German anti-aircraft ship moored in a Norwegian harbour. It was originally the *Tordenskjold*, a coastal defence ship captured from the Norwegian Navy in 1940. It served both in Norwegian waters and in the air defence of Kiel. It survived the war but ran aground only a week or so after and was scrapped. (NHHC)

Zielschiffe (Target Ships)

At the end of World War I, Germany was permitted to retain a small number of obsolete pre-dreadnoughts. Some ultimately served in the Kriegsmarine though not in their original role, but rather as radio-controlled target ships for gunnery training under the control of the Inspectorate of Naval Artillery.

Hessen was a Braunschweig-class battleship displacing some 13,300 tons. It was withdrawn from service in 1934, the year before the Reichsmarine transitioned into the Kriegsmarine. Most of its subsequent career, stripped down and with armament removed, was spent as a target ship though it did undertake some icebreaker duties in the Baltic. *Hessen* did survive the war and was handed over to the Soviet Union in 1945 and served on until 1960, a longer career than some of the more illustrious Kriegsmarine warships.

A Wittelsbach-class battleship, *Zähringen* originally displaced 11,774 tons. Stripped down and with much of its superstructore and all turrents removed, like *Hessen* it served as a radio-controlled target ship. In 1944 it was sunk in Gotenhafen by a British bombing raid. The Germans raised it then sank it again in the harbour mouth as a blockship, where it remained until finally broken up in 1950.

Flakschiffe (Flak Ships)

A small number of obsolete or captured vessels were converted to flak ships and armed with both heavy and medium anti-aircraft guns. These were positioned near naval ports to give added firepower to land-based flak batteries.

Arcona was an elderly Gazelle-class light cruiser from the Imperial Navy. It was fitted out with five 10.5cm heavy anti aircraft guns, two 3.7cm guns and four 2cm guns. Defending Brunsbüttel, it was scuttled at the end of the war to prevent capture.

Medusa was another Gazelle-class cruiser. It was given similar armament to its sister, and was used in the defences around the naval base at Wilhelmshaven. Like *Arcona*, it was scuttled at the end of the war to prevent capture.

Niobe was formerly the Dutch navy cruiser *Gelderland*. It was captured in 1940 and after use as a training vessel was converted to a flak ship. It carried eight 10.5cm heavy flak guns, four 40mm Bofors and four 2cm guns. Based in Kotka harbour in Finland, it was sunk by Soviet aircraft in July 1944.

Nymphe was formerly *Tordenskjold*, a coastal defence ship of the Royal Norwegian Navy. It was armed with six 10.5cm heavy flak guns, two 4cm medium flak guns and 14 2cm guns.

Attacked by British aircraft at its moorings in Svolvaer, Norway, it was beached to prevent it sinking. Surviving the war, it became an accommodation ship before being scrapped in 1948.

Thetis was formerly the Norwegian coastal defence ship *Harald Haarfagre*, and sister to *Nymphe*. It was given the same armament as its sister. It too survived the war and was scrapped in 1948 after a brief period as an accomodation ship.

Hospitalschiff (Hospital Ship)

Built in 1939 as a cargo liner for the commercial shipping company Neptun Line, *Mars* was requisitioned by the navy in 1940 and converted for use as a designated hospital ship. Although damaged during a British air raid on Bremen in December 1943, *Mars* survived the war and after a spell in British hands was handed to the Soviet Union where it eventually became the research ship *Vityaz*. It still exists and is now a museum ship.

Wetterschiffe (Weather Ships)

The Kriegsmarine operated in excess of 20 weather ships during World War II. These were predominantly vessels which were originally built as deep-water trawlers and requisitioned by the navy for use on weather reporting duties. Although generally given names, they were officially known by their number, prefixed by WBS (*Wetterbeobachtungsschiff*).

Most were lost due to enemy action or by being scuttled but a few survived. One, WBS11 *Externsteine*, was captured by the US Coastguard Cutter *Eastwind* and subsequently commissioned first into the coastguard as USCG *East Breeze* and then into the US Navy as USS *Callao*.

Typically these converted trawlers would have a crew of around 20–30 and be armed with a bow mounted 2cm canon.

BELOW The *Externsteine* was a purpose-built German weather-reporting ship which was captured in October 1944 by the US Navy when it became trapped in the ice near Greenland. Thereafter it served with the US Coastguard as USCG *East Breeze* before being transferred to the US Navy as the USS *Callao*. (USCG)

Kleinkampfverbände der Kriegsmarine

The *Kleinkampfverbände* (K-Verbände) was formed in April 1944 under the command of Vizeadmiral Helmuth Heye, former commander of the heavy cruiser *Admiral Hipper*. Acting as his Chief of Staff was U-boat ace Fregattenkapitän Fritz Frauenheim. The Kleinkampfverbände was effectively a 'special forces' type organization using midget submarines, combat frogmen and assault boats loaded with explosives. The men were tough, fearless characters who served, in a similar manner to many elite formations, with a much-reduced level of formality and discipline. The men were recruited from all branches of the Wehrmacht, but significantly Dönitz refused to

Principal Active Units of the K-Verbände	
Lehrkommando 200 (Priesterbeck)	K-Flottillen 215–221 (*Linse*)
Lehrkommando 250 (Schlutup)	K-Flottillen 261–270 (*Biber*)
Lehrkommando 300 (Neustadt/Holstein)	K-Flottillen 312–314 (*Seehund*)
Lehrkommando 350 (Suhrendorf)	K-flottillen 361–366 (*Neger/Marder*)
Lehrkommando 400 (Suhrendorf)	K-Flottillen 411–417 (*Molch*)
Lehrkommando 600	K-Flottillen 611–613 (*Linse*)
Lehrkommando 700 (Sylt)	K-Flottillen 702–704 (*Kampfschwimmer*)

permit Heye to recruit men from his U-Bootwaffe, considering his U-boat men to be indispensable.

A total of five K-Verbände command staff units were established: West, Süd, Holland, Norwegen and Skagerak. In addition, six K-Verbände divisions were formed: 1 K-Division (Narvik), 2 K-Division (Trondheim), 3 K-Division (Bergen), 4 K-Division (Holland), 5 K-Division (Holland) and 6 K-Division (Italy).

The K-Verbände also contained support elements such as training, transport and flak to defend their unit locations.

Midget Submarines

A number of midget submarine types were produced. The following vessels are some of those. A number of other types were designed and reached prototype stage, but were never used in action or put into full scale production.

Type XXVIIA – *Hecht* (Pike)

The *Hecht*, officially known as the Type XXVIIA, was a two-man submarine. Electrically powered, it could achieve a top speed of some six knots and could dive to 50m.

The *Hecht* (officially the Type XXVIIA) one-man submersible being lowered into the water. The markings on the nose of the torpedo (red and white quarters) indicate that this is a training mission with a dummy warhead. The crew figures clearly show the tiny size of the entry hatch. (DUBM)

A single torpedo was carried, slung beneath the hull. A total of 53 *Hecht* were built, by Germaniawerft in Kiel, though the type does not seem to have been particularly successful, mostly being used for training purposes.

Hecht Specifications			
Displacement	12 tons	**Speed**	5.7 knots surface 6 knots submerged
Length	10.4m	**Range**	78 nautical miles
Powerplant	1 x 12hp AEG electric motor	**Armament**	1 x G7e torpedo

The Type XXVII B5 or *Seehund* was the largest of the midget submersibles. This is a surviving example at the naval museum in Wilhelmshaven. This shot clearly shows the arms protruding from the hull side which carried the torpedoes, one either side. Note also the shroud protecting the propeller. (Author's collection)

Type XXVII B5 – *Seehund* (Seal)

The largest of the midget submarines, *Seehund* was a direct descendant of the *Hecht*, but longer, and heavier. *Seehund* was equipped with a diesel engine for surface travel, and an electric motor, for submerged travel. Two torpedoes were carried externally, slung against the lower hull, one to each side. With excellent handling characteristics, and capable of diving to 50m, this was by far the best of the German midget submarines. It has been estimated that up to 90,000 tons of enemy shipping were sunk in operations using the *Seehund*. Some 137 of this type entered service, built at Germaniawerft in Kiel and Schichau in Elbing.

Seehund Specifications			
Displacement	17 tons	**Speed**	7.7 knots surface 6.0 knots submerged
Length	12m	**Range**	300 nautical miles
Powerplant	1 x Büssing NAG diesel motor 1 x 25hp Siemens electric motor	**Armament**	2 x G7e torpedoes

A *Biber* one-man submersible. A diminutive vessel with a tiny conning tower, this type suffered extremely high losses for little or no operational success. Several survived the war and may be seen in various museums, including the Imperial War Museum, Duxford, UK. (DUBM)

Neger/Marder

This was effectively a manned torpedo, using the body of a standard torpedo, with a small cockpit covered by a plexiglass dome, in the nose. Under this was slung a live G7e torpedo. When nearing the target, the operator would start the G7e torpedo, point at the target and release the torpedo.

Around 200 were manufactured. The *Neger* was not a submersible. When loaded with its torpedo payload, it ran partly submerged, with only the dome above water. The low position made it very difficulty for the operator to see and any oil or scum on the water could soon obscure vision through the plexiglas dome.

The *Neger* did see some successes. One cruiser, one destroyer and three minesweepers fell victim to *Neger* attacks. However, the *Neger* was dreadfully unstable. On its first use, from a force of 30, a total of 13 capsized when lowered into the water. The fatality rate for the *Neger* was around 80 per cent.

One *Neger* operator, Schreiberobergefreiter Walter Gerhold, was decorated with the Knight's Cross of the Iron Cross for destroying the Polish cruiser *Orp Dragon* off the Normandy coast on 6 July 1944.

Neger Specifications			
Displacement	4 tons	**Speed**	4 knots
Length	7.6m	**Range**	48 nautical miles
Powerplant	1 x 12hp electric motor	**Armament**	1 x G7e torpedo

Schreiberobergefreiter Walter Gerhold in his *Neger* one-man torpedo. This weapon was probably more dangerous to its operator than to the enemy. Gerhold was awarded the Knight's Cross of the Iron Cross in July 1944 as a *Neger* operator and promoted to Schreibermaat. (DUBM)

A variant known as the *Marder* was produced. It was slightly longer at 8.3m and was fitted with a ballast tank which allowed it to submerge, but only for a very short period and limited depth.

Biber (Beaver)

The *Biber* had a cylindrical hull with a small observation tower just forward of midships, and was propelled by a petrol-driven Opel Blitz truck motor for surface travel and a battery-powered electric motor for submerged travel. The *Biber* carried two torpedoes slung externally in concave indentations in the lower hull. Around 320 *Biber* were produced. Although they scored no sinkings in their first action on the Normandy invasion front in August 1944, all the vessels that took part returned to base safely, itself quite an achievement. Subsequent operations, however, saw heavy losses incurred. Around 320 were produced, mostly by Klöckner-Humboldt-Deutz.

Mini Submarine Crew

(1)

(2)

(3)

(1) Crewman of *Neger* one-man torpedo from Lehrkommando 350, with grey green overalls over his blue inform, a Tauchretter rebreather and a canvas helmet plus an oxygen mask to connect to the *Neger*'s supply. (2) *Kampfschwimmer*, wearing a so-called 'Belloni' suit, with cargo pockets at the hips and a close-fitting hood. He has canvas and leather deck shoes and large rubber flippers as well as an Italian made rebreather. (3) *Sprengboot* crewman from Lehrkommando 200, with black rubber diving suit, standard *Kriegsmarine* life vest and a distinctive paratrooper style helmet. (Mike Chappell © Osprey Publishing)

Biber Specifications			
Displacement	4 tons	**Speed**	6.5 knots surfaced 5.3 knots submerged
Length	9m	**Range**	125 nautical miles
Powerplant	1 x Opel Blitz 32hp petrol motor 1 x 13hp Siemens electric motor	**Armament**	2 x G7e torpedo

Molch (Salamander)

The *Molch* was a one-man vessel with a cylindrical hull, the forward three-quarters of whose length was packed with batteries to power the motor. In the rear was the pilot's compartment, with hatch and periscope.

Unlike most similar vessels, *Molch* was capable of diving. One torpedo was slung on each side of the lower hull. Almost 400 of these craft were built by AG Weser in Bremen, and were used at Anzio and along the Dutch and Belgian coasts. They had very poor handling characteristics, however, and were far from successful, suffering losses disproportionate to their rare achievements. First used in September 1944, a flotilla of 12 suffered ten losses with no successes recorded.

During 1945 they took part in 102 combat missions, in which they lost 70 of their own number and sank only seven small relatively unimportant vessels.

Molch Specifications			
Displacement	11 tons	**Speed**	4.3 knots surfaced 5 knots submerged
Length	10.7m	**Range**	125 nautical miles
Powerplant	1 x 13 hp Siemens electric motor	**Armament**	2 x G7e torpedo

Kampfschwimmer (Combat Frogmen)

Although combat frogmen had been utilized earlier in the war on relatively rare occasions, they were to become part of the K-Verbände. The men were organized into *Marine Einsatzkommandos* (MEK) consisting of one officer and 22 men.

The first significant operations came in June 1944 when frogmen towed torpedo-shaped containers full of explosives along the River Orne through the Allied lines in Normandy, and secured them to bridge supports. The charges were then detonated by automatic timers.

Locations of Marine Einsatzkommandos	
MEK 20 in Cavella (Italy)	MEK 65 in Boulogne
MEK 25 in Bergen	MEK 70 in Brest
MEK 30 in Molde	MEK 71 in Toulon
MEK 35 in Horstadt	MEK 75 in Anzio
MEK 40 in Denmark	MEK 80 in Meina
MEK 50 in Germany	MEK 85 on Oder Front
MEK 60 in Le Havre / Rouen	MEK 90 in Dubrovnik

On 26 August 1944 frogmen were landed near Le Havre by Linsen boats, evaded Allied sentries and sneaked into a captured coastal artillery battery whose guns had been turned to attack the German garrison. They successfully placed charges which destroyed the battery.

A further successful raid took place on 15 September 1944 when frogmen landed once again from Linsen boats succeeded in demolishing the lock gate at Kruisschans in Allied-occupied Antwerp. An attempt on the bridges over the Waal at Nijmegen was successful in that the frogmen succeeded in reaching the bridge and attaching their explosives which detonated, but proved to be insufficient to destroy the bridge. Now fully alerted, the Allies were able to prevent subsequent attempts to finish the job.

In the closing stage of the war combat frogmen, often working with Linsen, were active on the Eastern Front, predominantly in attacks on bridges aimed at slowing the Soviet advance. Bridges at Eisenhüttenstadt, Kalenzig, Rebus, Zellin, Dievenow, Nipperweise and Fiddichow were all destroyed or put out of action by units of the K-Verbände.

Sprengboote

In addition to midget submarines, the K-Verbände used surface boats. These were known as *Sprengboote* and consisted of small, fast motor launches known as *Linse*. These were first manufactured in early 1942 for use by Regiment Brandenburg zbV 800, a German Army commando unit. In April 1944, the Oberkommando der Wehrmacht authorized the transfer of such vessels to the K-Verbände. The version built for the K-Verbände in 1944 was produced by a number of yards and a total of 1,200 were built.

These were organized into flotillas, each with 48 boats: 16 as command boats and 32 as demolition boats.

Each demolition boat had the stern packed with explosives and was driven by a pilot who would steer it at the target and jump overboard at the last possible moment. The control boat would then steer the *Linse* by radio control for the last stage of travel. A bar around the forward part of the boat would, when compressed by the boat hitting the target, set a fuse which would cause detonation.

In many cases, *Linsen* operated alongside *Neger/Marder* types as well as E-boats. In the confusion of battle it was often impossible to determine which type of German vessel had scored a torpedo hit.

As well as carrying out attack missions, the *Linsen* also carried out support tasks. On 17 April 1945, *Linsen* succeeded in penetrating the Allied blockade around the beseiged port of Dunkirk and brought much needed food and ammunition to the beleaguered German garrison.

Linsen also operated in the Mediterranean and Adriatic but with little success there, many of the boats being destroyed in Allied air raids or lost in heavy seas. On 17 April 1945, however, *Linsen* succeeded in sinking the French destroyer *Trombe*.

A number of Linse-type Sprengboote moored at their base. By October 1944 at least 385 had been produced from a target of over 1,200. Although successes were achieved, they had little effect on the outcome of the war. (Narodowe Archiwum Cyfrowe)

Linse Specifications			
Displacement	2 tons	**Speed**	31 knots
Length	5.75m	**Range**	80 nautical miles
Powerplant	1 x 3.6 litre V8 petrol engine	**Armament**	300–480kg explosives

CHAPTER FOUR

SERVICE IN HITLER'S NAVY

At the outbreak of World War II, on 1 September 1939, the Kriegsmarine had a total personnel strength of only 78,000. By 1943, the number of personnel serving in the Kriegsmarine had risen to its wartime peak of 22,000 commissioned officers, 613,000 petty officers and seamen, and 14,000 officials (*Marinebeamte*). By now, the surface fleet was a spent force, and the U-boat war had turned in favour of the Allies. However, during the closing months of the war, the Kriegsmarine personnel played a vital role in transporting troops and refugees from eastern provinces to the West across the Baltic, saving hundreds of thousands of lives.

Kriegsmarine personnel can be grouped into five basic categories: *Matrosen* (enlisted personnel, usually serving for a short term); *Maate* (technical specialists/petty officers); *Feldwebel* (senior NCOs); *Seeoffiziere* (officers); and the

The end for the U-boats, like this Type XXIII, came with Operation *Deadlight* when the Royal Navy took surrendered U-boats far out to sea, and sank them with gunfire or explosives. Only a few were retained as war reparations or for testing purposes. (Getty Images)

Admiräle (flag officers). Not all served at sea – and some Kriegsmarine personnel never served at sea at all.

SEAMEN, NCOS AND OFFICERS
Training

Enlisted Men Training

The sailor's pools for the Kriegsmarine came under the command of the Second Admiral of the North Sea or Baltic commands (*2.Admiral der Nordsee* or *2.Admiral der Ostsee*). All sailors were allocated to one of the two main naval commands, the North Sea or Baltic, and were posted to the appropriate *Schiffsstammdivision* (sailor's pool).

Wartime expansion and reorganization saw this structure change from the basic division into six regiments (three each in the Baltic and North Sea commands) with further subdivisions into a final total of 31 training detachments (the *Schiffsstammabteilungen*) where sailors carried out their initial basic training.

Schiffsstammabteilung Locations	
Kiel (Ostsee)	Schiffsstammabteilungen 1 and 3
Wilhelmshaven (Nordsee)	Schiffsstammabteilungen 2, 4 and 6
Eckernförde (Ostsee)	Schiffsstammabteilung 5
Stralsund (Ostsee)	Schiffsstammabteilungen 7, 9 (for NCO Training)
	Schiffsstammabteilungen 11 (for NCO Training) and 32
Leer (Nordsee)	Schiffsstammabteilung 8
Wesermünde (Nordsee)	Schiffsstammabteilung 10 (NCO Training)
Brake (Nordsee)	Schiffsstammabteilung 12 (NCO Training)
Sassnitz (Ostsee)	Schiffsstammabetilung 13
Glückstadt (Nordsee)	Schiffsstammabteilung 14
Beverloo in Belgium (Nordsee)	Schiffsstammabteilungen 15 (NCO Training) and 22
Bergen in Norway (Nordsee)	Schiffsstammabteilung 16
Memel (Ostsee)	Schiffsstammabteilung 17
Buxtehude (Nordsee)	Schiffsstammabteilung 18
Diedenhofen (Ostsee)	Schiffsstammabteilung 19
Norden (Nordsee)	Schiffsstammabteilung 20
Leba (Ostsee)	Schiffsstammabteilung 21
Deutsche-Krone (Ostsee)	Schiffsstammabteilung 23 (Naval Artillery)
Groningen in Holland (Nordsee)	Schiffsstammabteilung 24 (Naval Artillery)
Pillau (Ostsee)	Schiffsstammabteilung 25 (Naval Artillery)
Wazep (Nordsee)	Schiffsstammabteilung 26
Ollerup in Denmark (Ostsee)	Schiffsstammabteilung 27 (Naval Artillery)
Sennheim (Nordsee)	Schiffsstammabteilung 28 (for foreign volunteers)
Wittmund (Nordsee)	Schiffsstammabteilung 30
Windau (Ostsee)	Schiffsstammabteilung 31

(The numbering sequence ran up to 32, but Schiffsstammabteilung 29 was never made operational).

Initial basic training for sailors consisted of the same common military syllabus through which army infantry soldiers were processed. All sailors had to don field grey uniform and participate in drill exercises, exhaustive physical training, assault courses, gunnery and bayonet practice, route marches and the general range of whatever delights might be dreamed up by their training NCOs. Once deemed fit to pass out as soldiers (the German custom is to refer to all servicemen as 'soldiers', whether from the army, air force or navy), the recruits would pass to specialist training schools that would teach them the trade relative to the *Laufbahn* (military speciality) to which they had been allocated.

Major Kriegsmarine Training Schools	
Marinesanitätsschule	Navy Medical School, at Kiel
Torpedoschule	Torpedo School, at Mürwick
Schiffsartillerieschule	Ships Artillery School, at Kiel
Kustenartillerieschule	Coastal Artillery School, at Swinemünde
Steuermannsschule	Helmsman/Navigator School, at Mürwick
Marineflugabwehrschule	Navy Anti-Aircraft Defence School, at Swinemünde
Marinesportschule	Navy Sports School (for PT Instructors), at Mürwick
Marinegasschutzschule	Navy Gas Defence School, at Kiel

NCO Training

After the reintroduction of conscription in 1935, vast increases in NCO grades required put the training establishments under considerable strain. The existing NCO school at Friedrichsort could not cope with the influx, so a new, second NCO training school was opened at Wesermünde (Bremerhaven), the two becoming known as Marineunteroffizierlehrabteilung 1 and 2. In 1938, a new purpose-built NCO training school was opened at Plön, which exists to this day. Unlike officers, who could apply to join the navy as such, NCOs were chosen by selection from the ranks. Their own officers kept a close eye on high-quality sailors with several years experience to identify suitable future NCOs. Indeed, the practice of promoting NCOs from the ranks was not new, but the old procedure of simply promoting a senior rating who had given good service and leaving him to acquire gradually the skills of the higher rank had proven far from satisfactory. The difference with the new system was that once selected, the new NCO would be required to sign on for a spell of at least 12 years service and was then put through extensive professional training to ensure that he would have all the skills needed as an NCO. This meant that by the time a sailor was selected, he was already highly experienced, fit and well motivated.

Once selected, he would be sent for advanced technical training for the trade relevant to his *Laufbahn*, and this could take anything from three to ten months, before moving on to NCO school. At NCO school, he would once again don field grey, and go through further intensive training, both on the drill square and in simulated combat training where he would gain the confidence required to give clear, concise, well thought out orders under all sorts of adverse conditions. Given all this, as well as the advanced technical specialisation skills of his *Laufbahn*, there were few NCOs in any other branch of the armed services with such a high multi-skill level as those of the Kriegsmarine.

Officer Training

The initial part of officer training was common to all branches, before splitting into various specialist training paths. Line officers had the suffix '*zur See*' appended to their rank, engineer ranks were followed by the abbreviation (*Ing.*), for *Ingenieur*, weapons officer ranks were followed by the letter (*W*), for *Waffen-offizier* and administrative staff by (*V*) for *Verwaltung*.

The initial training was as follows:
- Induction and basic training: 5 months
- Practical training: 4 months (sail training for line officers, workshop training for engineers or weapons officers)
- Promotion to Cadet Service on a training ship: 9 months
- Examinations followed by promotion to *Fähnrich*
- Home leave: 15 days

Thereafter, more specialized training commenced (Mürwick refers to Marineschule Mürwick, the premier German Naval Academy), as below:

Line officers: Mürwick, 7 months; Weapons, 5 months; Fleet service, 6 months; Promotion to *Leutnant zur See.*

Engineers: Mürwick, 7 months; Engineer exams; Workshop, 5 months; Fleet service, 6 months; Promotion to *Leutnant (Ing).*

Gunnery: Ships Artillery School, 6 months; Shipyard, 6 months; Mürwick, 7 months; Weapons, 5 months; Fleet service, 6 months; Promotion to *Leutnant (W).*

There were clearly several common elements even in the second part of training, but these were interspersed with more role-specific training. Officer training began at Danholm on the Baltic, where they were put through a two-day induction course comprised almost entirely of extremely strenuous physical training and interviews which would weed out one in every four applicants. Those who passed were issued uniforms and allowed to continue training. At each stage of training, it was official policy to mix recruits continuously so that they did not always work alongside friends they had made and that cliques therefore would not be formed.

The training itself was extremely arduous, with the training NCOs putting the potential officers through the mill. Unscheduled route marches could be sprung on the trainees any time of the day or night. Kit and uniform inspections found fault with the slightest imperfection, and those unfortunate enough to be found wanting would be given extra fatigue duties or drill exercises during what should have been free time. The inevitable 'show parades', known and hated by soldiers the world over, could involve cadets struggling on to the parade square carrying the steel locker cabinets from their quarters to show their instructor that everything inside was spick and span, then having to stagger back and replace the locker and rush back to the parade square, all within a few minutes. Failure to get back in time resulted in even more fatigues.

Recruits were chased around the drill square in full combat kit with heavy pack, steel helmet and wearing gas marks, all at double time, until they were ready to drop from sheer exhaustion. At Mürwick, there is a sandy headland which ends in a precipitously steep slope running down to the water's edge. Recruits were chased headlong down the slope to the water's edge, only to have to turn around and run up the slope again, in full battle kit and often wearing gas marks, until they were almost in a state of collapse.

Whatever might be felt about officers by the lower ranks, it must be said that the physical aspects of their training were every bit as hard as, if not harder than, that suffered by lower grades.

Naval officers did their shipboard training on sail trainers, the best known of which is probably the *Gorch Fock*. This was extremely tough training before the mast, and deaths in training were not unknown, the training weeding out those who did not possess the required determination, physical ability and strength of character. This exhausting training was generally followed (in peacetime at least) by a goodwill cruise into foreign waters aboard a major surface warship. This was also very hard work, but gave many young officers their first chance to see the world. Tough examinations, followed by promotion to Officer Cadet for those who passed, would in turn be followed by a welcome two-week leave. Thereafter, training would differ depending on the career path the cadet wished to follow, but one common feature was the obligatory seven-month course at Marineschule Mürwick, the most famous of all the German naval academies, located in a hugely impressive Gothic-style building built near Flensburg on the orders of Kaiser Wilhelm II and first opened in November 1910. Due to the high degree of technical specialization within the navy, most ranks had some form of advance training, certainly more so than in the other branches of the armed forces. By the latter part of the war, however, the Kriegsmarine, with the exception of the U-boats, was a spent force. Many experienced and highly trained sailors, including U-boat crews, were transferred to the army or Waffen-SS, or were thrown into the Kriegsmarine's own infantry units formed in the closing months of the war. The 'conversion training' for infantry duties was rudimentary to say the least. One former

Naval troops wearing field grey uniforms undergoing rifle training. All Kriegsmarine sailors, irrespective of which branch they would ultimately serve, underwent basic combat training in field grey uniform. Some would remain in field grey for the entire war. (DUM)

U-boat crewman commented that he received but one day's infantry 'refresher' training, one day being instructed on how to use the *Panzerfaust* anti-tank weapon, and one day on small-arms training. On the fourth day, he was in action against British armoured units near Hamburg. Unsurprisingly, losses were heavy, though the former sailors did give a good account of themselves. A recent detractor of Grossadmiral Dönitz criticized this 'desperate idea', but the fact remains that these navy tank hunters destroyed over 40 armoured vehicles in just two days of fighting between 18 and 20 April, halting a British offensive in their sector. So, although the conversion training was less than intensive, the quality of the men themselves showed through.

Belief and Belonging

A particularly significant factor in understanding the high morale, sense of honour and devotion to duty in the German Navy, is that it was by far the least politically involved of all the branches of the German military and paramilitary forces. Hitler was a poor sailor, who is said to have once been seasick simply visiting a ship tied up in port. Whilst he was interested in the propaganda value any victories by his navy would bring him, he had no real interest in ships or in the navy and its traditions. Naval regulations were quite strict in that membership of a political party was prohibited. There are many examples of well-known and highly decorated Kriegsmarine sailors who had to give up membership of the Party before taking up their commissions with the navy. This of course does not mean that there were no Nazis in the Kriegsmarine, one source estimating that over 40 per cent of new officer recruits were former Party members. However, it certainly seems that once in the navy, it was the code of ethics of the Kriegsmarine, not of the Party, that was adhered to. The navy was very much a conservative, not to say right-wing, organization, but could never be considered 'Nazi'.

Many former Kriegsmarine personnel have gone on record to say that they honestly believed that the navy shielded them from National Socialist ideology. Where Nazi ideals were foisted upon the navy, they tended to be paid lip service, but were rarely treated with any serious interest.

In some cases, such as when the Nazi-style salute was introduced throughout the armed forces following the abortive attempt to assassinate Hitler in July 1944, the rules tended to be obeyed on formal or public occasions, but ignored when it was felt safe to do so. Certainly, there seems to have been no shortage of occasions when naval personnel clashed with the political authorities, with U-boat men being the worst offenders.

Throughout the entire war, the Kriegsmarine adhered to its own moral codes and sense of honour. It must be reasonable to suggest that there is some link between the fact that the navy is generally considered as being the least political of the German armed forces, and the fact that the war at sea was far more cleanly fought than the war on land. Again,

Morale was generally excellent in the navy and much effort was made to maintain this. Welcomes were laid on for ships returning from missions, especially successful ones, with senior ranks, sometimes Dönitz himself, amongst the welcoming committee. (DUBM)

there is no shortage of incidents of Kriegsmarine personnel acting with great chivalry towards wounded or captured enemy, and there seems to have been considerable mutual respect between the sailors of both sides.

Although the German Navy was a fairly young organization, it had a fiercely proud tradition. Of course, there were still many rather antiquated vessels in the Kriegsmarine. In fact, as noted earlier, the first shots of World War II were fired from the old pre-dreadnought *Schleswig-Holstein*, a relic of the Kaiser's days, when it shelled the Polish fortress at Westerplatte on 1 September 1939, and its sister ship, the *Schlesien*, was still in action against the Soviets in the battle for Gotenhafen in April 1945. The loss of the High Seas Fleet, scuttled at Scapa Flow in 1919, had forced Germany to build anew, so that many of the Kriegsmarine's ships were fast, powerful and ultra-modern.

The typical German sailor serving on one of these modern vessels was immensely proud of his ship, and every effort was made to encourage unit pride. Ship's crews from the great battleships which bore the names of famous historical individuals such as *Bismarck*, *Tirpitz*, *Scharnhorst* and *Gneisenau*, found that a great deal of tradition was inherited along with the ship's name. Often, descendants of these historic individuals were invited to the official launching ceremony to foster these bonds.

The crews of such ships as the light cruisers that were named after major cities usually formed close relationships with the city for which they were named, and the actions involving these ships were keenly followed by the local press. Even smaller ships such as destroyers were named for heroes of World War I, including those such as Bruno Heinemann and Wolfgang Zenker who were killed resisting the so-called sailors' revolution of November 1918. The naming of ships was a matter of no small importance to naval pride. Many of the names used were those of well-known heroes within Germany, little-known, then or now, outside the Fatherland. Thus, the men of the Kriegsmarine, though serving in a young branch of the services, had no shortage of the traditional links that are so important to any fighting force.

Although the naming of smaller vessels ceased with the onset of war (only the first 22 of the Kriegsmarine's destroyers were named, the others all being simply numbered), every effort was made to instil *esprit de corps* at flotilla level with the introduction of unofficial cap insignia (particularly widespread in the U-boat service) or small honour pins (the so-called *Ehrennadel*, which was typically in the form of a small enamelled lapel pin), which were usually accompanied by an elaborate award document.

The uniform worn by a serviceman also played an important part in maintaining morale and instilling pride. There can be no doubt that the service dress worn by the typical German sailor during the life of the Kriegsmarine was particularly elegant. It drew on the best elements of the Royal Navy uniform, and then added its own uniquely German touches to produce an eminently suitable form of naval dress. One of the most important factors in maintaining morale and a sense of belonging was certainly the award of the appropriate 'war badge' to an active-service sailor. A plethora of badges and insignia was produced during the period of the Third Reich, where even the most humble

On long cruises, where space and time permitted, sailors practised the ancient maritime art of model building. This crewman of the auxiliary cruiser *Orion* has created a beautiful model of a galleon. Such hobbies kept the men busy and avoided boredom. (DUBM)

of jobs seemed to have its own special range of uniforms and insignia. The difference, however, between impressive badges such as the Pilot's Badge of the Luftwaffe and the Fleet War Badge of the navy was that the former was simply a qualification badge, but the latter had to be earned through wartime combat service.

Top designers, such as Wilhelm Ernst Peekhaus of Berlin, were commissioned to create a range of awards to recognize the participation of sailors in a set number of war cruises. Separate badges were created for the crews of U-boats, destroyers, minesweepers, capital chips, S-boats, auxiliary cruisers, blockade breakers and coastal flak units. Early examples of such badges were made in the best-quality expensive materials, and finely fire-gilded to give a most attractive appearance. Even later in the war, although the use of cheaper materials was necessary, the quality of the strikings themselves remained high. In some cases, special versions of the badges were manufactured in real silver, gilded and with the swastika held by the eagle national emblem studded with diamonds. These beautiful awards were bestowed, as personal gifts by the *Oberbefehlshaber der Kriegsmarine* (Commander in Chief Navy), upon a number of sailors who had been decorated with the Oak Leaves to the Knight's Cross of the Iron Cross.

The German fashion was for the full-size original version of most military decorations to be worn at all times, even in combat, so a decorated soldier could be easily spotted, and a combat veteran would wear his war badge with great pride. As well as providing the individual with a visible reward for his active service, the war badge would also help maintain morale amongst other, less experienced sailors who could take comfort from the presence of easily identifiable, seasoned combat veterans in their midst.

Many vessels and shore establishments created their own local news-sheets or newspapers with unit news, reports on unit members who had been decorated or specially commended etc. All of this helped to build and maintain morale and a sense of kinship, and most of all a deep sense of pride in having served with the Kriegsmarine. A number of highly active veterans' associations for former crew members of various ships and flotillas were formed, indicating that despite the difficulties in being seen to commemorate anything connected with that period in Germany today, the bonds of comradeship formed during service with the Kriegsmarine are as strong as ever for the few that still survive.

OTHER SERVICE ROLES
Marineartillerie (Naval Artillery)

Often overlooked when considering the performance of the Kriegsmarine in World War II, a significant number of naval personnel were clad not in dark naval blue uniform, but the same field grey as the army. All sailors wore field grey when they went through basic military training before being allocated a posting, but some remained in field grey throughout the war, serving in the *Marineartillerie*, *Marineinfanterie*, Engineering units, Fortress units, Transport units and others.

The *Kriegsabzeichen für Marineartillerie*, or War Badge for Naval Artillery, was instituted on 24 June 1941. Designed by Otto Placzek, it was awarded on a shared points basis to those shooting down enemy aircraft, also to those detecting enemy aircraft by searchlight as well as naval land artillery units. (Author's collection)

The Marineartillerie manned the massive coastal artillery emplacements along the coasts and on the much vaunted 'Atlantic Wall'. They also manned a huge number of anti-aircraft positions not just around the coasts but in naval ports and bases. Those on the coast can be said to have formed Germany's first line of anti-aircraft defences and indeed the Naval Artillery Badge shows what is obviously an anti-aircraft gun. There were well over 120 *Marineartillerieabteilungen* spread around the German coast and in occupied areas.

Naval artillery also took part in land operations in the opening days of World War II, during the attack on Poland. The main duty of this branch, however, was to defend naval establishments from the far north of Norway down to the North African coast, from the Atlantic Wall to the Baltic and Black Seas in the East.

Marinehelfer/Marinehelferinnen (Youth Auxiliaries)

In January 1943, the Kriegsmarine published regulations governing the employment of male youths as auxiliaries. They initially wore the uniform of the *Marine Hitlerjugend* though this was soon replaced by regular naval dress, sometimes with Hitlerjugend sleeve insignia but just as often not. They wore a sleeve band with the legend '*Marinehelfer*' in yellow on blue. Senior auxiliaries, those with at least nine months service, were authorized a sleeve band '*Marineoberhelfer*' in May 1943.

As well as assisting flak artillery units, these boys also served in command posts, as guards at supply or ammunition stores, as telephonists and even as guards for foreign labourers.

During the last few weeks of the war, some of these flak units saw action against enemy ground forces and a number of these youths are known to have earned combat decorations including the Iron Cross.

The navy had always employed civilians for simple tasks such as cleaners, canteen staff etc. and from April 1941 had used females as Aircraft Reporting Auxiliaries (much in the same way as female auxiliaries were used in a similar role by the RAF) but in mid 1942 it created its own corps of female auxiliaries, the *Marinehelferin* with their own special uniform including a sleeve band with the legend '*Marinehelferin*' in yellow on

ABOVE LEFT Polish prisoners guarded by the *Marinestosstruppe* (a secret Kriegsmarine formation of troops) after the surrender of the Westerplatte fortress, Poland, September 1939. After defending bravely, the Germans accorded the surrendering Poles considerable respect, standing to attention as they left the battered fortress and allowing the Polish commander to retain his sword. (Narodowe Archiwum Cyfrowe)

ABOVE A naval officer, and holder of the Iron Cross First Class, commanding a coastal artillery unit on the Atlantic coast is seen using range-finding optics. Note on his pocket the War Badge for Naval Artillery, indicating he has already seen combat action. (Josef Charita)

ABOVE Members of the Marine Hitlerjugend or Naval Hitler Youth were often conscripted for service as naval auxiliaries. The youth at left wears the Hitlerjugend armband on the naval uniform along with the cuffband *'Marinehelfer'*. (Culture Club/ Getty Images)

FAR RIGHT An award document for the Naval Artillery Badge. Interestingly, the award is to a member of the Hitlerjugend serving as a naval auxiliary with the flak branch. Many of these young boys served as *'Flakhelfer'* and won combat awards. (Author's collection)

CENTRE A number of naval auxiliaries welcome a returning U-boat crew. The cuffband on the individual at right bears the inscription *'Marinehelferin'*. They also wear the insignia of their branch, a small brooch embossed with an anchor, on their tie. (DUBM)

blue, plus a brooch bearing an anchor to be worn on the knot of the neck tie. They were employed in clerical roles, administration, communications, signals etc. and ultimately even with the flak artillery assisting with searchlight duties, sound detector equipment etc., though it tended to be males who operated the gun itself.

In November 1944, the female auxiliaries of all branches of the armed forces were combined to create the *Wehrmachthelferinnen*.

Marinebeamte (Functionaries)

Formed in 1934, the *Wehrmachtbeamte* were specialist officials serving in the armed forces. They were effectively the Civil Servants of the military. They wore uniform, and held military ranks broadly equivalent to the ranks of the regular armed forces, but had their own unique insignia.

Those serving with the navy, the *Marinebeamte*, carried out a wide range of administrative tasks relating to their area of expertise such as meteorology, engineering, dentistry, pharmacy and training. They also provided judicial expertise (though the Kriegsmarine also had its own regular judicial officers) and provided personnel for the Chaplaincy of the navy.

The majority of Marinebeamte were of officer equivalent rank, but there was also a smaller number of the most senior NCO ranks. All wore regular naval uniform in dark blue or field grey but with a subtle difference in that all insignia and buttons were in a silver colour rather than traditional naval gilt. Embroidered insignia worn just above the naval sleeve rank rings indicated their particular career branch. Rank banding was decided upon by the educational and/or professional qualifications of the individual. Generally, there were three grades, Intermediate, Advanced and Higher grade. Officers could hold ranks up to the equivalent of an Admiral. Ranks would generally indicate trade so that the equivalent of a regular navy *Oberleutnant zur See*, in the administrative branch might be referred to as an *Oberverwaltungssekretär*.

The silver rather than gold insignia resulted in some sailors referring to them somewhat pejoratively as '*Silberlinge*'. (A Silberling was reputed to be the silver coin Judas received for betraying Christ.) It should be said, however, that these Marinebeamte were not all 'desk jockeys' serving out the war in safe office jobs. Those in the engineering branch often went to sea and experienced the same dangers and privations as their regular navy comrades, some even earning war badges and decorations. In any case, they performed essential administrative tasks which eased much of the burden on regular navy personnel.

Marineküstenpolizei (Water Protection Police)

During peacetime, the policing of Germany's waterways was carried out by the *Wasserschutzpolizei* (WSP), a branch of the civilian police. During wartime, however, a new military branch of the Kriegsmarine was created. On 20 April 1940, the Marineküstenpolizei was created, under the control of the *2.Admiral der Nordsee/Ostsee*. The *2.Admiral* was the flag officer in command of administration as opposed to operations.

Staffed initially by a tranche of manpower transferred from the WSP, the Marineküstenpolizei was part of the Kriegsmarine, not the police, in the same way as the *Feldgendarmerie* was part of the army, not the police.

Within the Reich itself, the authority of the Marineküstenpolizei extended over the inshore coastal areas and ports whilst inland rivers etc. were controlled by the *Wasserschutzpolizei*. In occupied countries their authority extended also to inland rivers and lakes. Its areas of responsibility included the security of rivers and river mouths, protection of fisheries and controlling order and discipline of personnel onboard ships whilst in port, and also of naval land units in coastal areas.

Duties included the arrest of miscreants and their delivery to either the military justice system if a court martial was appropriate, or to a responsible civilian court in other cases, the monitoring and observing of coastal areas, prevention of the escape of wanted persons by sea from occupied areas and general assistance to the military authorities.

It can be seen that whilst some of their duties might seem similar to 'Shore Patrol' personnel in the US Navy or Royal Navy, the range of duties they carried out was far wider than what might be considered their Allied equivalents.

The Marineküstenpolizei were effectively a naval version of the military police though with their own very specific tasks. Compared to the Wehrmacht Feldgendarmerie however, they perhaps performed a function closer to that of a Customs/Coastguard force.

Initially, transferees wore their original *Wasserschutzpolizei* uniforms but they were later issued with full naval kit on which a special police style eagle was worn on the left sleeve together with a cuffband bearing the title '*Marineküstenpolizei*' in yellow thread on blue. A special duty badge in the form of a crescent shaped gorget was worn on the right breast. Personnel used the same ranks as the regular navy, but with the suffix '*der MKP*'.

As stated in the original regulations for the creation of the Marineküstenpolizei, they were as a rule not formed up as self contained units as were their *Feldgendarmerie* counterparts. Instead, a small handful of Marineküstenpolizei personnel would be allocated to the office of the local *Hafenkommandant* (Harbour Commander) who

ABOVE LEFT A Kriegsmarine administrative official (*Marinebeamte*) from the technical branch giving advice to the engineering officer on a U-boat. The silver braid officer cap cords identify him immediately as an admin official; regular naval officers wore leather chinstraps. (DUBM)

ABOVE RIGHT An NCO from the Marineküstenpolizei. He wears a naval cap, with a civilian water-police jacket 'militarized' by the addition of a naval breast eagle. As time progressed, full naval issue uniform would be adopted. (Author's collection)

BELOW An original example of the special badge worn by members of the Marineküstenpolizei. It was worn pinned on to the jacket immediately below the breast eagle. Identifying the wearer's police authority, it was worn only on duty. (Author's collection)

would typically hold the rank of *Fregattenkapitän* (Middle Field Officer) in smaller ports or *Korvettenkapitän* (Lieutenant Commander), or even *Kapitän zur See* (Captain at Sea), in larger ports.

Late-War Land Units

Formed in February 1945, the *Marine-Panzervernichtungsbataillon* was a short-lived unit created around a group of naval personnel, predominantly U-boat men, who had formed the personal guard unit of Grossadmiral Dönitz. Commanded by U-boat ace Korvettenkapitän Peter 'Ali' Cremer, formerly of U-333, it went into action south of Hamburg in the closing days of the war and achieved some success as a tank-hunting unit against British forces, including 11th Armoured Division.

Marinepanzerjagdregiment 1 was a tank-hunting unit, but little is recorded of it other than it was commanded by another former U-boat ace, Korvettenkapitän Robert Gysae of U-177, and that it consisted of two battalions.

1.Marine-Infanterie-Division was formed in January 1945 in Stettin from redundant ships' crews and those from shore establishments, ships replacement pools and the like. It fought on the Oder Front in the closing stages of the war. In late April 1945 it was virtually wiped out in fighting near Kasekow. Fragmented sub-unit survivors did not reform but operated individually, some fighting alongside Waffen-SS troops near Seehausen. Withdrawing westwards, the survivors crossed the demarcation line between the Soviets and Western Allies and surrendered to British forces on 2/3 May 1945.

2.Marine-Infanterie-Division was formed in March 1945 in Schleswig-Hosltein from surplus ships crews and was deployed in defensive actions on the Western front. It saw action around Bremen and surrendered to British forces in May 1945.

1.Marine-Infanterie-Division's Commanders	
January–February 1945	Konteradmiral Hans Hartmann
February–May 1945	Generalmajor Wilhelm Bleckwenn

1.Marine-Infanterie-Division Main Sub-units

Marine-Infanterie-Regiment 1
Marine-Infanterie-Regiment 2
Marine-Infanterie-Regiment 3
Marine-Infanterie-Regiment 4
Marine-Artillerie-Regiment 1
Divisions-Füsilier-Kompanie 1
Marine-Panzerjäger-Abteilung 1
Marine-Pionier-Bataillon 1
Marine-Nachrichten-Bataillon 1
Marine-Feldersatz-Bataillon 1
Marine-Versorgungs-Regiment 1
Marine-Sanitäts-Kompanie 1

2.Marine-Infanterie-Division's Commanders

February–April 1945   Vizeradmiral Ernst   April–May 1945   Oberst Graf von
Scheurlen   Bassewitz

2.Marine-Infanterie-Division Main Sub-units

Marine-Grenadier-Regiment 5   Marine-Panzerjäger-Abteilung 2
Marine-Grenadier-Regiment 6   Marine-Pionier-Bataillon 2
Marine-Grenadier-Regiment 7   Marine-Nachrichten-Bataillon 2
Marine-Artillerie-Regiment 2   Marine-Feldersatz-Bataillon 2
Divisions-Füsilier-Bataillon 2   Marine-Versorgungs-Regiment 200

3.Marine-Infanterie-Division Main Sub-units

Marine-Grenadier-Regiment 8
Marine-Grenadier-Regiment 9
Marine-Grenadier-Regiment 10
Marine-Artillerie-Regiment 2
Marine-Feldersatz-Bataillon 3

8.Marine-Infanterie-Division's Commander

March–May 1945   Kapitän zur See Hans Ahlmann

8.Marine-Infanterie-Division Main Sub-units

Marine-Schützen-Regiment 111
Marine-Schützen-Regiment 112
Marine-Schützen-Regiment 113

16.Marine-Infanterie-Division's Commander

March–May 1945   Kapitän zur See (Marineartillerie) Hollweg

16.Marine-Infanterie-Division Main Sub-units

Marine-Schützen-Regiment 161
Marine-Schützen-Regiment 162
Marine-Schützen-Regiment 163

Superficially similar to the uniform of the army, the naval version features anchor motif buttons. A national emblem woven in golden yellow thread, and wide shoulder straps embroidered here with crossed anchors and the letter 'O', indicate that this male is part of a ships cadre unit under the Baltic command. (DUBM)

3.Marine-Infanterie-Division was formed in early 1945 in Itzehoe. It saw action around Prenzlau and at the Hohenzollernkanal. Although it surrendered to American forces the survivors were handed over to the Soviets. This unit was commanded by officers from the army.

8.Marine-Infanterie-Division was formed in March 1945 with personnel from 2.Schiffsstammregiment. It served with army units in the Netherlands.

16.Marine-Infanterie-Division was formed in March 1945 with personnel from 4.Schiffsstammregiment. It too served with army units in the Netherlands.

ABOVE Members of the Marine-Panzervernichtungsbataillon in 1945. At left is U-boat ace Peter 'Ali' Cremer wearing a Luftwaffe camouflage jacket over his naval uniform. From his badges, the officer in field grey to the right is a former U-boat officer. (DUBM)

ABOVE RIGHT Easily mistaken for army infantry soldiers, these are sailors in field grey, on combat manoeuvres. All except the NCO giving directions are in full combat kit, with bread bags, gas masks and canteens, as well as two sets of ammo pouches for the Kar98k rifle. (DUBM)

ABOVE Towards the end of the war, large numbers of surplus sailors were transferred to infantry units. These men had already had an element of basic infantry training, and were retrained in only a few rushed days in the latest combat techniques and new weapons, such as the *Panzerfaust*, before being sent into action. This group of sailors represents a tank-hunting team, near Hamburg in the closing days of the war. One sailor, sporting the Wound Badge and Fleet War Badge on his left breast pocket, is being questioned by a British military policeman. His interrogation is watched by his squad commander, a junior officer who wears a combination of whatever clothing was available. (John White © Osprey Publishing)

CONCLUSION

Having lost virtually its entire fleet at the end of World War I, Germany was forced to start rebuilding with only a tiny naval force, composed mainly of obsolete vessels. However, this meant it began the war in 1939 with a fleet which was composed predominantly of relatively new, modern warships. The problem was that there were so few of them compared to the vast number of ships available to its primary opponents, the Royal Navy and Commonwealth. In addition, many of its ships were using new and untried technology, something which would cause innumerable problems. Many of Hitler's warships spent a significant amount of time in port undergoing repairs or modifications to their engines. Indeed, many of its relatively new warship types were relegated to training duties for most of the war.

The British also had the advantage of being able to call upon the navies of the Commonwealth for aid. The Royal Canadian Navy was heavily involved in supporting British naval forces during the Battle of the Atlantic and was responsible for sinking 27 U-boats and sank or captured over 40 surface vessels. In addition, of course, it helped prevent the destruction of countless merchant ships by U-boats. Even Australia, though obviously heavily committed to actions in the Pacific, also contributed warships to serve in the Mediterranean, the North and South Atlantic and even the Arctic convoys. New Zealand too, from the other side of the world, contributed to the forces available to the Royal Navy, with HMNZS *Achilles* being part of the force which caused the scuttling of the pocket battleship *Graf Spee*. South Africa, though unable to supply ships, did supply men and virtually every major warship in the Royal Navy had a contingent of South Africans in its crew. In addition, several ships from countries attacked by Germany escaped destruction or capture, and made their way to British-controlled ports to subsequently serve alongside the Royal Navy.

Germany on the other hand could call on very little useful naval assistance having been denied the chance to gain control of the major French heavy units by the British bombardment of Mers-el-Kébir, in French Algeria, on 3 July 1940, where one battleship was sunk and two damaged. Then, on Germany taking control of Vichy France, the subsequent scuttling of the bulk of the remainder of the French fleet at Toulon also prevented key ships from falling into Hitler's hands. In fact, two of the major units which did survive, *Bretagne* and *Provence*, found their way into Free French hands and served alongside the Royal Navy, as did the giant submarine *Sourcouf*.

Grossadmiral Dönitz often took the time to personally welcome returning U-boats, and was quite happy to crack a joke with his men. The smiling face of the crewman being poked with the ceremonial baton of his commander in chief speaks volumes of the regard in which he was held. (DUBM)

To all intents and purposes, the Kriegsmarine would fight the bulk of the naval war against the Allies in the Atlantic on its own, a battle it could never hope to win – at least on the surface. Only by attempting to destroy ships carrying vital supplies to Britain could they hope to exert pressure on the British to seek peace terms.

Germany's Italian allies did posses some fine modern warships but, apart from providing convoy escort operations in the Mediterranean bringing much needed supplies to Rommel's desert army in North Africa, its heavy warships spent much of the time sheltering in port due to severe fuel shortages. After Italy's surrender, the Luftwaffe actually sank one of Italy's newest battleships, *Roma*, with aircraft-launched guided bombs. Italy's modern heavy cruisers did see frequent action, but although fast and well armed they were weakly armoured and fared badly when up against British heavy units. During the Battle of Cape Matapan, the three sisters *Zara*, *Pola* and *Fiume* were all sunk by a force including three battleships, *HMS Barham*, *HMS Valiant* and *HMS Warspite*. The Italians did, however, contribute a number of submarines to assist Germany's U-boats. Italy in fact was far better equipped than Germany in terms of submarines, with 116 in service on the outbreak of war. Most of these operated in the Mediterranean where they achieved moderate success, but suffered heavy losses due to improving Allied anti-submarine warfare techniques – Italian submarines were technically inferior to the German types and suffered from slow diving speeds. A small number did serve in the Atlantic, operating from the Kriegsmarine base at Bordeaux and succeeded in sinking 109 Allied merchant ships totalling some 593,864 tons. This compares with around 5,000 ships sunk by U-boats in the Atlantic.

It can be seen then that Germany was forced to fight the war at sea, for which it was woefully unprepared, with only a very modest amount of support from its allies and in that sense was at a huge disadvantage when compared to the massive naval strength available to the Royal Navy, and even more so once the United States entered the war.

Technical problems with weaponry also caused major problems for Germany. The so-called torpedo crisis of 1939 through to 1942 saw many U-boat captains ready to tear their hair out in frustration as direct hit after direct hit came to nothing when the new G7e torpedoes failed to detonate. The number of occurrences was so great that an enquiry was rapidly launched. At first the inexperience of some commanders was blamed, but when some of the leading aces reported the same problems, it became obvious that the real problem was something more serious. As many as 25 per cent of hits were failing to detonate. Sabotage was feared. The head of the torpedo directorate was sacked and his replacement, Admiral Kummetz, swiftly determined that a technical fault was to blame. Ultimately it was found that faulty contact pistols, and not sabotage as many had thought, lay behind this. Depth-keeping devices were also causing problems, with torpedoes running too deep and passing harmlessly under the target. Accusations of insufficient testing, negligence and incompetence followed, and resulted in courts martial and prison sentences. Dönitz himself commented, 'I do not believe that ever in the history of war, men have been sent against the enemy with such a useless weapon.' It would not be until late 1942 that the torpedo problems would eventually be completely solved. Considering the vast amount of tonnage sunk by U-boats during World War II, the devastation that might have been inflicted on Allied shipping had the Kriegsmarine possessed efficient torpedoes from the start can only be imagined.

Germany also made a significant error in failing to develop a naval air arm. Very little effort was put into the building of aircraft carriers. Even if the bulk of material genuinely was needed for the construction of U-boats and surface warships, Germany could have followed other nations by converting merchant vessels into small auxiliary aircraft carriers. They certainly achieved significant success in converting merchantmen into auxiliary cruisers, so why not aircraft carriers? Göring's insistence in demanding control of everything that flew would certainly have caused problems, but Göring could easily have been overruled by Hitler if he had chosen to do so. Differing priorities within naval high command, with Raeder focused on large battleships and Dönitz on submarines, and Hitler's well-known propensity for playing senior commanders off against each other as well as his ignorance of naval matters, probably all played a part. Whilst there were genuine strategic reasons for not investing huge amounts of resources and vast sums of money in the construction of large fleet aircraft carriers – which would then have been subject to constant attempts by the enemy to sink them (the Germans themselves torpedoed and sank six Allied aircraft carriers) – smaller amounts spent on converting merchants might have proven useful. One might imagine that had *Bismarck* and *Prinz Eugen* been accompanied by even a small auxiliary aircraft carrier, a handful of fighters would have seen off the elderly Swordfish aircraft which sealed *Bismarck*'s fate. Though efforts were made to produce carrier-based versions of the Bf 109 and Ju 87, these came to nothing, with the few that were built reverting back to regular land-based use, and spotter floatplanes such as the Arado Ar 196 and Heinkel He 60 were the only types to be carried on German warships.

Initially, the limited range capabilities of Allied aircraft meant that there was a large 'gap' in the mid-Atlantic through which ships had to pass without air cover, giving the U-boats the opportunity to attack with much less risk to themselves. Overwhelming Allied superiority in air power and the advent of long-range anti-submarine aircraft and auxiliary aircraft carriers providing air coverage across the full width of the North Atlantic, vastly reduced the effectiveness of the U-boats.

Along with having to serve throughout the first half of the war with faulty torpedoes, the Allied cracking of the Enigma codes was probably the biggest single factor in the Germans losing the Battle of the Atlantic. Based on a commercially available coding machine, the military Enigma used by the German Army had already been partially cracked by the Poles before the outbreak of war and this information, which proved crucial, was swiftly passed on to the British along with a Polish version of the machine based on the information they had gathered. Luftwaffe codes were the

Sailors whose performance and devotion to duty had been brought to the attention of Dönitz would often receive a personally dedicated photograph, often in a real silver frame. These U-boat crewmen are admiring the gift presented to their comrade. (DUBM)

first to be broken, with their messages being intercepted as early as 1940. In February 1940, Enigma rotor wheels were found on some of the survivors of U-33 when it was sunk, providing the British with more vital information. Catastrophe struck for the Germans in May 1941, however, when U-110 was depth charged and forced to the surface during an attack on convoy OB 318. A British boarding party was able to recover not only a complete Enigma machine but more importantly a full set of current codebooks. The recovery was kept secret and the Germans had no idea that the highly secret material had been captured. On 27 August 1941, U-570 was captured and along with it a further Enigma machine and its codebooks.

The Kriegsmarine introduced a more complex version using four coding rotors rather than the three used on army machines in early 1942, this variance gave a far greater number of possible coding combinations. For nine months the British were unable to crack messages sent on this new four-rotor machine. This all changed on 30 October 1942 when U-559 was attacked and forced to the surface by British warships. The boat was boarded and codebooks for the new four-rotor machine were seized. By 1943 the British were able to break the coding of virtually all German messages and U-boat movements were assiduously tracked.

On 4 June 1944, U-505 was captured by the US Navy in the South Atlantic and its Enigma machine and codebooks seized. The Kriegsmarine's secret coded messages by then were no longer secret. To make matters worse, Dönitz refused to believe that the Enigma codes had been cracked and insisted they were unbreakable; Kriegsmarine High Command preferred to believe Allied successes were down to spies and to advanced air-to-surface radar equipment. Even after the war, Dönitz refused to believe the Enigma codes had been decyphered.

Many of his commanders were not so sure and used extreme caution, maintaining radio silence as much as possible. The U-boats suffered terrible losses which can be directly attributed to the cracking of the Enigma codes. With the Allies often knowing exactly where and when U-boats would attack, Allied warships could be lying in wait. Almost all of the U-boat tankers, the *Milchkühe*, essential to supporting U-boat operations in the Atlantic, would be destroyed in ambush scenarios.

Political interference from Hitler, who knew little of naval warfare or strategy, also proved a major hindrance to the Kriegsmarine. From the point of view of a supreme commander, he was far too timid in the use of his major units for fear of losing any of them, something which only increased over time after the loss of major vessels like *Graf Spee*, *Blücher*, *Bismarck* and *Scharnhorst*. The *Tirpitz* was hidden away in a Norwegian fjord for fear of meeting the same fate. Intended primarily as commerce raiders, his heavy units, however, did serve a useful purpose in tying down a significant number of warships hunting for them and thus leaving merchant shipping more open to attack by U-boats. Heavy units were as often as not ordered to avoid contact with enemy equivalents.

Working in the close confines of any ship, but more so in submarines, of course, with relaxed discipline and no strict dress regulations, engendered a close bond of comradeship of the type common amongst elite forces. (DUBM)

The navy's relationship with politics was a complex one. Political influence over the navy was limited at least in the early days. Membership of political organisations was prohibited to officers. At least one well known U-boat ace was forced to cancel his Party membership in order to achieve a commission in the

navy. So-called *Nationalsozialistische Führungsoffiziere* (National Socialist Leadership Officers) were introduced in early 1944. Recruited from specially selected serving officers, usually the younger types, who were dedicated to the Nazi cause, these officers can be considered somewhat similar to the Soviet Political Commissars in the Red Army. Some 43,000 of them served in the Heer (Army), 3,452 in the Luftwaffe, but only 900 in the Kriegsmarine. Even when ultimately forced to accept National Socialist Leadership Officers in the Kriegsmarine, Dönitz ensured that none were permitted to serve on U-boats, one place where it was essential that the crew could trust and rely on each other without an atmosphere of suspicion and fear that some innocent, off-the-cuff, comment could be misconstrued and reported.

This of course does not mean that there were no naval personnel who supported the Nazi regime. In fact, many were fiercely loyal, without being Party members. Naval representation in the military resistance to Hitler was almost non-existent, yet a well known but true anecdote has U-564 arriving in port at the end of a long war cruise and its commander Reinhard Suhren shouting through a megaphone 'Are the Nazis still in charge?' and when the reply 'Yes' came, ordering his boat to reverse away from the quay. Such jokes could be extremely dangerous, but seem to have been more likely to be tolerated in the navy. Despite many instances of obvious antipathy towards the Nazis, the only naval individual associated with the plot against Hitler was Admiral Canaris, head of the *Abwehr* and even here there was no specific evidence, only strong suspicion. We therefore have a navy which Hitler himself considered 'Christian' rather than National Socialist, that avoided political involvement with the Nazis, yet took no part in any of the serious resistance and remained remarkably loyal.

We have seen that even when the Kriegsmarine was involved in an otherwise successful campaign, the cost in losses was sometimes enormous. Significant victories often came at huge cost. The sinking of HMS *Hood* also saw the loss of the *Bismarck*. Victory at Narvik involved the loss of a major part of the destroyer fleet.

In effect, apart from some minor successes by medium to large surface vessels, the war at sea would be left to the U-boats. Dönitz's submarines certainly achieved phenomenal success during the Battle of the Atlantic, but ultimately the principal weapons available to him, the Type VII and Type IX, reached the limit beyond which they could no longer be further improved and developed, and the introduction of the superb Type XXI came too late. Even these advanced machines were beset by technical and quality control issues. Although they finally provided the Kriegsmarine with a vessel which could overcome much of the Allied anti-submarine measures, by then the Kriegsmarine had lost all its bases in occupied France. In the end only two were to undertake active service operations before the war ended.

Ultimately, towards the end of the war, many thousands of trained sailors, their ships laid up, would be squandered as cannon fodder on land on the Eastern and Western fronts in the conflict's closing stages, both in rapidly formed ill-trained Marine Infantry Divisions, Alarm Battalions, Assault Battalions, Festungs Battalions or even transferred to the Waffen-SS to make up for combat losses. The Kriegsmarine fought bravely, and in the vast majority of cases, honourably, but could never realistically have overcome the naval power of Great Britain supported by the Commonwealth and the US Navy.

The Kriegsmarine, however, though under a different name, continued to serve after the end of the war when, in June 1945, the German Mine Sweeping Administration (GMSA) was formed under the control of the Royal Navy. Using surviving German minesweepers and with German crews, and initially still wearing their original uniforms but with the eagle and swastika insignia removed, they carried out mine-clearing operations in the North Sea. They continued its work until January 1948 when it was replaced by a civilian organization still under British control. Thus, the Kriegsmarine carried out the first major action of the war with the attack on Westerplatte and was still serving nearly three years after the war ended.

One of the greatest achievements of the Kriegsmarine took place in the closing days of the war when many vessels, including the liner *Deutschland* shown here while serving as a naval accommodation ship, saved over 800,000 German civilians from areas about to be overrun by the Red Army. (Library of Congress)

FURTHER READING

Asmussen, John, *Bismarck, Pride of the Germany Navy*, Fonthill Media, Stroud, (2013)

Breyer, Siegfried & Koop, Gerhard, *The German Navy at War, Vol 1*, Schiffer Publishing, Pennsylvania (1989)

Breyer, Siegfried & Koop, Gerhard, *The German Navy at War, Vol 2*, Schiffer Publishing, Pennsylvania (1989)

Breyer, Siegfried & Skwiot, Miroslaw, *German Capital Ships of the Second World War*, Seaforth Publishing, Barnsley,(2012)

Chazette, Alain & Reberac, Fabien, *Kriegsmarine*, Editions Heimdal, Bayeux (1997)

Delgado, Eduardo, *Deutsche Kriegsmarine*, Andrea Press, Madrid (2016)

Elfrath, Ulrich & Herzog, Bodo, *Battleship Bismarck*, Schiffer Publishing, Pennsylvania (1989)

Forczyk, Robert, *German Commerce Raider vs British Cruiser*, DUE 27,Osprey Publishing, Oxford (2010)

Greentree David & Campbell, David, *British Destroyer vs German Destroyer*, DUE 88, Osprey Publishing, Oxford (2018)

Knowles, Daniel, *Tirpitz*, Fonthill Media, Stroud (2018)

Koop, Gerhard & Schmolke, Klaus-Peter, *Battleships of the Scharnhorst Class*, Greenhill Books, London (1999)

Koop, Gerhard & Schmolke, Klaus-Peter, *Pocket Battleships of the Deutschland Class*, Greenhill Books, London (2000)

Koop, Gerhard & Schmolke, Klaus-Peter, *Heavy Cruisers of the Admiral Hipper Class*, Greenhill Books, London (2001)

Koop, Gerhard & Schmolke, Klaus-Peter, *German Light Cruisers of World War II*, Greenhill Books, London (2002)

Kuhn, Vollmar, *Schnellboote im Einsatz*, Motorbuch Verlag, Stuttgart (1976)

Lardas, Mark, *Battle of the Atlantic 1939–41*, ACM 15, Osprey Publishing, Oxford, (2020)

MacLean, French L., *Dönitz's Crews*, Schiffer Publishing, Pennsylvania (2009)

Mallmann-Showell, Jak P., *The German Navy in World War Two*, Arms & Armour Press, London (1979)

Mallmann-Showell, Jak P., *U-Boats under the Swastika*, Ian Allan, Surrey (1998)

Mallmann-Showell, Jak P., *U-Boat Commanders and Crews*, Crowood Press (1998)

Mallmann-Showell, Jak P., *German Navy Handbook 1939–45*, Sutton Publishing, Stroud (1999)

Mallmann-Showell, Jak P., *U-Boats in Camera*, Sutton Publishing, Stroud (1999)

Mallmann-Showell, Jak P., *U-Boat Warfare*, Ian Allan Publishing, Hersham (2002),

Mulligan, Timothy, *Neither Sharks nor Wolves*, Chatham Publishing (1999)

Paterson, Lawrence, *Otto Kretschmer*, Greenhill Books, Barnsley (2018)

Pigoreau, Olivier, *The Odyssey of the Komet*, Histoire & Collections, Paris (2016)

Rössler, Eberhard, *The U-Boat: The evolution and technical history of German submarines*, Arms & Armour Press, London (1981)

Sharpe, Peter, *U-Boat Fact File*, Midland Publishing, Leicester (1998)

Stern, Robert C., *Kriegsmarine: A Pictorial History of the German Navy 1935–45*, Arms & Armour Press, London (1979)

Stern, Robert C., *Type VII U-Boats*, Arms & Armour Press, London (1991)

Whitley, M. J., *German Cruisers of World War Two*, Arms & Armour Press, London (1985)

Whitley, M. J., *German Capital Ships of World War II*, Cassell, London (1989)

Whitley, M. J., *German Coastal Forces of World War Two*, Arms & Armour Press, London (1992)

Williamson, Gordon, *Wolfpack*, Osprey Publishing, Oxford (2005)

Williamson, Gordon, *Torpedo Los!*, Bender Publishing, San Jose (2006)

Williamson, Gordon, *War Badges of the Kriegsmarine*, Bender Publishing, San Jose (2010)

Williamson, Gordon, *Kriegsmarine U-boats 1939–45 (1)*, NVG 51, Osprey Publishing, Oxford (2002)

Williamson, Gordon, *Kriegsmarine U-boats 1939–45 (2)*, NVG 55, Osprey Publishing, Oxford (2002)

Williamson, Gordon, *German E-boats 1939–45*, NVG 59, Osprey Publishing, Oxford (2002)

Williamson, Gordon, *German Pocket Battleships 1939–45*, NVG 75, Osprey Publishing, Oxford (2003)

Williamson, Gordon, *German Battleships 1939–45*, NVG 71, Osprey Publishing, Oxford (2003)

Williamson, Gordon, *German Destroyers 1939–45*, NVG 91, Osprey Publishing, Oxford (2003)

Williamson, Gordon, *German Light Cruisers 1939–45*, NVG 84, Osprey Publishing, Oxford (2003)

Williamson, Gordon, *German Heavy Cruisers 1939–45*, NVG 81, Osprey Publishing, Oxford (2003)

Williamson, Gordon, *U-Boat Bases and Bunkers 1941-45*, Fortress 3, Osprey Publishing, Oxford (2003)

Williamson, Gordon, *Kriegsmarine Coastal Forces*, NVG 151, Osprey Publishing, Oxford (2009)

Williamson, Gordon, *Kriegsmarine Auxiliary Cruisers*, NVG 156, Osprey Publishing, Oxford (2009)

Williamson, Gordon, *German Seamen*, WAR 37, Osprey Publishing, Oxford (2001)

Williamson, Gordon, *Grey Wolf*, WAR 36, Osprey Publishing, Oxford (2001)

Williamson, Gordon., *U-Boat Crews 1914–45*, Elite 60, Osprey Publishing, Oxford (1995)

Williamson, Gordon *U-Boat Tactics in World War II*, Elite 183, Osprey Publishing, Oxford, (2010)

Williamson, Gordon, *E-Boat vs MTB*, DUE 34, Osprey Publishing, Oxford (2011)

Wynn, Kenneth, *U-Boat Operations of the Second World War, Vol. 1*, Chatham Publishing, London (1997)

Wynn, Kenneth, *U-Boat Operations of the Second World War, Vol. 2*, Chatham Publishing, London (1998)

ABOVE Adolf Hitler visits the heavy cruiser *Deutschland* in 1936, posing for a photograph with the crew. (Print Collector/Getty Images)

GERMAN NAVAL RANKS AND EQUIVALENTS

Enlisted

Seemann	Seamen
Matrose	Ordinary Seaman
Matrosen-Gefreiter	Able Seaman
Matrosen-Obergefreiter/Hauptgefreiter	Leading Seaman
Matrosen-Stabsgefreiter/Stabsobergefreiter	Senior Leading Seaman

NCOs

Obermaat	Chief Petty Officer
Bootsmann	Boatswain
Stabsbootsmann	Senior Boatswain
Oberbootsmann	Chief Boatswain
Stabsoberbootsmann	Senior Chief Boatswain

Officers

Fähnrich zur See	Midshipman
Oberfähnrich zur See	Midshipman
Leutnant zur See	Lieutenant
Oberleutnant zur See	Lieutenant (junior)
Kapitänleutnant	Lieutenant (senior)
Korvettenkapitän	Lieutenant-Commander
Fregattenkapitän	Commander
Kapitän zur See	Captain
Kommodore	Commodore
Konteradmiral	Rear Admiral
Vizeadmiral	Vice Admiral
Admiral	Admiral
Generaladmiral	—
Grossadmiral	Admiral of the Fleet

INDEX

Page numbers in **bold** refer to illustrations.

In the compilation of this volume we relied on the following previously published Osprey titles, all by Gordon Williamson : NVG 51: Kriegsmarine U-boats 1939–45 (1), NVG 55: Kriegsmarine U-boats 1939–45 (2), NVG 59: German E-boats 1939–45, NVG 75: German Pocket Battleships 1939–45, NVG 71: German Battleships 1939–45, NVG 91: German Destroyers 1939–45, NVG 84: German Light Cruisers 1939–45, NVG 81: German Heavy Cruisers 1939–45, NVG 151: Kriegsmarine Coastal Forces, NVG 156: Kriegsmarine Auxiliary Cruisers, WAR 36: Grey Wolf, WAR 37: German Seaman 1939–45, DUE 34: E-Boat vs MTB, ELITE 177: German Special Forces of World War II.

Maps by Bounford.com, previously published in CAM 171: River Plate 1939: The sinking of the Graf Spee (p 19), CAM 183: Denmark and Norway 1940: Hitler's boldest operation (p 21), CAM 232: The Bismarck 1941: Hunting Germany's greatest battleship (pp 26, 29 and 30), CAM 356: North Cape 1943: The Sinking of the Scharnhorst (p 37), RAID 51 Tirpitz in Norway: X-craft midget submarines raid the fjords, Operation Source 1943 (p 38).

Artworks previously published in NVG 71: German Battleships 1939–45, (pp 47, 49, 51, 55), NVG 75: German Pocket Battleships 1939–45 (pp 57, 59, 64), NVG 81: German Heavy Cruisers 1939–45 (pp 67, 68, 69, 71, 72), NVG 84: German Light Cruisers 1939–45 (pp 75, 76, 77, 84, 86), NVG 91: German Destroyers 1939–45 (pp 100, 102, 108, 110–111, 112), NVG 59: German E-boats 1939–45 (pp 173, 175, 176, 178, 179), NVG 151: Kriegsmarine Coastal Forces (pp 184, 204), NVG 156: Kriegsmarine Auxiliary Cruisers (pp 87, 90, 93, 95), NVG 51: Kriegsmarine U-boats 1939–45 (1) (pp 115, 126, 128, 130, 138), NVG 55: Kriegsmarine U-boats 1939–45 (2) (pp 140, 141, 143, 160), Elite 177: German Special Forces of World War II (p 222), DUEL 34: E-Boat vs MTB: The English Channel 1941–45 (pp 40, 62–63), Warrior 36: Grey Wolf: U-Boat Crewman of World War II (p 150), Warrior 37: German Seaman 1939–45 (p.240).